In 1971, a man  a
jetliner, demanded s,
and bailed out somewhere over Oregon, never to be seen
again. He became a folk hero to hippies, survivalists, liber-
tarians, and anarchists, who admired the man who had,
apparently, beat the system. However, his jump, in brutally
cold weather and in the midst of a major storm, left one
question unanswered: where was he?

George C. Nuttall, with his best friend, also a trained
policeman and investigator, began to poke around in the
mystery of Cooper's disappearance. The resulting book,
D.B. Cooper Case Exposed: J. Edgar Hoover Cover-Up? is
a record of his investigations, which turn up some results
implicating far more powerful people than D.B. Cooper,
whoever he was.

Nuttall and his crony found poor police work, missing
documents, and outright lies everywhere they looked, and
began to smell a cover-up. The two men were convinced
that there was no possibility that Cooper survived the jump,
although they never definitively proved this. More puzzling
is the unmistakable FBI fingerprint they find at every turn.

Now, decades later, Nuttall has written an exposé, linking
an astonishing cast of characters: cops, congressmen, FAA
officials, and Mafia dons. The common thread is that, one
way or the other, they were all linked back to Washington,
to the powerful, corrupt, and perverse head of the FBI, J.
Edgar Hoover.

Other books by George C. Nuttall

Cops, Crooks and Other Crazies

D.B. Cooper Case
EXPOSED

J. Edgar Hoover Cover Up?

· George C. Nuttall ·

VANTAGEPress
NEW YORK

Cover design by Michael Fusco
Interior design by Neuwirth & Associates, Inc.

Vantage Press and the Vantage Press colophon are registered trademarks
of Vantage Press, Inc.

Published by Vantage Press, Inc.
419 Park Ave. South, New York, NY 10016

Manufactured in the United States of America

ISBN: 978-0-533-16390-8

Library of Congress Catalog Card No: 2010908175

0 9 8 7 6 5 4 3 2 1

ABOUT THE AUTHOR

GEORGE C. NUTTALL was born into a second-generation San Diego family on August 6, 1930. His father, George Patrick Nuttall, was a San Diego City fire captain, and his maternal grandfather, John Andrew Wood, was a fire department battalion chief. They both contracted pneumonia at the same fire, and died three days apart when George was five months old.

His mother, Fern Wood Nuttall, never remarried and raised George and his two older brothers on meager city and veterans' survivors' pensions. His father was a World War I Navy veteran.

Their next-door neighbors were childless veteran San Diego Police Officer John Edward Golden and his wife Ida, and they were like family to the Nuttalls. By age five, Officer Golden became George's surrogate father, and George started learning firearms safety and police work from Officer Golden at that very early age.

Although George's mother and Fire Chief George Courser wanted George to become a fireman, at age nineteen, George decided that he wanted most of all to be a California Highway Patrol officer, as they were then called, "The Princes of the Highways" by many Californians and out-of-staters alike.

But George was ten months too young to take a Highway Patrol test in October 1950, so he took the San Diego Police Department test in December 1951. He was hired by the San Diego Police Department on July 14, 1952, along with twenty-five other recruits.

In his fifth month on the San Diego P.D., George was partnered with Officer Harry L. Grady for two months, and their complete compatibility quickly prompted them to become lifetime friends.

After walking foot beats alone in San Diego's skid row in the patrol division, he was assigned to the traffic division, and was ultimately assigned to motorcycle duty for six months just prior to leaving the SDPD and joining the California Highway Patrol.

On the CHP, George served in nine varied assignments, including two at the CHP Academy as an instructor, and rose through the ranks to captain. His last assignment was as the Santa Barbara office area commander and CHP Coastal Division Protective Services Coordinator to coordinate with the Service Service for the protection of President Reagan and other dignitaries when on public highways. In that capacity, he served as the CHP commander of the Queen of England's motorcade when she and Prince Philip met with President and Mrs. Nancy Reagan for their heads-of-state meeting on March 1, 1983. This was reported to be the most complex operation in Secret Service history due to an El Niño winter and the geographical limitations, as fully explained in George's first book, *Cops, Crooks and Other Crazies*.

George then retired from the CHP, five months later on August 7, 1983.

CONTENTS

DEDICATION

HARRY L. GRADY

3/17/21 – 9/10/09

This book is dedicated to the memory of Harry L. Grady, who passed away on September 10, 2009, at the age of 88. Harry L. Grady was the most dedicated, tenacious, persistent, knowledgable, insightful, humorous, and humanitarian officer I ever had the honor and pleasure of working with. It was indeed a blessing to have him as a close friend for fifty-seven years. He began to pursue solving the D.B. Cooper skyjacking case on his own, soon after he moved back to his homestate of Washington in 1986.

Then, seven years later in, 1993, he graciously invited me to join him to confirm his conclusion of where Cooper's wild-life scattered remains were located. Needless to say, that was the opportunity of a lifetime for an old retired cop, to get involved in one of the most publicized crimes of the twentieth century. And the only reason that this book could be written and published about our solving the reportedly unsolved 1971 D.B. Cooper skyjacking case.

The only dishonest act Harry ever committed that I ever knew of was when he was so eager to become a policeman that he lied about his age when he was twenty years old to join the San Diego Police Department, since the legal age was twenty-one years.

So, this is rightfully Harry L. Grady's story, and a tribute to his entire adulthood of pursuing criminals and justice.

INTRODUCTION

"This work gets in your blood real fast and spoils you for any other kind of work."

THERE ARE ANY NUMBER of highly publicized criminal cases that are reportedly unsolved in addition to other mysterious cases still open to speculation and debate. Some of the most famous or notorious are as follows:

Jack the Ripper: Who was he, and was he a physician?
Amelia Earhart: Was she captured and killed by the Japanese?
Lindbergh baby kidnapping and killing: Was the man convicted of this crime the actual perpetrator?
Black Dahlia case: Who was the killer, and was he a physician?
Roswell aircraft crash: Was it a UFO?
President Kennedy assassination: Were there two or more shooters?
Robert Kennedy assassination: Were there two shooters?
Dr. Martin Luther King assassination: Was it a conspiracy?

Jon Benet Ramsey Murder: Who was the killer?

D.B. Cooper Skyjacking Case: Who was Cooper, and why is his the only skyjacking case of the over 2,111 skyjackings in the 1960s and 1970s that has not been reportedly solved by the FBI?

Of these high-profile cases, and many more, it was my good fortune to be invited by my old 1952-to-1953 San Diego Police Department partner, Harry L, Grady, and friend since that time, to join him in his investigation of the D.B. Cooper case. As my first San Diego Police Department training officer told me on my first day in that department, on July 14, 1952, "This work gets in your blood real fast and spoils you for any other kind of work." He was so right! It was like a gift from above to be invited to get involved in one of the most publicized and confused criminal cases in U.S. history, and as an old retired cop.

Many, most, or all may think we were crazy to take on such a case, just like the parachute rigger who owned the chutes provided to Cooper. His first comment to us when we sat down in his home to interview him was, "You're both crazy for getting involved in the Cooper case." He was probably right at that time, but four years later, all of the missing pieces of this mysterious case clearly fit together, and proved otherwise.

Amazingly, one of the integral facts was known to Harry and me in the 1940s and 1950s in San Diego, but was of no consequence until I discovered the key connection in 1998.

Up until Harry's passing on September 10, 2009, he and I completely agreed that we had solved the case, but the only way it could be officially solved would be by a county grand jury in Washington, Oregon, California or Nevada. And in the context of an investigation of the state crimes of grand theft and kidnapping, not the federal crime of skyjacking.

We agreed that an attorney general of any one of those states or district attorney of any of the many counties that Cooper's skyjacked plane passed over between Seattle and Reno would have jurisdiction in this case.

Harry and I agreed that it was not likely that a federal grand jury or a congressional committee would investigate this case, because I had already attempted to get six congressional members and one U.S. Attorney to investigate the case, and I was stonewalled by all of them. Even though I mailed my complete summary of the case to the congressional members via certified and return receipt requested U.S. mail, and the return receipts were signed by an aide and returned to me, I got no further response.

I have compiled a list of over twenty-five potential material witnesses and secured it with my attorney, and with a notarized waiver of my attorney/client privileged communication to allow it to be subpoenaed by any attorney general or district attorney with jurisdiction in this case.

If any of those prosecutors should pursue a county grand jury investigation, I believe it would be necessary for some of those listed to be granted immunity from prosecution for the obstruction of justice in order to get the truth, whole truth, and nothing but the truth of this suspicious case.

In order to clearly note the many reported omissions, discrepancies, contradictions and oversights in the reported

FBI investigation of this case, and suspicious events that Harry and I experienced during our investigation, each will be followed with a (WHY?). With these noted, readers should be able to act as unofficial interim judges and jurors of this case.

If readers arrive at the same opinions and conclusions that Harry and I did, they should contact their state attorney general and district attorney by phone or mail, and demand a complete grand jury investigation. In doing so, it might bring an end to this decades-old suspicious case and put a stop to any further waste of taxpayers' money and FBI manpower.

I must say that any person with average intelligence and common sense should be able to come to the same opinions and conclusions that Harry and I did, despite our over seventy-two years of combined law enforcement investigative experiences.

All of the reports, known facts, and our experiences in investigating this case are circumstantial, but when they are as overwhelming in numbers as they are, they are not disputable and are sufficient to conclude and convict. And so much so, that less-compelling circumstantial evidence has been solely used to convict numerous suspects for major crimes, and even to send many to death rows for murder.

Many homicide investigators have proclaimed that there are no coincidences of evidence in investigations. I did experience a couple in investigations, but they were insignificant and did not influence the outcome and successful conclusion of the investigation. This notwithstanding, Harry and I noted all of the strange events that occurred during our investigation and carefully weighed them for their relevance, even if they appeared to be coincidental.

Also, it must be understood by readers that the underworld, and particularly that of the Mafia, is a very small world, so much so, that it is not difficult to track their well-known, age-old traditional operations and methods solely with a paper trail.

With all of these combined, the D.B. Cooper case was not difficult to solve, after we had uncovered all of the reported known facts and the strange events that we encountered, and put them together piece by piece from 1986 to 1998.

So, please read this true story with an open mind and form your own independent opinions and conclusions.

Special note: All of the newspaper articles reported herein could not be included due to the refusal of some publishers or editors to grant permission to reproduce and include their copyrighted material.

D.B. Cooper Case
EXPOSED

[ONE]

Once a Cop, Always a Cop

The Pit Bull Cop

My 1952-TO-1953 SAN DIEGO Police Department partner and training officer, friend since that time, and investigation partner in the reportedly unsolved D.B. Cooper case, Harry L. Grady, was born in Everett, Washington, on March 17, 1921. When he was nine years old, his family moved to San Diego on a doctor's advice to be in a milder climate, because his father was still suffering from the affects of being mustard-gassed in World War I. Then tragically, five years later, his father was killed while working on the merry-go-round in Balboa Park when it collapsed on him.

At age nineteen, Harry became a San Diego City lifeguard. Then in 1941, he lied about his age and joined the San Diego Police Department along with two other lifeguards, just days after the city fire and police retirement system was amended from twenty to twenty-five years of required service to retire. This obvious intentional delay in the hiring of Harry and the other two lifeguards was still a very sore subject with Harry when I worked with him in 1952 and 1953.

Then, when he and the other two former lifeguards who had joined the P.D. with him had twenty years of service, in 1961, they got a bright idea. The lifeguard service had been a part of the police department when they were lifeguards, so they sued to bridge that service with their P.D. time. They won, and all three retired with great joy, because the San Diego Police Department had become a full-blown traffic-ticket-writing agency for the collection of half of the fine money for the city coffers.

With Harry's well-known enviable, reputation as an expert investigator, he was quickly recruited by Naval Intelligence as an investigator, where he remained for eleven years, then again retired.

About the time he became a Naval Intelligence investigator, a Japanese/American ensign went on leave and did not return to duty. It was reported that the ensign had received a less than satisfactory employee evaluation. A few days later, the missing ensign's car was found hidden among some trees by a California Highway Patrol officer near Campo Lake in the Laguna Mountains in the southeast part of San Diego County.

The Navy searched the area two times with over fifty sailors, including frogmen (now Navy SEALs) searching Campo Lake, but did not find any trace of the ensign.

Knowing the Japanese sense of honor, Harry strongly

suspected he had committed suicide because of his employee evaluation, and he repeatedly urged his supervisor to renew the search, but in a much wider area. But his supervisor rejected all of his requests, saying it would be futile and a waste of manpower and money, and the case was closed, listing the ensign as missing.

Then after fifteen months of believing the missing ensign had committed suicide, Harry recruited five of his fellow rank-and-file co-workers to join him in an extended search of the most logical area on a day off.

Harry told me when they reached the location where the ensign's car had been found, he carefully looked around, and his instincts told him where the ensign would have gone to conceal his suicide. And his search partners were quite willing to follow him and his hunch.

About ninety-five minutes after starting their search, and about a mile from where the ensign's car had been found, and far beyond where the Navy had originally searched, they found human bones scattered over a quarter-mile area. They then found the ensign's wallet and a razor blade.

In one of the several newsclippings Harry sent to me about the amazing discovery, there was a photo of Harry sitting on a large rock with a smug look on his face. He told me he was "gloating" over his supervisor and his repeated rejections of a new and wider search. Not only because of the supervisor's resistance, but also because Harry was not favorably impressed with the "elitist" supervisors as he called them. He said they were all college graduates with absolutely no street cop experience, and he was recruited to do their heavy work. In my first book, *Cops, Crooks and*

Other Crazies, I repeatedly stressed that true police work is learned solely on the street, not in college or other classroom. And Harry's extensive experiences with the white-collar, college-degreed, political supervisors confirmed my conviction that one has to get one's hands dirty to really, truly know police work and how to do it with any degree of success.

If it hadn't been for Harry, his street-learned cop instincts and persistence, the ensign's wildlife-scattered remains would probably still be in the Laguna Mountains, unless some hunter or other outdoorsman stumbled across them.

And finding the ensign's remains gave Harry the know-how and confidence to try to locate Cooper's wildlife-scattered remains, believing they would be scattered over a wide area, making them much easier to find than an intact body.

In his usual humorous way, Harry told me during one of our many phone conversations that if he found Cooper's remains, he would then go after "Bigfoot."

Then after retiring from the Naval Intelligence, having been a Mafia expert since before I worked with him in 1952 and 1953, Harry was hired by the San Diego D.A.'s office in its Organized Crime Unit. There, he built an airtight case and successfully prosecuted a younger, hot-headed Mafia hood, who had the same surname as a well-known Mafia godfather of the 1940s and 1950s. And the younger hood was much like "Sonny" in *The Godfather*. As such, the renegade Mafia hood did not conform to the age-old Mafia code of never harming an honest law enforcement officer, which existed for one apparent reason, because it could ignite an all-out war between law enforcement and the Mafia.

Despite the deadly consequences of violating any Mafia code, the pathological younger street hood seriously threatened to kill Harry. Knowing the sneaky, sadistic, torturous methods of Mafia hits, and the psychopathic nature of his tormentor, Harry took him at his word.

With that, Harry created his own witness protection program when he moved to Washington, years before the psycho hood was to be released from prison. Harry had an unlisted phone number, and years later when "Caller ID" was initiated, he subscribed to the "Star 82" protection that requires that it be dialed prior to dialing the phone number so any caller's blocked number would appear on the caller ID screen. And Harry did not have an answering machine/message recorder.

Also, when I stayed with Harry and his wife of over fifty years in 1994 to search with him and complete my investigation to confirm his theory of where Cooper's remains were located, he had his home well posted with warning signs. On all exterior doors and some windows there were signs that read: THIS PLACE PROTECTED BY COLT, WINCHESTER, REMINGTON, AND SMITH & WESSON.

Accordingly, in my first book, *Cops, Crooks and Other Crazies*, I referred to Harry Grady as "Gary Gray." But now that Harry is safe in his final resting place, his true name should be used to let it be known that he was solely responsible for this book, and hopefully the final official solving of the D.B. Cooper case. May he rest in peace!

[TWO]

Partners Again

"You're the analytical one, so you figure it out."

SHORTLY AFTER RETIRING FROM the California Highway Patrol in August 1983, I attended an annual San Diego Police Department Veterans' Luncheon to see as many of my old friends and associates that I hoped were still alive and would be there.

There, I was lucky enough to see my old friend Harry Grady, whom I hadn't seen for twenty-nine years since I left the P.D. in 1954 and joined the CHP. As always, we had an enjoyable discussion bringing each other up to date, and with many laughs about our old San Diego P.D. days that weren't very funny at the time. Harry was retired after forty-one years in law enforcement, and then had his own private investigation business. We then bid each other fond farewells and went on our own ways.

Then, about nine years later, in 1992, I learned from

another old P.D. friend that Harry had moved back to his homestate of Washington, and I was entrusted with his highly confidential home address and phone number.

I phoned Harry to see how he was, then we started exchanging letters to bring ourselves up to date on everything from our past police experiences to current activities. This went on for over a year. Harry openly admitted that he hated to type, and his handwriting was bad, so it usually took about a month for him to answer my letters, which I always sent to him a few days after receiving his delayed responses.

Then, running out of much to write about in March 1993, I asked, off-the-wall, in a letter if he lived near where D.B. Cooper bailed out of a plane and if he knew anything about the case. I said that bizarre case had fascinated me for decades. In less than a week, I received an all-time-record response from Harry. He started with, "You're a man after my own heart, because I've been working on that case since I moved up here seven years ago."

Then about a week later, there was a parcel post box at my front door. It contained Harry's seven-year collection of D.B. Cooper books, newsclippings, and related maps and Columbia River tide tables. About a week later, I received a follow-up letter in which Harry wrote, "You're the analytical one, so you figure it out."

There were two copies each of four books about D.B. Cooper's skyjacking case. One was so fictional that I disregarded it, as Harry later told me he had done. The other three contained so much conflicting and contradictory information that I seriously questioned my ability to be analytical. One attempted to prove Cooper was Richard Floyd McCoy, Jr., who skyjacked a plane for $500,000 ransom on April 7, 1972, and bailed out over Provo, Utah. But the book did have some critical information.

The most valuable and believable book was entitled, *D.B. Cooper: Dead or Alive*, authored by Richard T. Tosaw, a five-year-term FBI agent in the 1950s, turned attorney, then turned author of interesting stories. The second was entitled, *NORJAK*, authored by retired Portland FBI special agent Ralph P. Himmelsbach and a Thomas K. Worcester. And the third is entitled, *D.B. Cooper: The Real McCoy*, authored by Bernie Rhodes, former chief Utah probation and parole officer, and researched by Ralph P. Calame, former special agent in charge of the Salt Lake City FBI office.

Because Tosaw's book appeared to be the most factual, and was written much like a police report without digressions, I studied it intently for all of the facts I could compile. The only major disagreement I had with his writings was his theory that Cooper had landed safely in the Columbia River, was pulled under by the twenty-one-pound weight of the money bag, and had drowned.

To test this theory, I placed a sheet of dry twenty-pound bond typing paper in a pan of water. It floated until it became saturated, then slowly sank. Then in discussing Tosaw's drowning theory with Harry, he said he had rejected it from the beginning of his investigation. He said he knew from his lifeguard days that the bodies of drowned persons always become bloated from bacterial action and float to the surface in a number of days, depending on the temperature of the water. Harry also said he followed the TV and newspaper reports of persons drowned or missing in the Columbia River, and in his seven years in the area, the bodies of all of those victims had surfaced and been recovered.

Then jumping ahead, in the early 2000s, there was a TV reenactment of Cooper's jump by two men. One jumped off of a high diving board into a swimming pool with a twenty-one-pound of dry paper enclosed in a cloth bag simulating Cooper's money bag. The dry paper bundle floated on top of the water much like a beach ball.

With Harry's lifeguard experiences, the news reports he had followed for seven years, my paper test, and the TV demonstration, we had to conclude that Cooper had not drowned in the Columbia River.

Thus, this being disregarded was more support of Harry's theory of where Cooper's remains were located—and on a Columbia River island.

As I analyzed the conflicting information in Tosaw's and Himmelsbach's books, I phoned Harry a few times to offer my not-too-bright opinions. He patiently listened, rejected my ideas, then said, "You have to come up here to get to know the lay of the land to understand what could or couldn't have happened." He was so eager for me to come up to Washington to confirm his Columbia River island theory, he offered to pay half of my airfare, which he did when I flew up there. My eager agreement to fly to Washington to become oriented to the area, and to try to confirm Harry's conclusion about where Cooper's remains are located, inspired Harry to actually start searching the peninsulas and islands of the Columbia River for anything related to Cooper, especially his remains. In one of our early phone conversations thereafter, months before I flew to Washington, Harry said, "It really gets the juices flowing."

In that the Columbia River islands are owned and controlled by the Port of Portland, and are public access by issued permit only, Harry applied for permits and was issued some, including one for Hayden Island. The peninsulas did not require permits as they were free access with public parking lots for visitors.

Harry told me that the Port of Portland employees who issued the permits to him were very interested in his searching, and even somewhat excited about his possibly finding Cooper's remains. In appreciation of their cooperation, Harry told me he prepared written reports of his findings on Hayden Island for the Port of Portland employees and delivered the reports to them. Most encouraging for Harry was his finding the bones of a steer scattered over an area of about fifty yards by wildlife, as he had speculated Cooper's remains would be scattered and easy to find.

With that discovery, Harry was more confident than ever that he could find Cooper's remains spread over a wide area.

Exhibit A

May 31, 1994

[redacted]
Senior Development Manager
Port of Portland

Attention –
Mr. [redacted]

Sir:

I would appreciate permission to conduct a walkin search of the Ports property on Hayden Island from the railroad tracks west to the west end. My search would involve only the dense wooded areas and there would be no digging or interference with the ecology of the area. I believe at my slow pace it would take me several months to complete. My target is to locate the remains of a hyjacking suspect known as Dan Cooper (an alias). This would include of course his skeletal remains as well as one parachute and part of another. I mean by my presence on Port property to present no legal liability for injuries or for whatever might happen to me.

I am a retired lawenforcement person with 41 years of expierence and have been working the Cooper case since 1986 because of the challange of an unsolved case. I would hope to complete the search before the Port commences developing the area. This area, in my opinion, is a very probable landing zone (in the forest area) of Cooper.

②

I work alone searching but for 4 days my partner in this venture Mr. GEORGE C. NUTTALL, retired Captain (40 years) of the California Highway Patrol and former San Diego Police officer, wants to join me for four days searching the area between June 15-22, 1994. His address is ▓▓▓▓▓▓▓▓▓▓▓▓▓▓▓▓▓▓▓▓ Telephone (714) ▓▓▓▓▓▓▓▓ He will also execute a non-liability statement if necessary.

I would appreciate permission to carry out this search that could possibly answer the questions concerning COOPERs success or failure in this 1971 crime.

I remain,
Sincerely yours

Harry L. Grady   wife Ruth

Vancouver, WA ▓▓▓▓▓▓▓▓▓▓▓▓▓▓

Enclosures

DPOB: 3-17-21 EVERETT, WA
SSN: ▓▓▓▓▓▓▓▓   (GREY 6'3" 200)
Retired - San Diego Police Dept (1961)
Office of Naval Intelligence (1972)

CERTIFICATE OF INSURANCE

This certifies that   ☒ STATE FARM FIRE AND CASUALTY COMPANY, Bloomington, Illinois
     ☐ STATE FARM GENERAL INSURANCE COMPANY, Bloomington, Illinois
Insures the following policyholder for the coverages indicated below:

Name of policyholder   *Grady, Harry L & Keith H*

Address of policyholder   *Vancouver, Wa 98665*

Location of operations

POLICY NUMBER	TYPE OF INSURANCE	POLICY PERIOD Effective Date : Expiration Date	LIMITS OF LIABILITY
	☐ Comprehensive General Liability		Dual Limits for: BODILY INJURY
	☐ Manufacturers and Contractors Liability		Each Occurrence $ _____
	☐ Owners, Landlords, and Tenants Liability		Aggregate $ _____
This insurance includes:	☐ Products - Completed Operations		PROPERTY DAMAGE
	☐ Owners or Contractors Protective Liability		Each Occurrence $ _____
	☐ Contractual Liability		Aggregate* $ _____
	☐ Professional Errors and Omissions		BODILY INJURY AND PROPERTY DAMAGE
	☐ Broad Form Property Damage		☐ Combined Single Limit for:
	☐ Broad Form Comprehensive General Liability		Each Occurrence _____
			Aggregate _____

POLICY NUMBER	TYPE OF INSURANCE	POLICY PERIOD Effective Date : Expiration Date	CONTRACTUAL LIABILITY LIMITS (if different from above) BODILY INJURY
			Each Occurrence _____
			PROPERTY DAMAGE
			Each Occurrence _____
			Aggregate _____

POLICY NUMBER	TYPE OF INSURANCE	POLICY PERIOD Effective Date : Expiration Date	LIMITS
	EXCESS LIABILITY		BODILY INJURY AND PROPERTY DAMAGE (Combined Single Limit)
44-09-3662 5	☒ Umbrella ☐ Other _____	7/25/86 : 7-25-95	Each Occurrence $ 1,000,000 Aggregate $ 1,000,000
	☐ Workers' Compensation and Employers Liability		Part 1 STATUTORY Part 2 BODILY INJURY Each Accident $ _____ Disease Each Employee $ _____ Disease - Policy Limit $ _____

*Aggregate not applicable if Owners, Landlords, and Tenants Liability Insurance excludes structural alterations, new construction, or demolition.

THIS CERTIFICATE OF INSURANCE IS NOT A CONTRACT OF INSURANCE AND NEITHER AFFIRMATIVELY NOR NEGATIVELY AMENDS, EXTENDS, OR ALTERS THE COVERAGE APPROVED BY ANY POLICY DESCRIBED HEREIN.

Name and Address of Certificate Holder

Port of Portland
Box 5529
Portland, Or 97208

Signature of Authorized Representative

Title *Agent*

Date *6/29/94*

Agent's Date Stamp

Port of Portland

PERMIT AND RIGHT-OF-ENTRY

No. _____ 11-160

Date Issued: _____ 6/16/94

PERMITTEE:

Barry L. Grady

Vancouver, WA

The Port of Portland hereby grants to Permittee the right to enter upon and use the below-described premises in accordance with the terms and conditions set forth below and printed on the reverse side of this document.

Premises and Permitted Use: Hayden Island west of the Burlington Northern rail tracks. Search for the remains of D.B. Cooper. See Attached Exhibit "A". If any suspected remains are found, Permittee shall notify the Port and all appropriate legal authorities prior to any removal. No digging on the Premises shall be permitted. **

Term of Permit: The effective date of this Permit and Right-of-Entry shall be from _____ June 14 _____ 19 94,

to _____ May 31 _____ 19 95, unless terminated as provided herein.

Special Insurance Requirements: _____ None

Compensation to be Paid by Permittee: _____ No permit fee is payable under the terms of this permit.

** All search activities shall take place between the hours of 8am and 5pm M-F

Both parties agree to be bound by the terms and conditions of this Permit and Right-of-Entry.

PERMITTEE

By: _____

Typed Name: Barry L. Gray

Title: Private citizen

Date: 6-13-94

Address: _____

PORT OF PORTLAND

By: _____

Title: Sr. Director

Date: 6/16/94

Address: P.O. Box 3529

Portland, OR 97208

This form has been approved as to Legal Sufficiency by the Port's Legal Counsel. Any Special Insurance required by this Permit and Right-of-Entry shall be determined by the Port's Risk Management Division. All terms and conditions printed on the reverse side of this document are incorporated by reference herein and shall apply to this Permit and Right-of-Entry.

Form No. 138

THREE

The Key Missing Link

Where Did Cooper Bail out?

THE FIRST TIME I phoned Harry after receiving his parcel post package with his seven-year collection of D.B. Cooper material, his first exclamation was, "Why is there no report of Cooper's skyjacked plane being tracked on radar by the Portland Airport air traffic controllers?"

Of course, I hadn't even started to read any of the three books I intended to use in my investigation, but knowing Harry's investigative skills, I took notice. Then in the following weeks when I read Tosaw's and Himmelsbach's books and used a Hi-Liter felt-tip pen to highlight all information I thought was important or critical, I clearly saw that there was no mention of radar tracking of Cooper's skyjacked Flight 305 by Portland International Airport air traffic controllers. And if Flight 305 had been on automatic pilot course Vector-23, it would have flown only about five miles or less west of the Portland International Airport air traffic control tower, and about one mile east of the I-5 Freeway.

Shortly after Harry was discharged from the Navy after World War II, he took flying lessons on the G.I. Bill. He earned his pilot's license, and was well aware of FAA rules and radar tracking procedures. So, he knew radar tracking requirements. It was well reported in Tosaw's and Himmels-bach's books that on February 10, 1980, $5,800 of Cooper's ransom money was uncovered on a bank of the Columbia River known as Tina's Bar. Eight-year-old Brian Ingraham was digging a small pit to roast wieners on a family picnic when he uncovered the money packs. Two days later, on Tuesday, February 12, 1980, the Ingrahams took the money packs to the Portland FBI field office, and Special Agent Himmelsbach confirmed from the list of serial numbers that the money was indeed part of Cooper's ransom money.

Although Himmelsbach did not report it in his book, one of the newsclippings Harry had sent to me in his collection, and dated November 24, 1988, the seventeenth anniversary of Cooper's skyjacking, included some critical information. It reported that on February 29, 1980, over two weeks after the money find, copilot Rataczak visited Himmelsbach. (Note: Himmelsbach always spelled it "Radaczak" in his book, and Tosaw, the FAA and Northwest Airlines consistently spelled the copilot's name Rataczak). When Rataczak told Himmelsbach he had flown the plane manually, not on automatic pilot, and had drifted east of Vector-23, and probably over the Washougal River watershed, Himmels-bach learned for the first time that the FBI and two hundred or four hundred Fort Lewis soldiers (Tosaw reported four hundred and and Himmelsbach reported some 200 troops) had searched the wrong area, and at immense expense to the taxpayers. However, despite this seemingly new discovery, there was never any report of any later searches for Cooper's remains.

Himmelsbach repeatedly reported in his book that he was the Portland FBI field office case agent. He also reported that he had been an aircraft pilot since World War II, and still owned his own personal plane, a Beechcraft Bonanza. With that flying experience, and being appointed the Portland FBI field office Cooper case agent, Harry and I thought he should have known Cooper's skyjacked Flight 305 should have or would have been tracked on radar by the Portland International Airport air traffic controllers. But it has never been reported. (WHY?)

Furthermore, Tosaw reported that the entire six-member flight crew of Cooper's skyjacked Flight 305 was debriefed at Reno, just hours after the plane landed at that airport. In that Harry and I had conducted thousands of interviews and interrogations in our combined seventy-two years in law enforcement, it was obvious to us that none of the FBI special agents debriefing Co-pilot Rataczak and the other flight officers had asked them anything about how the plane was being flown, on automatic pilot or manually, to determine if it was on Vector-23 when Cooper jumped at 8:13 P.M. And Rataczak's report seventeen years later proved it had not been asked. (WHY?).

In that only the newsclipping reported Co-pilot Rataczak visiting Himmelsbach, and in that there were so many conflicting and contradictory reports between Tosaw's and Himmelsbach's books, I decided to try to personally contact the three flight officers to get the best information and specific details from the most reliable first-hand sources.

So, on March 1, 1994, I wrote to the Northwest Airlines headquarters in Minneapolis requesting the home addresses of the three flight officers of Cooper's skyjacked plane. On April 6, 1994, a law clerk sent me a letter stating that they had forwarded a copy of my letter to the flight officers, and if they wanted to get involved in my investigation, they would contact me directly. But I never heard from any of them. (WHY?).

Then, on April 29, 1994, I wrote to the FAA in Oklahoma City requesting the home addresses of Captain William A. Scott, Co-pilot William J. Rataczak and Flight Engineer Harold E. Anderson. Surprisingly, the FAA responded with the home addresses of Co-pilot Rataczak and Flight Engineer Anderson, but amazingly, they stated that they could not locate any information on Captain Scott. But it wasn't very important, because I knew from the books and 1988 newsclipping that Co-pilot Rataczak had flown the plane from Seattle Airport until Cooper jumped at 8:13 P.M., then all the way to Reno, where Captain Scott took over the controls to land at the Reno Airport.

Other than Tosaw's theory of Cooper landing safely in the Columbia River, being pulled under by the twenty-one-pound bag of money, and drowning, the only other flaw in his book that I could find was his two conflicting reports of who flew the plane starting at the Seattle Airport en route to Reno. On Page 9 of Tosaw's book, he reported that

THE KEY MISSING LINK [19]

Captain Scott would fly the plane, and Co-pilot Rataczak would handle the communications. Then on Page 33, he reported Co-pilot Rataczak was at the controls when the tower gave clearance to take off. Then on Page 38, he reported as they approached the Reno Airport, Captain Scott took the controls as they started their descent to land.

Not to criticize Tosaw for this minor conflicting report, because he did an outstanding job of reporting this confused case, and it was most valuable to us in our investigation.

I had to assume Co-pilot Rataczak had flown the plane, because on one of my several flights from Los Angeles LAX Airport to Sacramento Airport to instruct a class at the CHP Academy, I rode in the cockpit of a Pacific Southwest Airlines plane in 1972. I had to go into the cockpit to get the captain's approval to carry my off-duty gun on the plane. The captain turned out to be an old high school classmate of mine, and he told me to ride in the cockpit. I did, and as we talked, the co-pilot flew the plane until we started the descent nearing Sacramento. He then said we couldn't talk anymore, because this was the really hard part. He then took the controls from the co-pilot and made a perfect landing. As he maneuvered to land, the silence and tension in the cockpit was electrifying.

I was lucky enough to get Co-pilot Rataczak's home phone number from directory assistance, and I phoned his home on two Saturdays. Both times, a women answered, said he wasn't home, and said she didn't know when he would return home. It was quite obvious to me that he knew who I was from the copy of my letter sent to him by

Northwest Airlines, and he didn't want to, or for some reason couldn't, talk to me. (WHY?)

When I told Harry in a phone conversation of my efforts to contact the captain and co-pilot with no responses, he angrily said, "You would think everybody would want to solve this case, and especially them."

Harry was already irritated, because he had also had no response when he attempted to get in contact with flight attendant Tina Mucklow, who was probably the most critical witness to Cooper's attire, conduct and actions. Tosaw wrote in his book that Tina Mucklow had become a Catholic nun and was in the Carmelite Order Convent in Eugene, Oregon, and he had interviewed her. Harry had been a very devout Catholic all of his life, so he sent a letter to Sister Tina Mucklow at the convent on April 23, 1994, requesting an interview, or permission to send her a list of questions I had prepared for her to answer. He wrote that he and I were retired law enforcement officers with a combined total of over seventy years experience, that he was a Catholic, said if he could interview her, he would bring his wife with him, and he enclosed a self-addressed-stamped envelope. But he never received any response. (WHY?)

Harry and I were very puzzled about why Tosaw was so freely able to interview Sister Tina, when he had been an FBI agent for only five years in the early 1950s, not a career law enforcement officer as Harry and I had been, was an attorney, and a free-lance investigator. (WHY?)

To make it more suspicious about why there was no report of the Portland International Airport air traffic controllers radar tracking Cooper's skyjacked Flight 305, Rhodes wrote in his book, *D.B. COOPER: The Real McCoy*, that the Salt Lake City FBI field office had had a hijacking plan since 1970, the year before the Cooper skyjacking. That year, Director J. Edgar Hoover had directed all FBI field offices to develop hijacking plans for approval by headquarters. The Salt Lake City hijacking plan included three teams with two predesignated special agents assigned to each team. "Team One" was to go to the air control tower of any commercial airport that could be affected.

It was well known inside and outside the FBI that when Director Hoover gave any direction whatsoever, it would be complied with, or else! Hoover had the sole authority to hire, transfer and fire special agents, which he did with an iron fist.

With that reported directive, the Portland FBI field office must have had a hijacking plan as good or better than that of Salt Lake City, and if they did, why was there no report that it had been implemented? (WHY?)

Himmelsbach reported that when he arrived at the Portland International Airport, there were already FBI cars parked in the parking lot. He later reported many FBI agents were at the airport interviewing Northwest Airlines employees, baggage handlers, limousine drivers, and others to find out if they had seen Cooper, and if they knew where he had come from.

But he did not report any FBI agents being in the air controllers' tower, and this was before Cooper's skyjacked Flight 305 had taken off from the Seattle SEATAC Airport. (WHY?)

Rhodes also reported that the Federal Aviation Administration (FAA) had regional control facilities that had the responsibility of tracking all aircraft on airways from their point of origin to their destination. One was in Auburn, Washington, about one hundred miles north of Portland.

To further confuse the tracking of Flight 305, as soon as the flight officers were informed of Cooper's skyjacking, Tosaw reported that Co-pilot Rataczak immediately contacted Northwest Airlines headquarters in Minneapolis. He was transferred to Paul Soderlind, the company's Director of Flight Operations-Technical, and chief troubleshooter.

Then when Cooper jumped at 8:13 P.M., Soderlind drew an area map where he thought Cooper had jumped: it extended south for about twenty miles from Woodland, Washington to Portland. Relying on this information from over 1,500 miles to the east, instead of tracking Flight 305 on radar at the Portland International Airport, the area near Woodland was searched for weeks by numerous FBI special agents, local law enforcement, and four hundred or about two hundred Fort Lewis soldiers. But they did not find anything related to Cooper.

Tosaw reported that he began his investigation by interviewing Paul Soderlind and all members of the flight crew. He said Soderlind reviewed the flight data and drew a diagram. When Tosaw looked at the diagram, he was surprised to see that Cooper could have landed in the Columbia River.

In order for Cooper to land in the Columbia River, Flight 305 would have had to be south of the river, because it runs due east and west at the Portland International Airport, then bends to the north about ten miles west of the airport. That supported Harry's Columbia River island theory of where Cooper's remains are located.

Most interesting was that Tosaw reported when he interviewed the flight officers, they gave him the notes they had taken during the skyjacked flight. Cooper had given Flight Attendant Florence Shaffner two notes of demands to deliver to the captain. She took the notes to the cockpit, then when she started to leave to return to Cooper's location, Co-pilot Rataczak told her to stay in the cockpit and take notes, which she did.

That flight officers were still in possession of handwritten notes taken during the skyjacking over ten years after the skyjacking was incredible to Harry and me. All thorough, dedicated, competent investigators collect every piece, scrap, and bit of potential evidence as soon as possible that might be of value at a later time, regardless of how insignificant it may appear to be at the time of the initial investigation.

To make it more interesting, Tosaw was the only author who reported anything about the notes, and if it was true, which Harry and I had every reason to believe, because his book was the most complete and accurate, then the FBI had not taken possession of the notes during their investigation. (WHY?)

Also, Himmelsbach reported that the flight officers knew within two minutes after leaving the Portland terminal that they were being skyjacked. That was before the flight officers contacted Northwest Airlines headquarters by radio and were transferred to communicate with Paul Soderlind.

So, flying from Portland to Seattle, they most certainly had to stay in radio contact with one of those airport control towers at all times to comply with FAA rules. Cooper said he wanted to be flown to Mexico City, which would require refueling stops at Reno and Yuma, and would take Flight 305 over Portland, where Portland traffic controllers most certainly had to radar track Flight 305. But there was no report of that tracking. (WHY?).

Also, when Harry first told me about no reports of Cooper's skyjacked plane being radar-tracked by Portland International Airport traffic controllers, he said all commercial airports had to start tracking aircraft when it came within five miles of their air space. Although Harry had earned his pilot's license on the G.I. Bill in the 1940s upon being discharged from the Navy after World War II, he was no longer flying when I worked with him in 1952 and 1953. And about ten years later, commercial airlines converted from propeller-driven aircraft to jet aircraft, which is about three times faster than propeller-driven aircraft.

At the time I was authoring this book, that made me wonder if the FAA rules had changed to a greater distance for jet aircraft to be radar tracked when they entered an airport's air space. More important, I wondered what the FAA tracking rules were at the time of Cooper's jump in 1971.

So, I wrote a letter to the FAA in Renton, Washington requesting that information. The FAA was most cooperative and replied about a month later. They wrote that they had searched for 1971 records, but they had been destroyed. However, the 1971 rules were similar to those published in 1978, that stated in essence: in general, that Seattle Air

Route Traffic Control Center would hand off the aircraft to Portland Terminal Radar Approach Control about thirty to fifty miles out and they would transfer the flight to Portland Air Traffic Control Tower at about five to seven miles out. That confirmed Harry's FAA rules knowledge, and more!

March 1, 1994

Chief Executive ████████████,
Northwest Airlines
5101 Northwest Drive
St. Paul, Minnesota 55111-3034

Subject: D.B. Cooper Investigation.

Dear Mr. ████████:

In that the D.B. Cooper case has fascinated my 1950s San Diego
Police Department partner, Harry Grady, and me since the crime
was committed, we have collaborated in reviewing and analyzing
all of the available publications and media reports on the
subject. Furthermore, in that Harry has lived in Vancouver for
nearly ten years, within view of where Brian Ingram found $5,800
of the ransom money, he has been analyzing the case since moving
to that area.

With our combined eighty plus years of investigative experience,
analysis of the publicized data for over the past year, and
unpublished data and circumstantial evidence witnesses that
Harry has discovered, we are confident that we can bring the
case to a logical conclusion once and for all. Actually, with
Harry's systematic analysis of all of the data, information
from newly located witnesses, and his in-depth knowledge of
the area, we strongly believe that we may locate Cooper's
remains, the ransom money, and/or other evidence of D.B.'s fate.
Or in any event, we believe we can disprove the theories and
conclusions of Himmelsbach and Tosaw.

In early summer 1994, I will travel to Vancouver to spend as
much time as is necessary for us to isolate our search areas
and conduct a complete and systematic search.

However, due to incomplete and/or conflicting publicized data,
it would assist us greatly if we could contact the flight crew
members of Flight 305 from Portland to Seattle on 11-24-71,
scheduled departure time of 2:50 P.M. The flight engineer, if
one was aboard, was not mentioned in publications and should
be of great assistance. Those publicized, and some of their
reported areas of residence were:

Pilot: Captain William Scott, ████████████

Co-pilot: William Radaczak (or Rataczak), ██████████
            ████████

Flight
Attendants: Tina Mucklow, ██████████████████.
            Alice Hancock.
            Florence Schaffner.

1

We would greatly appreciate your providing us with a means of contacting all of the above listed crew members, including the unidentified flight engineer, if there was one on board. Or, forward a copy of this letter to each of them so they could contact me if they so desire.

Also, if you could provide the following information:
1. The name and address of Northwest Airline's insurance carrier who suffered the $200,000 D.B. Cooper loss.
2. If there is a reward for recovery of the balance of the lost money, or portion thereof.
3. If Northwest Airline or their insurance carrier that suffered the D.B. Cooper loss would assist in any manner whatsoever in our investigation and search of the very limited areas where Cooper most certainly landed.

In that the D.B. Cooper case is one of the major unsolved crimes of recent times, Harry and I are determined to put all of our combined expertise toward conclusively proving the fate of Cooper, and if possible, to recover what's left of the money. Actually, it's a personal and professional challenge that we can't overlook, and we will not give up until we have solved it or hopelessly exhausted every imaginable possibility. And if we do establish conclusive evidence of the fate of Cooper, or completely disprove other theories or conclusions publicized by others, I intend to author a script or book manuscript on the entire case.

We hope that you share our interest in this matter and can provide us with the above requested information and/or action.

In closing, I wish to express my greatest admiration for you for your refusing the $750,000 bonus. We need your kind of leadership and unselfishness from Washington down to the lowest level of management for our nation to survive economically and morally.

Most sincerely,

George C. Nuttall, Captain, California Highway Patrol, Retired.
                                California Private Investigator
                                License # ████████

Telephone: ████████████
Pager:

cc: file

[28]   G E O R G E   C.   N U T T A L L

April 29, 1994

FAA Airmen Certification Branch AVN-460
Box 25082
Oklahoma City, Oklahoma 73125

Subject: D.B Cooper Case - Flight Crew of Northwest Airlines
           Flight Number 305 - November 24, 1971.

To Whom It May Concern:

Hopefully, you will be able to provide the current addresses
or contact addresses for the below listed flight officers of
the much publicized Subject D.B. Cooper case. To do so would
greatly assist my over 40 year friend and 1952-53 San Diego
Police Department partner, Harry L. Grady, in our serious
investigation of this yet unsolved case. Combined, Harry and
I accumulated over 80 years of investigative experience, and
from our to-date review and analysis, are 90 percent certain
the man known as D.B. Cooper did not survive his jump and his
remains are somewhere to be found in the rugged country near
Harry's present residence of Vancouver, Washington.

However, the publicized data accumulated by us to-date is
somewhat conflicting and/or vague. Therefore, we are convinced
the flight officers could provide the best estimate of the data
needed to establish the most probable search areas where Cooper
would have landed, with or without the benefit of an open
parachute. With or without further data, we will initiate our
team search of the most probable landing areas in June 1994.

Although I lack birthdates for the below listed Northwest
Airlines Flight 305 Flight Officers, I hope the notoriety of
the case will be assist in lieu of DOBs. They are all believed
to reside in Minnesota and are:

    1. Captain/Pilot William A. Scott.
    2. Copilot William J. Rataczak.
    3. Flight Engineer/Second Officer Harold E. Anderson.

Any assistance you can provide will be greatly appreciated.

Most sincerely,

George C. Nuttall, Captain, California Highway Patrol, retired.

cc: file

May 4, 1994

Captain William A. Scott
Copilot William J Rataczak
Flight Engineer Harold E. Anderson

Dear Gentlemen:

Please pardon this imposition, but your assistance could be
critical to the very belated search for D.B. Cooper's remains
and remaining ransom money by my partner, Harry L. Grady, and
myself, starting in June of this year.

Combined, Harry and I gained nearly 80 years investigative
experience in varied law enforcement/investigative services,
and have been friends since we were partners on the San Diego
P.D. in 1952-53. I have enclosed a couple of documents to support
our past search accomplishments, and to prove to some degree
that we are serious and capable in the D.B. Cooper case. With
respect to the letter, I actually located the escapee, but let
the sheriff's captain apprehend Richardson because the captain's
career was on the line for letting the prisoner escape
in the first place. It saved the captain's career and he later
became the undersheriff of San Bernardino County. And that's
the teamwork attitude that Harry and I share for the public
good, regardless of the mission.

In the D.B. Cooper case, we believe even a late final solution
would be of some service to the public. Harry has been gathering
and analyzing all available data since he moved to Vancouver,
Washington, in 1986, then he invited me to join him as a partner
in this case a year ago. Since then, we have concluded that
there is a 90 percent chance that Cooper did not survive his
jump and his remains are out there to be found. The 1980 find
of the $5,800 by Brian Ingram strongly supports this conclusion
and indicates the general area of Cooper's landing. Even FBI
Agent Ralph Himmelsbach admitted in his book, NORJAK, that the
find proved to him that the FBI had searched the wrong areas
in 1971-72.

Therefore, in order to best calculate where Cooper may have
landed and to enhance our chances of success, your completion
of the enclosed questionnaire would of great assistance in
minimizing the target areas.

If Harry and I do locate conclusive proof of D.B. Cooper's
demise, we intend to co-author a book manuscript or movie script
covering the entire case, but with a definite conclusion - not
another unsolved mystery for publicity and profit.

1

With certain news media interest in any new conclusive discovery
in this well-publicized case, and our plans to author a script
or manuscript to explain our acquired investigative methods,
it presents the issue of including mention of those who
contributed to any success, or protecting from publicity those
who prefer anonymity.

In considering both of these possibilities with the utmost
respect, and our desire for any information that any of you
can provide, we ask that none of you positively identify
yourselves, if you complete and return the enclosed
questionnaire. If one or more did so, obviously, we could
possibly identify the other(s) by process of elimination.
However, if any or all would desire ackowledgement and credit
for contributions to any success that we may have, please enter
a random, confidential number/name on the line at the bottom.
Either way, it would help us to protect the confidentiality
of one or all of you, if that is what your responses indicate.

Regardless of your recollections of the requested data, etc.,
even the smallest details could help. Harry has located Tina
Mucklow at a Carmelite Convent in Oregon, but any response by
her will also be protected to the fullest, should she desire
it to be so, including whether she was ever contacted or
responded.

As nearly lifelong cops, the D.B. Cooper case is a serious
personal and professional challenge to Harry and me. Primarily,
because we have clearly identified many crucial parts of the
case that were missed, or discovered too late to be diligently
pursued because of the apparent loss of interest. And it is
obvious that the FBI focused on live leads, foot-searching the
wrong areas, and air-searches for an opened chute, rather than
intensely searching the most probable area(s) where Cooper would
have landed if his chute(s) did not open based on the most
precise calculations from where Cooper most likely jumped.

It is not our intention to embarrass anybody if we are
successful, including the FBI or Agent Himmelsbach. However,
we would let the facts of the entire case tell the story.

Thank you in advance for any information that you can provide.

Most sincerely,

George C. Nuttall, Captain, California Highway Patrol, retired.
███████████████████████████████.

Telephone: ████████████   enclosure
                                            cc: file

2

When Cooper was believed to have jumped at 8:13 P.M.:

1. Flight 305 was: A. On Victor-23 _____.

   B. West of Victor-23, approximately _____miles.

   C. East of Victor-23, approximately _____miles.

2. Compass heading was _____ degrees.

3. Were there any ground-based light reflections or other indications of location: No _____. Yes _____. If Yes, please describe:

_____

_____

_____.

4. Course was in line with the I-5 Freeway: Yes _____ No _____.

   If Yes, course was approximately _____ miles

      West _____ East _____ of I-5 Freeway.

5. Altitude _____.

6. Wind: Headwind of _____ knots at _____ degrees.

      Crosswind of _____ knots from _____ degrees.

7. Speed: Knots _____ or MPH _____.

8. Temperature: Celcius _____ or Fahrenheit _____.

9. Cloud cover ceiling of _____ feet.

Upon arriving at Reno:

1. Number and type(s) of parachutes found on plane:

   A. Two, neither marked with an "X" _____.

   B. Two, one marked with an "X" _____.

   C. Three, one marked with an "X" _____.

   D. Three, none marked with an "X" _____.

Please use reverse side for any additional comments.

CONFIDENTIAL CODE LETTERS OR NUMBERS _____.

July 14, 1994

Mr. William J. Rataczak

Dear Mr. Rataczak:

My past attempts to contact you through Northwest Airlines and
by phone have been unsuccessful, so I hope this last effort
will prove to be of benefit to all concerned.

My D.B. Cooper search partner and friend of over 40 years, Harry
Grady, and I can well appreciate that you have no doubt been
contacted far too many times about this case and are tired of
it. The number and frequency of persons pursuing the case was
explained to us by Earl Cossey, the parachute packer who packed
the Cooper chutes. However, Cossey was extremely helpful, as
was retired FBI Agent Ralph Himmelsbach, in providing us with
crucial facts to establish our search areas.

As you can see from the enclosed newsclipping, Harry Grady was
solely responsible for the eventual finding of one deceased
missing person through his acquired knowledge of human behavior
and innate tenacity. And that is what has spearheaded our efforts
to find Cooper's remains, or any conclusive proof of his fate.
We are not seeking the remaining ransom money because we are
certain it all fell into the Columbia River or is nearly totally
decayed if it fell on land.

Our sole purpose is professional in that solving cases was our
job for a combined total of nearly 80 years. If we succeed,
there would no doubt be a media frenzy that we have agreed to
deal with in a highly professional manner. And I believe it
would be worthy of publication, so I would try to author a book
manuscript detailing our research and analysis.

In that Harry is 73 years of age and lives in Vancouver,
Washington, he is searching on a regular schedule. However,
it would assist us greatly if you would provide us with your
best estimate answers to the questions on the enclosed
questionnaire. To do so could further isolate the most logical
search areas to prove in due time whether Harry and I are crazy
or not. Cossey started his very gracious personal interview
with us at his home by stating "I think you're both crazy."
We agreed that he could be right, but we later countered with
our opinions that anybody who would jump out of airplanes for
the fun of it had to be completely crazy. Thanks to Cossey,
it was a very enjoyable and enlightening experience. And from
what he explained to us about parachutes and parachuting, we

-1-

all share the opinion that Cooper did not survive the jump.
Ralph Himmelsbach also expressed this opinion.

Therefore, in that Harry and I are "Over-the hill" in age, we
could use your input to best isolate the most logical search
areas to minimize the time required to cover it thoroughly and
completely. We are also of the opinion that other unrelated
bodies or evidence of other crimes may be discovered in the
process, as was the case when the Army troops searched near
the Lewis River.

It may sound like we are crazy, but that's what police work
is all about. And we both became addicted to it as we grew up
in San Diego, long before we worked as partners on the San Diego
P.D. in 1952-1953. Everybody should have a hobby to enjoy life
to its fullest, and ours is trying to solve crimes as we did
for most of our lives as cops.

We fully realize that the weather, flying conditions and obvious
unusual distractions during the Cooper flight could have
detracted from your normal observations, but we would most
sincerely appreciate your providing your best estimate answers
to the questionnaire and returning same in the enclosed self-
addressed stamped envelope. To do so would make two crazy old
cops very happy.

Thank you in advance for your cooperation. And if you choose
not to respond, we completely understand and thank you for
reading this rambling mess, if you actually did so.

Most sincerely,

George C. Nuttall, Captain, California Highway Patrol, retired.

Telephone:

enclosure
cc: file
    Harry Grady

D.B. COOPER

1. What was your flight path in relation to Victor-23 at
   8:13 P.M. when Cooper was believed to have jumped?

   _____
   _____
   _____ .

2. Did Seattle Center Radar Control have Flight 305 on screen
   from Seattle to Portland?

   _____
   _____ .

3. Did Portland (PDX) have Flight 305 on their radar screen
   while in the PDX control Zone?

   _____
   _____ .

4. Did you see the glow of any city lights below at or near
   8:13 P.M. to indicate your location at that time?

   _____
   _____
   _____
   _____
   _____ .

5. The most important question: What is your best estimate of
   Flight 305's flight path in relation to Victor-23 when it
   passed over the Columbia River?

   _____
   _____
   _____
   _____
   _____ .

Department Number

A1170

Northwest Airlines Inc
5101 Northwest Drive
St Paul MN 55111-3034

NORTHWEST AIRLINES

April 6, 1994

George C. Nuttall

Re: D.B. Cooper Investigation

Dear Mr. Nuttall:

Your letter of March 1, 1994 to ███████ has been forwarded to
me for handling.

In response to your request for contact information for the flight
crew, I have forwarded a copy of your March 1, 1994 letter to three
of those individuals you identified: William Scott, William
Rataczak and Alice Hancock. If those individuals wish to become
involved in your investigation, they will contact you directly. We
are unable to locate addresses for Tina Mucklow and Florence
Schaffner.

In response to your request for the name and address of Northwest
Airline's insurance carrier, our records indicate that the
insurer's name was Global Indemnity. The bond policy number was
471954; the original claim was handled out of Global Indemnity's
New York Office located at 150 William Street. The current mailing
address is: Royal Insurance Group/Global Indemnity, P.O. Box 1000,
9300 Arrowpoint Blvd., Charlotte, NC 28273-8135.

Good luck in your investigation.

Sincerely,

NORTHWEST AIRLINES, INC.

Law Clerk, Labor Relations

**U.S. Department
of Transportation**

**Federal Aviation
Administration**

Office of
Aviation System Standards

P.O. Box 25082
Oklahoma City, Oklahoma 73125

JUN 0 1 1994

Mr. George C. Nuttall

Dear Mr. Nuttall:

Thank you for your letter of April 29, requesting
the current address of Harold Ellsworth Anderson,
William John Rataczak and William A. Scott.

Our records show Harold Ellsworth Anderson last reported
his address on April 29, 1982, as  and William John Rataczak
last reported his address on March 14, 1994, as

We have searched our files and are unable to find a record of
William A. Scott, based on the information provided. In order
to make positive identification on the airman, please provide
identifying information such as full name, date of birth,
certificate number, social security number, etc., and enclose
a copy of this letter with your response.

If you require further assistance, please contact the Airmen
Certification Branch at (405) 954-3261.

Sincerely,

Manager, Airmen Certification Branch

CONFIDENTIAL - QUESTIONS FOR SISTER TINA MUCKLOW.

MONEY BAG:
1. Did the money bag have zipper, straps, buckles, ties, etc., to keep it reasonably securely closed during the fall in an up to 300 mile per hour wind?

2. If yes to #1, did Cooper secure the closing device in your presence?

3. Describe how Cooper tied the money bag to his waist.
   A. Was he tying the money bag tightly to his waist, or was he tying a tether cord from his waist to the money bag as shown on page 26 of Tosaw's book?

MONEY:

1. Did Cooper offer some of the ransom money to Alice Hancock and/or Florence Shaffner as they deplaned at Sea-Tac?

2. If yes to #1, how many bundles did he offer to them? Could it have been three bundles of $2,000, the same as was found by Brian Ingram in February 1980?

3. If yes to #1, did Cooper return the bundles to the money bag and secure them therein with the rest of the ransom money?

CHUTES:

1. Did you observe Cooper sort out the chutes or attach any of them to his person?

2. Did you personally observe and identify any of the chutes that remained on the plane after landing at Reno?

3. If yes to 1 and/or 2, how many chutes remained on the plane at Reno?

1

4. If yes to any or all of the above, was the dummy chute marked with an "X" still on the plane in Reno?

5. If yes to any or all of the above, can you describe the chutes that were still on the plane in Reno?

FLIGHT CABIN (ABSOLUTELY AND COMPLETELY CONFIDENTIAL):

1. Was the plane being manually flown by Captain Scott or Co-pilot Rataczak?

2. Was Second Officer Anderson involved in any way in the flight operation? And if so, to what extent?

3. Were all of the flight officers, Scott and Rataczak in particular, calm, rational, and completely in control of their emotions with respect to the situation? (Please describe the tense atmosphere and its affect on the flight officers with respect to their being aware of their flight course, speed, altitude, etc.).

4. Were you watching any of the flight instruments to confirm the flight course, speed, altitude, etc.).

5. Did you observe any light reflections from below to indicate your location at any time prior to or at the time Cooper was believed to have jumped?

6. Was the flight officer piloting the plane trying to follow the course of the I-5 Freeway to any extent?

7. Did any of the flight officers indicate in any way that their flight course was to the east or west of the Victor 23 automatic-pilot course?

8. Was there an indication by instrument or cabin pressure
   change that Cooper's body weight lowered the rear staircase
   two times, including the time he went to the bottom of
   of the staircase to jump? (If so, the first time may have
   been to throw the attache case with the reported dynamite
   out of the plane before he jumped).

9. Do you believe the rear staircase indicator light change
   and change of cabin pressure at approximately 8:13 P.M.
   was the definite signal that Cooper had jumped at that
   time?

10. If yes to #9, did you see any ground light reflections
    or anything whatsoever that gave an indication of the
    the planes location and course at that time?

11. Prior to, or at the time of Cooper's jump, was there any
    indication in any way that the flight officer piloting
    the plane had changed course from southeast to southwest
    over Battle Ground or Ariel to follow flight course
    Victor 23?

12. Was there ever any mention by any of the flight officers
    that the flight instruments were not accurate or were
    malfunctioning?

13. Was there any mention by any of the flight officers that
    they were or were not heading at 148 degrees before or
    after passing over Battle Ground or Ariel?

14. Was there any mention of the headwind speed of the wind
    from the southwest at the time Cooper was believed to
    have jumped (from 10,000 feet ?) and the speed of the
    headwind or crosswind?

15. From all of your observations in the flight cabin, what was your best calculation of Flight 305s location, direction and altitude when Cooper was believed to have jumped?

COOPER:

1. From all of your observations of Cooper, did you ever form the opinion that he was of sound mind? Or that he was so desperate that he would face about a 90-95 percent chance of death to escape with the ransom money?

2. Did you ever perceive from your observation of all of the other 36 passengers that one of them could have been a Cooper accomplice who may have brought foul weather clothing and jump boots on board in carry-on luggage for Cooper?

FBI DEBRIEFING AND CREW MEMBERS (ALSO, ABSOLUTELY AND COMPLETELY CONFIDENTIAL):

1. Did the FBI Special Agents conduct a well-organized, controlled, articulate, complete and comprehensive debriefing?

2. How many FBI Special Agents were involved in the Debriefing?

3. Were you and the three flight officers all debriefed at the same time in the same room by the same FBI Special Agents?

4. If yes to #3, were there any conflicting accounts, data, etc., given by different crew members regarding any specifics, especially flight course, altitude, location, times, etc.?

5. If yes to #4, who do you believe gave the most accurate data, or who agreed on what appeared to be the most accurate data?

4

6. If yes to #3, was the Debriefing confused by too many FBI Agents asking too many speculative questions without systematic control by one or more agents?

7. If yes to #3, did any one or more crew members dominate the answering of Debriefing questions at the expense of others who had more accurate data to present?

8. Did any personality conflicts appear to arise between crew members and/or FBI Agents during the Debriefing that could have hindered the gathering of the most accurate and valid investigative data?

9. Did you at any time during the Debriefing feel intimidated by the flight officers or FBI Agents during the Debriefing to the extent that you did not have the opportunity to present your most accurate and complete account of your observations and perceptions?

10. Were you ever extensively interviewed or debriefed by FBI Agents, alone, at any time after the initial Debriefing at Reno?

GENERAL:

Can you offer any opinions or conclusions regarding any issue or condition regarding your observations and perceptions of the D.B. Cooper Case, not covered in any or all of the above?

U.S. Department
of Transportation
**Federal Aviation
Administration**

Northwest Mountain Region
Office of the Regional Administrator

1601 Lind Avenue Southwest
Renton, Washington 98057

DEC 0 3 2009

CERTIFIED MAIL – RETURN RECEIPT REQUESTED

Mr. George C. Nuttall
Captain, California Highway Patrol, Retired
██████████████

Dear Mr. Nuttall:

Subject: Freedom of Information Act (FOIA) Request 2010-000819WS

This is a Northwest Mountain Region, Air Traffic Organization (ATO), Western Service
Area, no-records response to your FOIA request of October 31, 2009, made under the
provisions of Title 5 United States Code, Section 552. You requested a copy of records
regarding Federal Aviation Administration (FAA) rules governing air traffic control and
radar tracking.

A search for records was conducted at the Seattle Air Route Traffic Control Center
(ARTCC), the Portland Airport Traffic Control Tower (ATCT), the Portland Terminal Radar
Approach Control (TRACON) facility, the Seattle TRACON facility, and with the archivist
within the Western Service Center on various dates in November of 2009. The search
revealed no records, documents, or files pertaining to your specific request.

While we were unable to locate any particular responsive records, we were able to determine
that FAA Order 7110.65, *Air Traffic Control*, was first published in January of 1978, long
after the incident to which your request referred. In trying to locate responsive records, we
were informed that the "rules" in 1971 were similar to those in effect today. You may
research a current copy of Order 7110.65 on the FAA website. In general, the ARTCC
would hand off the aircraft to the TRACON about 30 to 50 miles out and the TRACON
would transfer the flight to the ATCT about 5 to 7 miles out.

Any Orders pertaining to your request covering air traffic control from 1971 have been
destroyed in accordance with FAA Order 1350.15C, Records Organization, Transfer and
Destruction Standards.

Your request qualifies for the "All Other" fee category whereby you are not charged for the
first 2 hours of search time, any review time, and the first 100 pages of documents. There is
no charge to process this request.

The undersigned and John Warner, Acting Director, ATO, Western Service Center, are responsible for this no-records response to your request. You may request reconsideration of this determination by writing to the Assistant Administrator for Regions and Center Operations, Federal Aviation Administration, 800 Independence Avenue, S.W., Washington, D.C. 20591. Your request for reconsideration must be made in writing within 30 days from the date of this letter, state that it is an appeal from an adverse determination made under FOIA, and include all information and arguments relied upon. Please include your assigned FOIA control number and mark the envelope "FOIA."

If you have questions, please contact ██████████, FOIA Officer, ATO, Western Service Area, at ████████

Sincerely,

Regional Administrator
Northwest Mountain Region

FOUR

D.B. Cooper Skyjacking

The Desperation, Death-Defying Jump

B ASED MOSTLY ON TOSAW'S book, because of some
conflicting and contradictory reports in the other
books authored in part by retired FBI special agents, and
because his was the most concise, specific, and thorough,
the D.B. Cooper skyjacking can be recounted as follows:

On Wednesday, Thanksgiving Eve, November 24, 1971,
shortly before 3:00 P.M., a man reported by witnesses to be in
his mid-forties approached the Northwest Airlines ticket
counter at the Portland International Airport and ordered a
one-way ticket to Seattle. He gave his name for the flight manifest as "Dan Cooper," and paid for the $20 ticket with a $20
bill. He then asked the ticket agent if his Flight 305 was a 727.
The ticket agent replied that his flight was a 727.

Cooper carried a brief case (or attaché case as described
by others), and he was later described by witnesses as

wearing a dark or black, narrow-lapelled business suit and lightweight raincoat (some witnesses reported dark and others reported black); a white dress shirt; a narrow, black tie; and slip-on loafers, and he was not carrying any luggage other than a briefcase (or attaché case). And Himmelsbach reported Cooper was wearing a pearl stickpin in his tie, that he was the last of thirty-six passengers to board Flight 305, and he that sat in seat 18E, (Himmelsbach reported he sat in seat 18C) the middle seat of the last row to the right of the aisle, and nobody sat in either seat to the right or left of him.

Because of the short, thirty-minute flight to Seattle, drinks were being served while the plane was still at the gate, and Cooper ordered two bourbon-and-water high-balls. He was served by flight attendant Florence Shaffner. The drinks were a dollar each. He paid her with a $20 bill, and she gave him $18 in change.

While the flight officers were waiting for clearance from the tower to take off, Florence sat in a folding seat attached to the rear door a few feet from Cooper. He held out an envelope to Florence and said it was for her. Florence thought it was just another attempt to strike up a conversation for whatever reason, and she wasn't interested. Cooper insisted, and when she took it and read the note inside, it read that he had a bomb in his brief case, he was hijacking the plane, and for her to sit next to him.

When Florence was seated next to him, he told her he wanted $200,000 in used bills in a knapsack, and two-chest pack and two backpack parachutes; he would release the other passengers after refueling (he released the other passengers before refueling); he then wanted to take off from Seattle by 5:00 P.M.

Florence wrote his demands on the back of the envelope
he had given to her and started to go to the cockpit to
deliver his demands to Captain Scott. Cooper had seen
Florence slip his note to flight attendant Tina Mucklow,
and he told Florence to take that note to the captain also.

As soon as Florence was seated next to Cooper, he had
reached under his seat and pulled his briefcase up and onto
his lap. He opened it up and showed her what he claimed to
be a bomb. She saw several red cylinders that looked more
like highway flares than dynamite, and they were about the
same color as her uniform, which was burnt-red. But she was
not about to challenge the authenticity of his claim, so she
took the two notes to the cockpit as directed. When she told
the flight officers the color of the alleged explosive sticks,
they agreed with her that they would not question his claim.

Flight 305 became airborne at 2:58 P.M., and in those
days, banks closed at 3:00 P.M., except on Fridays, when
they remained open until 6:00 P.M., because most workers
were paid on Fridays.

For that reason, Cooper's demand to leave Seattle SEATAC
Airport by 5:00 P.M. was not realistic or rational, because
the FBI would have to get one or more banks to open for
them after closing to get $200,000 in used bills, and also
locate a knapsack and four parachutes in less than two
hours. Being Thanksgiving Eve, many or most bankers and
parachute services and sporting goods store operators were
most likely more interested in an early Thanksgiving cele-
bration than working.

One of the many contradictory reports in the two primary books I referred to was Cooper's choice of parachutes.

Tosaw reported that three civilian chutes and one military chute, an NB-8 emergency military chute, were delivered to Cooper, and that he jumped with the NB-8 military chute. When Harry and I interviewed Earl Cossey, the parachute rigger who owned the chutes provided to Cooper, he told us the only chute not returned to him was the NB-8 military chute. He also said one of the three civilian chutes returned to him had shroud lines cut from it, and one was missing the canvas cover case.

Conversely, Himmelsbach wrote that Cooper demanded civilian chutes because he apparently knew the military chutes suggested would open automatically after two hundred feet. (WHY?) It was and still is inconceivable to me how an inanimate chute can know when it has fallen two hundred feet or is on a garage shelf, in the trunk of a car, or anywhere else in the world, moving or stationary.

Cooper had demanded that they not land at Seattle Airport until the money, knapsack and chutes were there and ready for delivery to him. Being Thanksgiving Eve and after banks had closed, at 3:00 P.M., only two minutes after Flight 305 had airlifted from the Portland Airport, they had to go into a holding pattern, over Puget Sound in case they went down. With the frantic search and collection to meet Cooper's demands, Flight 305 landed at the Seattle Airport at 5:43 P.M., forty-three minutes later than Cooper had ordered them to take off from the Seattle Airport.

Tosaw reported that the $200,000 was obtained from the Seattle First National Bank, because the FBI knew that bank had prerecorded the serial numbers of $240,000 on microfilm in the event of a ransom kidnapping when all of the banks were closed. SEATTLE FIRST NATIONAL was printed on the bank money bag. However, Himmelsbach reported that the money had to be obtained from several banks. (WHY?)

After Flight 305 had landed, Cooper directed Tina Mucklow to bring the money, knapsack, and parachutes to him. After Tina struggled to deliver the demanded items to him, he checked the money bag for the amount in it, then inspected the parachutes. He then complained that there was no knapsack and the parachutes did not have "D" rings.

Despite those failures to meet his demands, Cooper then gave his permission for the other thirty-five passengers and flight attendants Alice Hancock and Florence Shaffner to deplane, but he ordered Tina Mucklow to remain on board in case he needed any help with anything.

As Alice and Florence were leaving, Cooper reached into the money bag and pulled out two $2,000 packets of money and offered the $4,000 to them, saying he hadn't tipped them for the drinks they had served him, and he didn't want the money. They refused the money and quickly deplaned. They later regretted not taking the money when they realized his fingerprints might have been detectible and identified on the money packets.

Although I am not a fingerprint expert, I have my doubts that any discernible fingerprints could have been lifted from the old bills, which they were, after being handled by thousands of people.

When Florence Shaffner delivered Cooper's notes to the flight crew, they asked her about his state of mind. She said that he was calm and relaxed. But he later became angry when there was a delay in refueling at the Seattle Airport. The first tanker developed a vapor lock and departed. The flight officers called Tina on the interphone and told her why another would complete the refueling. When she told Cooper of the problem, he became angry and yelled, "They're stalling, dammit. Tell them to get with it. Dammit, I won't take this." Then when he saw they had again started refueling, he calmed down. That was the only report in Tosaw's book that Cooper had used any foul or profane language.

Before taking off, Cooper was asked where he wanted them to take him, and he replied "Mexico City." That puzzled the FBI because it would require two refueling stops, which were determined by Northwest Airlines officials to be at Reno and Yuma. They first offered to make refueling stops in San Francisco and Los Angeles, but Cooper rejected those locations. As soon as the passengers and Alice and Florence were in the airport terminal, FBI agents checked the IDs of all of the passengers against the flight manifest. The only name not accounted for was "Dan Cooper." That name was phoned to the Portland Police Department for a criminal records check. A UPI reporter overheard an officer say the name of D.B. Cooper, a local man who had been arrested for a minor offense. As a good reporter seeking a scoop, he put it out on the UPI wire, and Dan Cooper, or whoever he was, forever became the legendary "D.B. Cooper."

After identifying all of the other passengers, the FBI agents questioned them and Alice and Florence about Cooper's personal appearance and characteristics. One

passenger said he was thirty to fifty years old, which would
describe almost half of the adult Caucasian men in the U.S.,
all of the others, including a college student who had been
seated across the aisle from Cooper, and in the same row
said he was in about his mid-forties. The student also said
Cooper was wearing socks or long underwear that did not
match his shoes or trousers. Cooper was also described as
being about 5'10"; 160 to 170 pounds with an athletic
build; dark brown, piercing eyes; dark, short hair; swarthy,
olive complexion; a raspy voice; and wore bubble-type,
wrap-around sunglasses most of the time.

Also, before takeoff, Cooper ordered the plane be flown
with the landing gear down, flaps down fifteen degrees, and
at 10,000 feet altitude.

The plane was a Boeing 727, which was the only commercial aircraft with a rear staircase that could be used for
jumping off. That was the obvious reason why Cooper had
asked the ticket clerk if his flight was a 727. He had Tina
call the cockpit and ask if they could take off with the rear
staircase down. They asked Paul Soderlind in Minneapolis
if they could take off that way, and he replied that it would
not be safe. When Tina told Cooper that it wouldn't be
safe, he responded that it would be safe, but he did not
pursue the matter.

Tina Mucklow watched Cooper as he examined the chutes,
placed the bank money bag in a canvas chute case he had
removed from one of the civilian chutes, because bank money
bags are like pillow cases without a securing device, and cut a
shroud line from a chute and tethered the canvas chute case
to his waist with about a six-foot of the shroud line.

It was reported that paratroopers tether loads to their waists with about a six-foot line so the load will hit the ground before they do to lessen their overall weight when they land.

Despite Cooper's demanding they fly him to Mexico City, before Flight 305 took off from the Seattle Airport, the pilots observed the light come on that indicated the rear door to the aft stairwell had been opened. That was the second indication to them that Cooper did not plan to go to Mexico City. After Cooper had donned the NB-8 chute and tethered the money bag to his waist, he told Tina to go to the cockpit and stay there, to close the curtain between the first class and coach sections, and to turn out the cabin lights. Just before Tina turned out the lights, she looked back at Cooper, and he waved his hand in a farewell salute to her. That was the very last time anyone ever saw "Dan Cooper," or whoever he really was by any other name.

It was 7:36 P.M. when Flight 305 finally charged down the runway and became airborne. At about 5,000 feet elevation, they broke through the layer of dense cloud cover of what was later described by a Continental Airlines pilot as being one of the worst storms he had experienced in his twenty-four years of flying.

Then at 7:45 P.M., five minutes after Tina had entered the cockpit, Cooper spoke on the "interphone" and told them to slow down a little, because he couldn't get the "airstairs" down.

Co-pilot Rataczak lowered the flaps down from 15 degrees to 30 degrees, which lowered the speed from 170 knots (195 mph) to 145 knots (167 mph).

The plane then leveled off at 10,000 feet and was on a heading of 148 degrees on automatic pilot course Vector-23, although Rataczak was flying manually, not on automatic pilot.

Then at 8:13 P.M., the four crew members in the cockpit felt a rush of air, and Rataczak said, "There he goes." When Cooper jumped, there was a forty-five miles per hour southwest wind at 10,000 feet, and the plane was traveling at 167 miles per hour, which made the headwind about 212 miles per hour, and the temperature at 10,000 feet was twenty-two degrees Fahrenheit. With that wind velocity and temperature, the wind chill factor would have been about thirty to forty degrees below zero, and about sixty to seventy-two degrees Fahrenheit below freezing. (Note: I had to calculate the wind chill factor temperature from a "New Wind Chill Chart" that went up to only sixty miles per hour. At that wind velocity and at twenty degrees Fahrenheit, the wind chill factor is 4 degrees below zero, or thirty-six degrees below freezing). And the wind at any velocity penetrates more than the same temperature in still air.

Cooper jumped in a business suit, light-weight raincoat, and slip-on loafers, and the shoes would have most certainly flown off of his feet as soon as he stepped off of the staircase into the 212 miles per hour headwind.

From all of these reported factors, I had to conclude that Cooper knew his odds of surviving the jump were about one in a hundred.

Whatever the odds, better or worse, Harry and I concluded that Cooper lost and crashed to his death at over 120 miles per hour.

New Wind Chill Chart

Temperature (°F)

Wind (mph)	Calm	40	35	30	25	20	15	10	5	0	-5	-10	-15	-20	-25	-30	-35	-40	-45
5		36	31	25	19	13	7	1	-5	-11	-16	-22	-28	-34	-40	-46	-52	-57	-63
10		34	27	21	15	9	3	-4	-10	-16	-22	-28	-35	-41	-47	-53	-59	-66	-72
15		32	25	19	13	6	0	-7	-13	-19	-26	-32	-39	-45	-51	-58	-64	-71	-77
20		30	24	17	11	4	-2	-9	-15	-22	-29	-35	-42	-48	-55	-61	-68	-74	-81
25		29	23	16	9	3	-4	-11	-17	-24	-31	-37	-44	-51	-58	-64	-71	-78	-84
30		28	22	15	8	1	-5	-12	-19	-26	-33	-39	-46	-53	-60	-67	-73	-80	-87
35		28	21	14	7	0	-7	-14	-21	-27	-34	-41	-48	-55	-62	-69	-76	-82	-89
40		27	20	13	6	-1	-8	-15	-22	-29	-36	-43	-50	-57	-64	-71	-78	-84	-91
45		26	19	12	5	-2	-9	-16	-23	-30	-37	-44	-51	-58	-65	-72	-79	-86	-93
50		26	19	12	4	-3	-10	-17	-24	-31	-38	-45	-52	-60	-67	-74	-81	-88	-95
55		25	18	11	4	-3	-11	-18	-25	-32	-39	-46	-54	-61	-68	-75	-82	-89	-97
60		25	17	10	3	-4	-11	-19	-26	-33	-40	-48	-55	-62	-69	-76	-84	-91	-98

Frostbite occurs in 15 minutes or less

Wind Chill (°F) = 35.74 + 0.6215T - 35.75(V$^{0.16}$) + 0.4275T(V$^{0.16}$)

Where, T = Air Temperature (°F)
        V = Wind Speed (mph)

[FIVE]

The Crucial Case Link

D.B. Cooper Profile

IN STUDYING ALL OF the Cooper material Harry had sent to me for over a year before I went to Washington to join him in his investigation, and from my own near-lifetime of observations, study, and experiences with criminal bahavior and motivations, I quite easily established a personal/psychological profile of Cooper. And Tosaw and Himmelsbach reported their Cooper profiles in their books.

Tosaw's book had a chapter entitled "Building A Profile." Based on Cooper's actions and his apparent knowledge of the Seattle area, Boeing 727 aircraft, and parachutes, he wrote that Cooper had most likely received parachute training in the military. And that most men of his age, in their mid-forties, had received their paratrooper training in the Commandos and later in the Green Berets. Also, that the type of bomb Cooper had constructed was like a military bomb and would not explode when it hit the ground. He also wrote that Cooper must have known many people, but nobody ever called the FBI with any promising leads that led to any positive identification of Cooper.

Tosaw did an excellent job of putting the known facts together to establish some clues about Cooper, but he did not speculate on where he came from or what would have motivated him to make his almost certain suicide jump.

Himmelsbach reported a few times in his book that Cooper must have been desperate. Of course, after reading all of the conditions that Cooper faced in his jump, that was obvious to me. But despite all of the information Himmelsbach must have had as the Portland FBI Cooper case agent, he profiled Cooper as an ex-con going for his last big strike, do or die. He had also referred to Cooper on a TV network as being a "rotten, sleazy crook."

Himmelsbach also reported that the FBI was developing a profile on Cooper. In his book, *Mind Hunter*, FBI Academy Behavioral Science Unit profiling pioneeer John Douglas wrote that in 1979 they had received about fifty requests for profiles. And that the following year that number of requests doubled, and then doubled again the following year.

Despite that reported volume of profiling requests, and Himmelsbach writing that Cooper's case was the most costly and highly publicized in FBI history, and that the FBI was the best investigative agency in the world, as of the writing of this book, I have never seen, read, or heard of an official FBI profile of Cooper. (WHY?)

Despite the numerous conflicting and contradictory

reports in all that I studied in the Cooper case, it was not difficult for me to profile Dan Cooper. First of all, as Tosaw had reported in his book, Cooper was most likely a former Green Beret. It was reported in Himmelsbach's book that Boeing 727s had been used by the CIA in Vietnam to drop agents and supplies behind enemy lines. I also learned from news reports that the CIA used Green Berets to assassinate foreign enemy leaders until 1976, when President Ford issued an Executive Order banning that clandestine activity. I also saw a TV documentary about the training of Green Beret trainee candidates; their final test was to bail out; of a plane at night in darkness, as Cooper had done. It also reported that Green Berets in combat jumped at an altitude of two miles, or 10,560 feet, just 560 feet higher than Cooper ordered Flight 305 be flown, and did not deploy their chutes until they had fallen forty seconds to minimize their exposure to enemy fire. From an altitude of 10,560 feet, and falling at about 120 miles per hour, it would take about sixty seconds to hit the ground. Therefore, they deployed their chutes just twenty seconds before landing.

Also, the Green Berets, as one of the most elite U.S. Army units, attracts what I would classify as young men who like to "live on the edge," and accordingly take great pride in their prominent, prestigious organization and themselves. I could easily identify with that type of personality, because my career dream since I was nineteen years old was to be a California Highway Patrol officer, when they were called "Princes of the Highways" by many Californians and out-of-staters alike. And despite an auto magazine publishing their study of the CHP a couple of years before I joined the

CHP in 1954 that classified the CHP as the most dangerous occupation in the U.S. That classification was based on the number of CHP officers to date and the number that had been killed. And during my twenty-nine years on the CHP, ninety-three officers were killed. Despite all of that, I wouldn't have wanted to do anything else for a living. But the excitement and thrill of chasing speeders and other violators in all conditions is a far cry from jumping out of an airplane at any altitude or in any condition, and I would not do that for any amount of money.

I then considered why Cooper skyjacked a plane on a usually busy Thanksgiving Eve with a takeoff time of 3:00 P.M., and with it always being on a Wednesday, when the banks closed at 3:00 P.M. If he had waited just two days, until Friday, the day after Thanksgiving, he would have a better chance of getting the seat he wanted, and the banks would be open until 6:00 P.M. That caused me to believe that he was in a rush, or in a panic, and had to get the money without even a two-day delay.

Then his wearing a dark (or black) narrow-lapelled suit; white dress shirt: and narrow, black tie made me think he was wearing a service uniform, such as worn by bartenders, limousine drivers, hotel employees, and other service personnel in higher class metropolitan cities, such as Las Vegas at that time.

I classified his attire as a service uniform because narrow suit lapels and narrow ties had gone out of style no later than the mid-1960s, and were not normal dress clothing. I was well aware of the current styles at that time, because I bought two suits, dress shirts and ties early in 1971, and the suits were medium blue and green, the dress shirts were pastels, and the ties were broad and with colorful designs.

In that it was easy to classify Cooper's jump as a desperate, almost-certain suicide caper, it caused me to believe he was trying to avoid a much worse death. The only other fate I could imagine would be a slow, torturous death at the hands of a sadistic Mafia hit man.

With that consideration, my curiosity compelled me to look in my big red dictionary to see if there were any definitions of Dan and Cooper. There are not many men's given names that have definitions, but Dan and Cooper both do have definitions. And the definition of Dan is: "a title of honor equivalent to master or sir." And the third definition of cooper is: "to furnish or fix (usually fol. by up)."

That confirmed my belief that Cooper was running from a certain slow, torturous death, and his concocted name was a coded message to his threatening or pursuing tormentor. Mostly because "honor" is one of the most revered terms in the Mafia codes in addition to family, loyalty and "omertà" (silence). So much so, that when a Mafia underling is initiated as a "made man," he is then known as "man of honor."

This personal profile of Cooper ultimately became the paramount crucial link in solving the case five years later when I discovered the missing, vital connecting link.

Because of Cooper's obvious haste to get the money, despite the day and hour that did not best accommodate his objective, and using the obviously coded message for the world to hear, although bungled by the UPI reporter, I had to believe his Mafia hit man had also threatened or was holding one of Cooper's friends, girl friend, wife, or other family member hostage, and Cooper was in a panic to get the message to him.

With that possibility, I later learned that Chicago Mafia enforcer/hit man Tony Spilotro had been moved to Las Vegas by the Chicago "outfit" to manage their affairs in that city. In the 1995 copyrighted movie *Casino*, Spilotro is played by Joe Pesci under the movie name of Nicky Santoro. One scene, showed Spilotro slowly squeezing the head of one of his victims in a large vise until one of his eyes popped out before he was reportedly killed. I had heard other reports of that same torture of that same victim by Spilotro, so it was not just a Hollywood concoction. And at the end of the movie, it was printed on the screen that it was a fictional story with fictional characters, but was based on a true story.

Cooper's apparent service uniform attire and his obvious panic skyjacking convinced me that he was a compulsive gambler over his head in debt to Las Vegas Mafia loan sharks who had given him his very last warning to pay up, "or else." Cooper's offering $4,000 of the $200,000 to Florence Shaffner and Alice Hancock was also very significant to me. I have known a couple of compulsive gamblers, and they do not have a sense of the value of money, no matter the amount. It becomes no more than their means of pursuing their craze to hit jackpots or other big winnings. And as they lose, they increase their bettings to win and make up for their past losses, and in extreme cases to pay off gambling debts. And if to Mafia loan sharks, to pay up, "or else!"

One I knew was a worthless partner I had to work with on the San Diego Police Department who gambled at legal poker parlors in San Diego and La Mesa. After I left the police department and joined the California Highway Patrol in 1954, he called in sick one afternoon shift and went to a poker parlor in La Mesa. When he had lost all of his money, he asked the female manager if she would cash a check for him. He showed her his driver's license, then for good measure, he showed her his San Diego P.D. ID card. Being suspicious of a policeman gambling and losing so much, she phoned the SDPD police station to verify his current employment. Her call was forwarded to his watch commander captain, who sent a sergeant to the poker parlor to verify that he was in fact there and playing poker. When he confirmed that he was there, he relieved him of his ID card, and he was fired from the P.D. on the spot. Even after being fired, he continued to gamble, and wrote bad checks to cover his continuing losses, and ended up in San Quentin. And he was married, had two small children, and was living in a $25 or $35 a month World War II Federal Housing Project unit. To make matters worse, he should have known that former cops are natural enemies and targets of the other prison inmates.

I also watched a documented TV production of a panel discussing compulsive (or addictive) gambling. One panel member was a Nevada casino owner, and another was a reformed compulsive gambler. The moderator told of an event when there was a fire in a casino, and one gambler at a slot machine would not leave his machine as ordered by firemen. Despite the danger, he refused to leave, so the firemen had to forcibly carry him out of the casino to safety. The moderator then asked the reformed compulsive gambler if he believed that story. He smiled, and said he did, because more than once he had urinated in his pants so he wouldn't have to leave his favorite, lucky slot machine.

Another of my considerations of compulsive gamblers is that they usually limit their personal contacts to others in the gambling world. And at that time, Nevada was the only western state that had legal gambling, mostly in Reno and Las Vegas. California had legal draw poker parlors, because draw poker was classified by the State as a game of skill, not chance. Ha-ha! Anybody who knows anything about poker parlors should know that poker parlors hire "shills" who play at the same tables with the "suckers" and play for the house.

That nobody reportedly contacted the FBI with a promising suspect in the Cooper case also supported my profile of Cooper, because those in the gambling world do not "rat" on each other.

Also, when I was a teenager, I was at an Italian friend's house, and for some childish reason, we were talking about gambling when his street-wise, bar-owner father walked in the front door. When he first heard us, he asked, "Are you talking about gambling?" When we replied that we were, he said, "Let me tell you about gambling. First of all, all casino owners know that gamblers can stand to lose, but they can't stand to win. If they win, then they keep playing until they lose all of it and more. And nobody can win in the long-run, because the house has millions to back up any short-term losses."

It has also been well reported that Mafia gambling genius Meyer Lansky always ran fair, honest gaming at

Mafia-owned casinos, even in Havana, because the house always wins in the long-run.

I also learned in 1998 that Chicago Mafia Godfather Sam Giancana was the boss of all Mafia loan sharks in the U.S., and had been living in Mexico City since 1966, when he fled Chicago because local law enforcement was on his case and hot on his tail.

So, considering all of the conditions of Cooper's jump that indicated it was nothing short of suicide, and all that was reported by Tosaw's and Himmelsbach's books, I had to conclude that Cooper's coded messages were, "I'm a man of honor and will pay up to Sam Giancana in Mexico City."

Although he wasn't going to pay directly to Giancana, as a Vegas gambler borrowing from Mafia loan sharks, he must have known that Mexico City was synonymous with Giancana, because Sam no doubt ultimately received some or all of the loan sharks' ill-gotten, immense-daily-interest profits for dispersal to the mob.

When I told Harry about my profile of Cooper, and his probable pursuer being Tony Spilotro, Harry agreed with me, because he had tailed Spilotro in San Diego in 1975 when he was an investigator in the San Diego D.A.'s Organized Crime Unit. Harry said Spilotro had gone to San Diego from Las Vegas, and he tailed him until he left San Diego, but Spilotro didn't do anything illegal, so Harry just filed a report.

Then later that year, on November 9, 1975, Tamara Rand was shot five times in the head, and her executioner was identified as Nicky Santoro (Tony Spilotro) in the movie *Casino*. Tamara Rand had filed a law suit against the Las

Vegas Mafia casino for some illegal activity, reportedly for skimming profits, that was well reported, and for which several Mafia figures were later criminally prosecuted.

Spilotro was reportedly in Las Vegas from April 1971, just seven months before Cooper's skyjacking, until about 1986. But while in Las Vegas, Spilotro blatantly violated some iron-clad Mafia dictates. One was that there shall not be any Mafia-type hits in Las Vegas, because they would indicate, or reveal, that the Mafia was operating in that otherwise fine, clean, recreational city. Disregarding that dictate, there were reports of nine bodies found in the surrounding desert, including five Mafia loan sharks, whom Spilotro apparently caught, or suspected, of skimming from the extremely lucrative profits. Another overall, general Mafia code Spilotro violated was having a sexual relationship with the wife of a Mafia member or associate. She was the wife of Frank "Lefty" Rosenthal, the front man who managed the Mafia casino, played by Robert DeNiro in the movie Casino. And other reportedly factual documentaries tell the same about Spilotro and Rosenthal. In addition to Spilotro's certain-death violations of Mafia codes in Las Vegas, he also reportedly openly bad-mouthed some Mafia bosses and Mafia codes.

Then, not long after Spilotro and his brother, Michael (Dominic in the movie Casino), left Las Vegas and returned to Chicago in about 1986, they were summoned to a meeting with Spilotro's close associates in an Indiana corn field. There, they were beaten to near death with baseball bats, then buried in shallow graves while still breathing. Their graves were later discovered by the corn field farmer.

With all of that, when I discovered Tony Spilotro had moved to Las Vegas from Chicago only seven months before Cooper's near-certain suicide jump into a 212 miles per hour headwind, in about a sixty-two to seventy-two degrees below freezing wind chill factor, in a reported worst storm in twenty-four years of flying, and wearing only a business suit; light-weight raincoat; and slip-on-type, loafers, I had to conclude that he had chosen that almost certain quick death to avoid being slowly tortured to death by psychopathic sadist Tony Spilotro.

Also, in that Cooper was described by the most reliable witnesses as having an olive or swarthy (dark) complexion, I theorized that he was probably of Italian or other Latin descent. And in that even some people with olive or darker complexions can pale if not regularly exposed to sunlight, and Las Vegas at that time was the only legalized gambling city in the desert, where the sun shines the year round, this again convinced me that Cooper had come from Las Vegas. And that was Tony Spilotro's home base from April 1971, seven months prior to Cooper's skyjacking, until about 1986.

In my studying and analyzing every D.B. Cooper book, and viewing numerous related TV documentaries for sixteen years, I am certain of this profile of Cooper, and why he committed his skyjacking when, why, and how he did it.

This profile of Cooper became the sole crucial link that ultimately resulted in my connecting it with the other key link in 1998 that solved this very mysterious, and shocking, case.

SIX

Cooper vs. McCoy

Richard Floyd McCoy, Jr. Skyjacking

O N FRIDAY, APRIL 7, 1972, Richard Floyd McCoy, Jr., a former Green Beret helicopter pilot and then an active Mormon Sunday School teacher, skyjacked United Airlines Flight 855 bound for Los Angeles. He boarded the plane at Salt Lake International Airport in Salt Lake City, Utah, with two pieces of luggage. Flight 855 made one scheduled stop at Denver's Stapleton International Airport, where McCoy deplaned and went to the United Airlines to pay for and get the ticket for Flight 855 that he had reserved a week before in the name of James Johnson.

Due to the crowded airport terminal, McCoy was delayed in getting his ticket, and had to rush to the men's restroom and change from his conservative suit into dark double-knit slacks; navy blue oxfords; green colorful shirt with a wide collar; a dark, wide, blue tie; and a royal blue, red-striped sport coat. And he donned mirrored sunglasses.

McCoy was first in line to board Flight 855, and he was the first passenger to board the plane. He then went straight to the aft restroom, where he applied dark makeup, curled his mustache, and put one of his wife's headbands over his large, protruding ears, then donned a wig over the headband.

When the second flight officer pounded on the restroom door and ordered McCoy to get out, because they were ready for takeoff, he quickly left the restroom and took seat 20D, an aisle seat to the right of the aisle, looking forward from the rear of the plane. Two brothers-in-law sat in the two seats to the right of McCoy, and there were eighty-five other passengers on the flight.

McCoy then scribbled a note on a 3″ x 5″ card, handed it to the man seated to his right, and told the man it was a hijack, and to move forward and get a stewardess. When the flight attendant came back to the rear of the plane where McCoy was seated, he handed her a white 5″ x 7″ envelope. Typed on the outside was "GRENADE-PIN PULLED PISTOL LOADED." Inside the envelope were two pages of typed instructions, a military grenade pin, and a .45-caliber cartridge. And the language in the two typed pages repeatedly referred to "WE," not "I." The instructions directed that the plane be flown to San Francisco, not Los Angeles, and with specific instructions which runway to land on, time to land, where to obtain parachute equipment, including a stop watch and wrist altimeter, along with some other demands, including $500,000.

As it continued, McCoy had brought his own parachute jump suit and boots and dressed in them before jumping over Provo, Utah, where he lived with his wife, two young children, and his sister-in-law, whom, for good reasons, he did not like.

Within days, he was identified as the skyjacker by a Utah Highway Patrol officer friend. A search warrant was issued, and nearly all of the $500,000 was found in McCoy's home.

McCoy was tried and convicted, and sent to prison. He later escaped with another inmate, robbed some banks, then was tracked down by the FBI and killed in a shootout with FBI special agents.

This summary of McCoy's skyjacking was taken from the aforementioned book, *D.B. COOPER: The Real McCoy*, authored by Bernie Rhodes, former chief federal probation and parole officer of the Utah district, and researched by Russell P. Calame, former agent in charge of the Salt Lake City FBI office.

Rhodes wrote that he started writing the book in 1985, the year after Tosaw's book was copyrighted, and it was copyrighted in 1991 by the Utah University Press. The book does not declare that it cannot be copied or photocopied, etc., as is common with nearly all other books.

The obvious intent of Rhodes' and Calame's book is to try to prove that 1971 skyjacker D.B. Cooper was also 1972 skyjacker Richard Floyd McCoy, Jr., which is clearly stated in the title of the book, *D.B. COOPER: The Real McCoy*.

But despite their extensive research and fine efforts, there were far too many differences between Cooper and McCoy for Harry and me to accept their theory that Cooper and

McCoy were the same person. And the significant differences are as follows:

1. Cooper was the last passenger to board Northwest
   Airlines Flight 305, and McCoy was the first
   passenger to board United Airlines Flight 855.
   McCoy then went straight to the aft restroom where
   he applied make-up to his face, a headband on his
   head to flatten his large ears, then donned a wig over
   the headband. Cooper went straight to seat 18E and
   remained there until the money and parachutes were
   delivered to him.

   Rhodes reported that McCoy's ears were so large
   and protruded so much that classmates at Brigham
   Young University (BYU) called him "Dumbo." Even
   the best witnesses did not describe Cooper as having
   unusual ears in any way whatsoever.
2. Cooper was described by the best witnesses as being
   in his mid-forties. McCoy was known to be twenty-
   nine years of age.
3. Cooper was described by the best witnesses,
   including the three flight attendants, as having dark
   brown, piercing eyes. Rhodes described McCoy's eyes
   as being light blue, and close together.
4. Tosaw reported that Cooper ordered two bourbon
   and water highballs and was a heavy smoker of
   Raleigh filter-tip cigarettes. McCoy was a Mormon
   Sunday School teacher, and Mormons do not smoke,
   drink alcoholic beverages or coffee, and do not
   gamble. Rhodes tried to connect McCoy to Raleigh

cigarettes because he was born in Raleigh, North
Carolina.

5. Cooper skyjacked Flight 305 on a Wednesday at
about 3:00 P.M. when the banks closed at 3:00 P.M.
McCoy skyjacked Flight 855 on a Friday when the
banks were open until 6:00 P.M.

6. Cooper jumped in a business suit; light-weight
raincoat; slip-on loafers, and into a raging storm in
about sixty-two to seventy-two degrees below
freezing wind chill factor, and over mountainous
forests of trees and thorny blackberry vines, lakes,
rivers, highways, high-tension power lines, and
heavily populated areas. McCoy jumped in clear,
warmer April weather over flat, level land, and in a
parachute jump suit and boots.

7. Cooper was described as having a raspy voice, with
no unusual characteristics. Rhodes wrote that
McCoy had been born with an oral defect that was
corrected by surgery, but left him with a lisp. Also,
Rhodes reported that when McCoy was young, he
had a noticeable southern accent.

With all of these reported comparative differences in the
three books, Harry and I completely disregarded any consideration whatsoever that Cooper and McCoy were the
same person.

Despite these differences, Rhodes reported that Cooper
had left a clip-on narrow, black tie and a mother-of-pearl
tie clasp on his seat on Flight 305. But in his interviews
with Tina Mucklow and the Reno FBI special agents that

searched Flight 305 at the Reno Airport, none of them could recall ever seeing those items, and there was not any written report of those items. Then years later, they mysteriously appeared at the Seattle FBI office. And when McCoy's much-hated sister-in-law, Denise, was shown a photo of them, she identified them as being McCoy's.

However, Denise had told McCoy's Utah Highway Patrol officer friend that McCoy was not at home when the very astute officer became suspicious that McCoy could be the skyjacker of United Airlines Flight 855. And when McCoy learned from Denise that she had told the officer that he was not at home, McCoy said he would kill her. Also, Rhodes reported that Denise was well aware of the $50,000 reward on McCoy's head, and she was very willing to testify at McCoy's trial. And so much so, that the FBI placed her in protective custody.

Rhodes' complete explanation of the relationship between McCoy and Denise made the McCoy household appear to be much more like the "Hatfields and McCoys" than *Father Knows Best*.

Accordingly, Harry and I did not believe Denise was an impartial, unbiased, credible witness with respect to her identifying the tie and tie clasp as being McCoy's.

Furthermore, Himmelsbach reported in his book that Cooper was wearing a pearl stickpin in his narrow, black tie, not a mother-of-pearl tie clasp.

Despite all of the differences between Cooper and McCoy, on January 9, 2009, there was a TV documentary about McCoy, entitled, *Flight from Justice, the Real Story of D.B. Cooper*.

Based on that TV show and numerous other D.B. Cooper episodes I have viewed, I take all of them with a grain of salt, because I have worked on the Cooper case for sixteen years, and know better.

Notwithstanding our disbelief of McCoy being Cooper, Rhodes did discover and secure some crucial evidence that could personally connect McCoy and Cooper as old Green Beret associates or buddies. They had obtained a copy of McCoy's BankAmerica credit card slip proving he had purchased 5.6 gallons of gas at a Las Vegas service station on November 25, 1971. And the FBI laboratory in Washington, D.C. had confirmed that the signature on the credit card slip was McCoy's. They also obtained a copy of McCoy's telephone records that listed a collect call from Las Vegas at 10:41 P.M. on November 25, 1971. The call was made from a pay phone in the lobby of the Tropicana Hotel, less than half a mile from McCarren International Airport.

Also, McCoy's same credit card was used in Cedar City, Utah, to buy gas on November 24, 1971. Cedar City is 182 miles from Las Vegas. He was driving a Volkswagen Bug that averaged about thirty-three miles per gallon, which would calculate to about 5.6 gallons, the same amount that was purchased in Las Vegas with his same BankAmerica credit card.

Long before I flew to Washington State on June 14, 1994, two days after Nicole Brown Simpson and Ron Goldman were brutally murdered, I profiled Cooper as a former Green Beret, which others had done as reported in Tosaw's and Himmelsbach's books, and a compulsive gambler over his head in debt to Las Vegas Mafia loan sharks, who had given him his very last warning to pay up—or else!

Green Berets are the elite of the U.S. Army, and much like U.S. Marines, they stick together and come to the aid of each other. "Once a Marine, always a Marine." They never leave a wounded comrade behind, even if they have to risk their own life under heavy enemy gunfire to rescue them and carry them to safety.

So, rather than trying to speculate that McCoy was Cooper, I theorize that McCoy had left his family on Thanksgiving Eve and all day of Thanksgiving Day to help Cooper in any way that he could to aid an old Vietnam buddy, and to wait for his return.

And a very strange event I report later herein supported my profile of Cooper being a former Green Beret and how they stick together and protect each other, and even after death.

In addition to that support of my profile of Cooper and a few other valuable items reported by Rhodes and Calame, it was very interesting to Harry and me that Rhodes reported that he had interviewed Tina Mucklow after he started his investigation in 1972. Calame provided the research in their investigation, and Calame retired from the FBI in April 1972. Then after Tosaw published his 1984 copyrighted book, Harry was unable to get any response from Tina Mucklow when he sent her his letter, and I did not receive any response from the flight officers after my letters and phone calls. Harry and I strongly suspected that the FBI had gagged the flight crew after Tosaw interviewed them and published his book.

SEVEN

The FBI Investigation

5,000 Men and Five Years

WITHOUT ANY REPORT OF Cooper's skyjacked Flight 305 being tracked on radar by Portland International Airport traffic controllers, Himmelsbach reported that someone, maybe his supervisor, suggested that they get a helicopter to stand by in case Cooper jumped in their area. Himmelsbach was asked if he could arrange it, and he said he would try.

Himmelsbach reported that he phoned the Oregon Army National Guard helicopter unit stationed in Portland. The helicopter pilots weren't there, so he called one at home. The pilot agreed to take Himmelsbach and another FBI agent up with him and another pilot. Himmelsbach and the other FBI agent met the pilots and took to the air in a "Huey" helicopter.

But it didn't go very well, because there were two serious

problems. One was that the Huey chopper had a top speed of 120 knots, and Tosaw reported that Cooper had asked the Flight 305 pilots to slow down, because he couldn't get the stairway down. So, Co-pilot Rataczak lowered the flaps from fifteen degrees to thirty degrees, which lowered the speed from 170 knots to 145 knots, twenty-five knots faster than the Huey. The other problem was that the cloud cover of the raging storm below 5,000 feet was so dense that Co-pilot Rataczak could not determine their location when Cooper jumped at 8:13 P.M. And if Rataczak and the other flight officers could not determine where they were when Cooper jumped, it's certain that those in the Huey could not either.

This futile attempt to determine Cooper's jump location again raises the key issue of no report of the Portland International Airport traffic controllers radar tracking of Flight 305.

And if Himmelsbach or any other FBI agents, such as "Team One," had gone to the air controller tower, they could have determined within a mile or so of where Flight 305 was located when Cooper jumped. Instead, Himmelsbach and another FBI agent flew over the area in a Huey helicopter in a raging storm with near zero visibility below 5,000 feet, and as possibly directed to do so by his FBI supervisor. (WHY?)

Himmelsbach reported that in 1975, about ten FBI special agents with skyjacking experience met to pool their expertise in a "brainstorming" session to come up with new ideas with respect to the D.B. Cooper case. The agents were from Portland, Seattle, San Francisco, Reno, Las

Vegas, Los Angeles, and Phoenix, and one Washington supervisor, who was an expert in skyjacking.

The list made me wonder why there was no Salt Lake City agent involved in the meeting. One who knew the McCoy copycat skyjacking case should have been able to contribute something of importance. (WHY?)

Himmelsbach reported that he was asked what it would take to do a complete search to determine once and for all where Cooper had landed. He replied, 5,000 men and five years, and he made reference to searching only the southwest portion of Washington.

When I searched with Harry for several days in June 1994, I quickly became oriented to the terrain and natural growth of trees, shrubbery and vines of southwest Washington. The trees are mostly spaced apart, and the borders of forested areas are mostly covered with very tall, dense, impassable, thorny blackberry vines that receive direct sunlight most of the year. But in the interior of the forested areas where the blackberry vines are shaded by the trees and never receive any sunlight, they are scraggly, puny, have little foliage, and are spaced far enough apart to walk in a zigzag mode between them. With that somewhat open and clear environment, there is a fairly clear view of at least twenty feet in all directions.

So, by spacing of searchers only ten feet apart, 5,000 men would span across 50,000 feet in a line, or almost ten miles. Or, if twenty feet apart, twenty miles. In that the FBI thought Flight 305 was supposed to be on automatic pilot course Vector-23, until 1980 when Co-pilot Rataczak told Himmelsbach he flew the plane manually, not on automatic pilot, the search area should have been no more than two hundred square miles, if Cooper had deployed his chute. Or, if he had not deployed his chute and plunged to his death, as many believed, the search area would be no more than five miles wide and twenty miles long. And that takes into account that Co-pilot Rataczak later told Himmelsbach in 1980 that they had drifted an unknown distance east of Vector-23 in the forty-five miles per hour southwest headwind at 10,000 feet.

So, even searching the larger area of two hundred square miles, about ten miles wide and twenty miles long, with one hundred men spaced twenty feet apart, spanning 2,000 feet, or over one-third mile, shouldn't take more than about ninety days. And that is an absolute maximum estimate, because there are expansive farming areas in and around Battle Ground, where Harry and I located the Vector-23 automatic pilot course facility, where the course changes directions from southeast to southwest, flying south.

Despite these logical calculations, Himmelsbach estimated it would take 5,000 men and five years to search. (WHY?)

Himmelsbach also reported that FBI agents had been reminding the Department of Justice of the five-year statute of limitations in the Cooper case, but they "waffled" until the very last day, November 24, 1976, to attempt to obtain a "John Doe" warrant to indefinitely extend the statute of limitations. (WHY?)

To complicate matters on that critical date, Himmelsbach reported that the Seattle federal grand jury was not sitting to hear the case to issue an indictment. But the jurisdiction in Cooper's case covered the states of Oregon, Washington, California and Nevada, because it was an interstate commerce crime. So, the case was heard by the Portland federal grand jury, and that body issued the needed no-time-limit "John Doe" warrant.

In Tosaw's and Rhodes' books, they reported that the list of 10,000 serial numbers of Cooper's $200,000 ransom money was released to the public, or press, but they did not state when it was released by the FBI. Then in Himmelsbach's book, he reported that J. Edgar Hoover released the list to banks, other financial institutions and money collection centers early in December 1971. Both Tosaw's and Himmelsbach's books include a copy of Director J. Edgar Hoover's written notice to those institutions, dated November 29, 1971, the Monday following the Thanksgiving weekend. He then reported that the list was not made "public" until November 1973 on the second anniversary of Cooper's skyjacking. He then wrote that the life expectancy of a $20 bill is eighteen months.

My son's next-door neighbor was a Secret Service special agent, so I asked him what the life expectancy of a $20 bill was. He replied that it was eighteen to twenty-four months.

The Seattle FBI agents had the list of the 10,000 ransom bills as soon as they picked up the $200,000, and before Cooper's skyjacked Flight 305 even became airborne from the Seattle SEATAC Airport. But they did not immediately release them to the press. (WHY?)

These mysterious reports, and some strange events that Harry and I experienced raised many questions in our minds.

OFFICE OF THE DIRECTOR

UNITED STATES DEPARTMENT OF JUSTICE

FEDERAL BUREAU OF INVESTIGATION

WASHINGTON, D.C. 20535

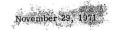

November 29, 1971

LIST OF RANSOM BILLS PAID IN AIR PIRACY CASE

Attached is a list of currency which constitutes the ransom paid to the hijacker of a commercial airliner in return for the release of the passengers and some of the stewardesses.

This currency is composed of $20 Federal Reserve Notes. The series year, if known, is shown after the serial number by the last two digits of the series year.

INSTRUCTIONS

It is requested that you examine all currency now in your possession to ascertain whether any of these bills have been received by you. It is further requested that you examine all currency hereafter coming into your possession for the purpose of locating any of the bills which are listed. In the event information is received concerning the location of any of this ransom money, it is requested that you immediately communicate by telephone collect with the nearest office of the Federal Bureau of Investigation. The location of the field offices of the Federal Bureau of Investigation, together with telephone numbers and addresses, is contained herein.

Your continued cooperation and assistance in this matter will be sincerely appreciated.

Very truly yours,

John Edgar Hoover
Director

Enclosure

EIGHT

Harry Grady's Investigation

Cooper's Remains
Are on a Columbia River Island

THE $5,800 OF COOPER'S ransom money was found on Tina's Bar by eight-year-old Brian Ingraham on February 10, 1980, just six years before Harry Grady and his wife, Ruth, moved back to Harry's homestate of Washington in 1986. Until that money was found, the 1971 Cooper skyjacking was truly a mystery of who he was and if he had survived his first-of-kind jump.

And with the confirmed money find, Harry Grady could not resist initiating his own personal investigation of the compelling case. Cracking difficult cases had been his love for over forty-one years, and he had been solely responsible for finding the wildlife-scattered remains of the missing U.S. Navy ensign, so he was confident he could find Cooper's remains that he was certain had been widely scattered by wildlife.

Using his acquired sense of logic, he set out to backtrack

from where Brian found the money on Tina's Bar. Like much that was written in Tosaw's and Himmelsbach's books, there were some so-called expert opinions on any number of issues in the case, including some on how the money ended up on Tina's Bar. One was that the banks of the Columbia River did not erode, they built up with sand by means of natural accumulation.

So, Harry went to Tina's Bar to start his investigation. In searching the area, Harry encountered an elderly couple that had lived near Tina's Bar for about forty years. They were very wary of Harry snooping around and didn't want to talk to him until he showed them his retired law enforcement ID cards and told them what he was doing there.

Even with that, they said they would talk to him only if he promised not to tell anyone they had helped him. He vowed to keep it all a secret, because he figured they had at least one good or valid reason for wanting to remain anonymous.

When Harry told me about the couple wanting to remain unknown, we laughed about it. We could only speculate that one or both of them might be wanted by the law, or they did not want to be in any way connected with finding Cooper or solving the case, because Cooper was a hero to the many anti-government militants in the Pacific Northwest who worshipped him for beating the system. It was probably the latter, because years later, I heard that the greatest concentration of anti-government radical activists are in the Pacific Northwest.

When the couple opened up to Harry, he asked them if they knew if the banks of the Columbia River eroded or built up with sand. The woman didn't hesitate to tell Harry that she had walked the banks of the river for forty years, including along Tina's Bar, and the banks did not build up, they eroded.

With that confirmation, Harry then knew the money did not just fall there and get buried by a build up of sand, as one so-called hydraulic expert had proclaimed. Being a fact-gathering enthusiast of all that interested him, Harry knew the flow of the Columbia River was regulated by the Bonneville Dam, more than forty miles upriver from Tina's Bar, and at a release flow of five miles per hour.

He also knew that dry paper, like currency, initially floated, then slowly sank as it became saturated. And Tina's Bar was about sixteen miles downriver from Government Island and the other river islands. So it would have taken a little over three hours for the bank money bag inside the canvas parachute case to become completely saturated, sink, and come to rest on the river bed in front of Tina's Bar.

Then, when the FBI had used backhoes to excavate Tina's Bar after Brian Ingraham found the $5,800 of ransom money, they discovered pieces of $20 bills about three feet deep. After the Army Corps of Engineers dredged the Columbia River in October 1974, a bulldozer followed and leveled the river banks back to their natural slopes.

Although some other so-called experts discounted the money being pumped onto Tina's Bar by the Army Corps of Engineers, Harry disagreed with the college-educated experts, and concluded with his high school education that it was the only logical explanation of how the money ended up there. I wholeheartedly agreed with Harry's conclusion, and we had to laugh, because we also had to conclude that the fish ate the rest of the money, after the gush of dredged water flushed most, or all, of the rest of the money back into the Columbia River, and it was carried about eighty miles downriver into the Pacific Ocean.

The irony of the loss of the remaining $194,200 of Cooper's ransom money is that all banks used cotton money bags until about 2005, when some, or all, switched to sealable, airtight/watertight plastic money bags. If plastic money bags had been in use at the time of Cooper's skyjacking, the entire $200,000 would have most likely floated down the Columbia River into the Pacific Ocean and washed up on a beach. Then, if an honest beach-goer found it, there would have been no loss to Northwest Airlines and its insurance carrier. But if found by a dishonest beach bum, there could have been a very rich thief in the Pacific Northwest.

All of Harry's Columbia River island theory made sense to me, and I completely confirmed it after going to Washington to conduct my own independent investigation.

Of the several Columbia River islands where Cooper could have landed, Government Island is the largest. It is about six miles long and about one mile wide in the middle, and tapered to narrow ends, and shaped much like a cheap cigar. And from all of our calculations, that's where Harry and I agreed Cooper's remains are most likely located.

Based on all of the reported facts, and mostly on the location of the money find, we concluded that Cooper had been unable to deploy his parachute and plunged to his death, being pushed about one-half mile to one mile to the northeast in the initial 45 miles per hour southwest wind at 10,000 feet. Then falling at about 126 miles per hour, or more, he struck the top of a very large tree on an island, causing the six-foot tethered money bag to break loose on impact and be launched as much as two hundred feet into the main channel of the Columbia River.

Then the money bag floated, slowly sank as it became saturated, and came to rest on the river bed in front of Tina's Bar when it became completely saturated. With the cotton bank money bag and the canvas parachute case rotting for almost three years until the Army Corps of Engineers dredged it unto the sandy bank, the bag and case fell apart when violently pumped onto Tina's Bar in October 1974.

Harry and I completely agreed for sixteen years until his passing in 2009, that this is the only logical, plausible explanation of how the $5,800 could have ended up where it was amazingly discovered by chance on February 10, 1980.

And that incredible discovery of the money was the sole key factor that convinced Harry that Cooper's wildlife-scattered remains are on a Columbia River island, with which I had to completely agree.

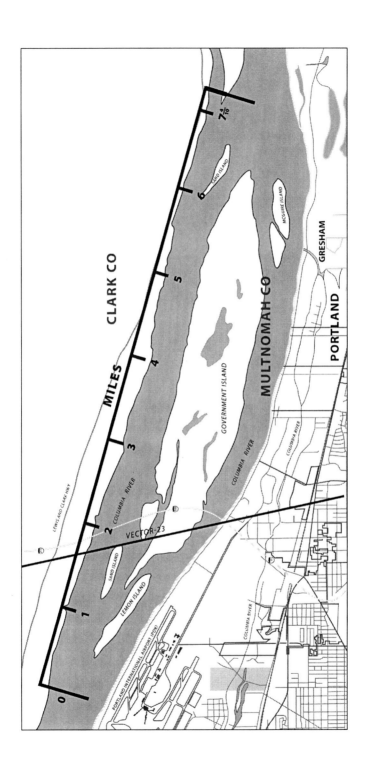

NINE

Harry's Mysterious Caller

You Could Get Shot

O N MAY 9, 1994, a little over a month before I flew to Washington, Harry sent a letter to retired Portland FBI Special Agent Ralph Himmelsbach at his business address in West Linn, Oregon.

In that letter, Harry explained his Columbia River theory to Himmelsbach, asking him for any information he could offer to minimize our search areas. Harry also gave a brief history of our law enforcement careers. Then at the bottom of the letter, Harry listed my P.O. box number, home phone number and date of birth, and his home address and phone number.

Harry did not receive any reply from Himmelsbach for about two weeks, so he got his business phone number from directory assistance. When he called the number, Himmelsbach's daughter answered. When Harry explained who he was and why he was calling, she told Harry that her father had been out of town for two weeks and would return the next day. Harry then thanked her.

The next day, Harry received a phone call from a complete stranger, who identified himself as a retired Green Beret sergeant, and gave his name, which I will reveal herein only as "J.T." (name on file with my attorney).

The mysterious caller told Harry that he was searching the Washougal River watershed area for Cooper's remains or anything related to him. He then told Harry that the area was heavily planted by marijuana growers, and they were like moonshiners and would shoot any strangers they did not know, but they knew him and what he was doing, so he was safe.

Harry said he almost laughed, because he followed all of the TV and newspaper reports, and had never heard or read of anybody being shot at or shot in the Washougal River watershed area. Also, Harry knew that the area was frequented by hunters, fishermen, hikers, and other outdoorsmen almost the entire year round.

Harry then told J.T. that he was not interested in searching the Washougal River watershed area, that he was searching the Columbia River areas. He told me that J.T. then said he had already searched all of the Columbia River areas and had not found anything related to Cooper. Harry then asked J.T. about landmarks and other distinguishing characteristics of the Columbia River, and J.T. responded with some answers that Harry described to me as "A bunch of baloney."

A few days later, Harry phoned me and told me that J.T. had phoned him a few nights before at 11:00 P.M., two hours after he and his wife had gone to bed, and were asleep. He said since then, he had phoned J.T. every day to ward off any more late phone calls from the pest. Harry then jokingly said he was going to give J.T. my phone number, because I was the one who spurred him on into this whole mess to begin with.

Harry also told me that when he called J.T., the background noise sounded like a hippie commune, and a couple of times, a woman answered the phone.

The first night I was at Harry's home in Vancouver, he asked me if I would like to talk to J.T. I said it should be interesting, so Harry phoned him. After greeting J.T., he told him that his partner would like to discuss the Cooper case with him; then Harry handed the phone to me. J.T started with his scare story about the deadly marijuana growers, then went on to tell me of his prize finds that he was certain were related to Cooper. When he described a pair of RayBan sunglasses with one lens missing, I had heard enough of his meaningless tales, and as politely as possible terminated the conversation.

Himmelsbach had described Cooper's sunglasses as being of bubble-type, wrap-around style. So, I had to assume that J.T. had not even read Himmelsbach's book, and didn't know anything about Cooper or his skyjacking case. Most of all, because RayBan sunglasses have light green lenses, or light yellow for night vision and target shooting, worn by aviators, and what I wore when riding police motorcycles.

A few years later when I was watching one of the many TV versions of the Cooper skyjacking, J.T. appeared on one with the same name he had given to Harry, and spoke of what he knew about the D.B. Cooper case and his investigation. So, I phoned Harry and told him about J.T.'s TV appearance. Harry phoned J.T.'s number, and a man answered and said there was nobody there by that name, and he had that number for about two years. J.T. had apparently moved to who knows where.

Being called by a complete stranger was disturbing to Harry. Because of the psychopathic Mafia hood who had threatened his life, Harry gave his phone number only to his family and close friends. But in entrusting it to Himmelsbach, a retired law enforcement agent, he thought it would be secure with him.

That was because after the Watts Riot in 1965, and ongoing anarchy, anti-police and anti-Vietnam demonstrations, bombing of police cars and stations and ambushing and shooting police officers that continued into the mid-1970s, law enforcement officers' home addresses and phone numbers became strictly confidential. So much so, that the California Highway Patrol issued an order requiring that all office rosters be shredded lengthwise at least four times before being trashed. And if anybody phoned a CHP office and asked for an officer, the receptionist would tell the caller that she would take their name and phone number and have the named officer call them back, and without telling them if the officer was on duty or off duty.

In addition to Harry giving his confidential phone number and home address to Himmelsbach in his letter to him, the fact that J.T. obviously called to try to scare him away from searching the Washougal River watershed and trying to discourage him from searching the Columbia

River islands made it crystal clear who had given him Harry's confidential home phone number, and why. (WHY?)

If it hadn't been for Harry's phone number being given to a somewhat strange, obviously uninformed stranger, Harry and I would have found it humorous. But giving his confidential phone number to such an amateur actor of sorts made it too serious to laugh about.

What made it more ridiculous was that Harry and I had ruled out Cooper or anything related to him being in the Washougal River watershed area. In order for Cooper to end up in the Washougal River watershed area, he would have had to deploy his parachute, because the nearest point of the Washougal River watershed area is the Little Washougal River, about eight miles east of the prolongation of automatic pilot course Vector-23. And Co-pilot Rataczak was flying Flight 305 manually, and would have been on the prolongation, instead of on Vector-23, where it turns southwest at Dollars Corner and a few miles southwest of Battle Ground. Even if Flight 305 had drifted as much as three miles east of the prologation in the forty-five miles per hour southwest wind, it would have been about five miles west of the closest part of the Washougal River watershed. Also, it was almost a certainty that Cooper had been unable to deploy his chute, as Earl Cossey had convinced Harry and me when we interviewed him at his home on June 18, 1994.

The fact that J.T. had so openly told Harry that he was a retired Green Beret sergeant caused me to wonder about a couple of possibilities. One being, that I knew Green Berets are much like U.S. Marines, who stick together to the extent of never leaving a wounded comrade behind, even if they have to risk their own life under heavy enemy gunfire to move them to safety. With that, I wondered, and still do, if J.T. knew Cooper as a Green Beret, and was trying to cover for him, dead or alive.

Whether J.T. knew Cooper and who he was, or not, his claim that he was a Green Beret and trying to scare us away and discourage us from searching, supported my profile of Cooper as being a former Green Beret.

Then the most revealing part of the J.T. scare event was that he told Harry in their first phone conversation that he had called Himmelsbach that morning, and Himmelsbach would call Harry in a few minutes. Harry then told me that Himmelsbach did call him a few minutes later at about 9:30 A.M. Harry told me that they had a very pleasant discussion and exchange of theories, but he did not learn anything he did not already know. J.T. and Himmelsbach working together as a team! (WHY?)

The number one issue in this entire scenario was that Himmelsbach had obviously, without any doubt whatsoever, given Harry's highly confidential phone number to J.T without Harry's permission.

This amateurish attempt to scare a seasoned veteran law enforcement officer away from searching the Washougal River watershed area and trying to discourage him from searching the Columbia River islands and surrounding areas was as glaringly obvious to us as the rising sun. However, we had to wonder who wanted to keep us from digging into the Cooper case, and why. (WHY?)

Then later in Himmelsbach's book, he wrote a comment that if anything of interest was found, to give him a call and the Bureau (FBI) would take it from there. This was interesting to Harry and me, because when human remains are found, the body cannot be touched or moved except by the county coroner, who must be immediately notified of the discovery of human remains.

Harry started searching weeks before I flew up to Washington on June 14, 1994. We had a phone conversation after he had searched some areas, and he told that if he found Cooper's remains, he would delay in notifying "The Heat," as he called police authorities, and he would immediately phone me. He said he would want me to get up there on the next flight I could catch, even if it was the "redeye." He said he did not want any public exposure of any kind on TV or any other news media for any reason. He made it clear that he would tell me where he found Cooper's remains or other related evidence and stay out of view of the TV coverage, and I would fake my big find.

My suspicions that J.T. may have known Cooper in the Green Berets and was trying to scare Harry and dissuade him from searching anywhere to cover for Cooper aroused another question in my mind. Himmelsbach wrote that the FBI had a decoding section in Washington, D.C., and they were the best in the world at breaking codes. He wrote that they were so good, that they broke the Japanese code during World War II. So, he sent a confused personal newspaper ad to them, but they couldn't make anything out of it. Himmelsbach later learned the ad came from the wife of a police officer, and because she couldn't make any sense of it, she speculated that it could be a coded message about, or from, Cooper. So, no discredit to the decoders on that one.

If the FBI decoders could break the Japanese code during World War II, I had to seriously wonder why they couldn't decipher Cooper's name as I did by just looking in a dictionary at "Dan" and "cooper." And it was reported that the FBI knew in the late 1960s that Sam Giancana was in Mexico City.

If I could put it all together with my high school diploma and mere sixty-nine-and-a-half law enforcement college units, it seems to me that the college-educated FBI specialists should have been able to do at least as well or better. But there has never been any report that I could find in my sixteen years of dabbling in this case that they decoded Cooper's obvious coded message. (WHY?)

Vancouver, Wa.
May 9, 1994

Mr. Ralph P. Himmelsbach

Dear Sir:

I am writing to seek your possible help in one area of the D.B. Cooper case.
Because of the challenge of an unresolved case, I began working on D.B.
Cooper in 1986 for my own satisfaction. By studying the weather in November
of 1971, the hydraulics of the Columbia River and interviewing knowledgeable
river people, I was hoping to determine what happened to him after he bailed
out.

In 1993 I joined forces with Mr. George C. Nuttall, a retired CHP captain,
of ████████ California. Our hypothesis of the Cooper disappearance
is that he jumped beside (not into) the Columbia River somewhere upriver
from Tina's Bar; that his chute did not open, for he would have been found
by now; that he landed in an area of heavy forestation where the public
would not normally penetrate. His body would have been stripped by animals
leaving skeletal remains scattered about 100 yards in all directions from
the point of impact. His bones, nylon chute and harness, from my past experience, are still materially intact and will remain so for many more years.

The money found on Tina's Bar became separated from his body either by
animals after impact or was lost while tumbling on the way down. We started
searching in forested areas along the Columbia in 1993 and are now working
along Columbia Slough, Kelley Point Park and the northwest end of Hayden
Island. We started this far downriver from V-23 because there seems to be no
solid information from the crew of Northwest Airlines Flight 305 as to
just where they actually crossed the Columbia that night. If we can pin down
this crossing more accurately, we can cut down our search area measurably.
Our written requests for this information was forwarded by Northwest Airlines
to the flight crew, but as yet we have no answers. We hoped perhaps you might
be willing to give us some specifics that would help in our search.

I retired from the San Diego Police Department in 1961 (20 years service),
Naval Investigative Service in 1972 (11 years service) and the San Diego
District Attorney's Organized Crime Unit in 1982 (10 years service). Both
Nuttall and I have had experience recovering bodies in wilderness areas.
Our efforts to locate Cooper's remains will take about 2 more years,
especially when we search selected areas east of V-23.

Any advice you may care to give will be greatly appreciated. Your book is the
best source we have to work with, and we thank you for this.

Sincerely yours,

Harry L. Grady

George C. Nuttall

DOB: 8-6-30

DPOB: 3-17-21-Everett.
SSN:
CSA: 2 ███ 809

TO Dear George: DATE May 26,1994
        After your phone call this morning I located the station and program
that played the D.B. COOPER case yesturday at 4PM. It was the A&E channel
and the title was IN SERCH OF 887748. The guy that is also searching for
COOPER is one   , ex Army Special Forces man
who says he is retired from the Army and doesn't work. His home number is
            And he lives in   WA. His search area is in the
Washougal River and creeks that lead into the Washougal River areas. He
claimed he has searched the NW forested ares of Hayden but when I pinned
him down about terrain of the area he is full of balony. Also, he would
not say how long the search took him (he works alone). He said he reached the
island by boat and did not get permission the search. Up till a few days
ago the east end of the wooded search area butting up against the xxxdxdx
raised RR tracks was owned by a large corporation and was patrolled
by Hayden Island Patrol with the entry gates locked. The Port Of Portland
owned the west half and , as I indicated before, recently purchased
the additional land for   was not together of the known facts
concerning the COOPER case at all. He called me after I talked to you this
morning and said he had called HIMMELSBACH this AM and that HIMMELSBACH
would be calling me in a few minutes. I left it with th mas that we had no
intention of searching in the Washougal River area but would continue to
work the Columbia River west of I-205 on both sides and in the middle islands
HIMMELSBACH then called me about 9:30 AM from his home in BEND, Oregon
                He was nice and seemed forthcoming. He guesses that
flight 305 was a little east of V-23 but in debriefing the pilots could
not say how far. Ue said the co-pilot did all the flying that night and
that the sdorm was severe with a strong wind coming at them from 245° There
was a cloud cover below them when they passed over Vancouver that was so thi
they couldn't see landmarks or even the glow of city lights. The pilot
maintained a speed of 170 knots at 10,000 feet. He went un in a Army helo
from PDX shartly after 305 passed over when movement by the extended ramp
indicated COOPER had jumped. He said is was a nasty storm going. He later
talked to RADACZAK the co-pilot about the time the money was discovered
on TINA's Bar or shortly thereafter. R said he was basicly on V-23 when he
passed over Vancouver, possibläy slightly east but he could not say how
far. There were not on automatic pilot but following there V-23 course
by instrumemts (VORTAC signals). R said he "was close to being right on
V-23 but possibly slightly to the left(east)" As I mentioned he was very

is his conversation. He said the breakdown in the debriefing of the pilots
was they were not interviewed by Agents that were also pilots s many of
the questions asked didn't cover navigation etc. When he retired shortly
after the COOPER case he recommended that the pilots be interviewed be
interviewed by pilot agents. I guess they later did this but I'm not sure.
Of course he later saw RADACZAK after retiring and gained a lot more
info. I told him we would continue tosearch our Columbia River areas west of
I-205 while   does his thing in the east. H says his best theory
is COOPER bailed out, the chute opened and he was blown so far east because
of that (Which is true, if the chute opened his drift would in my opinion
be considerable to the NE in that stang NE wind). Not knowing if or how far
flight 305 was east of V-23 this would explain COOPERS drift that far even
is they were right on V-23). He also xxxxxdxx be lieves its probable that
COOPER was unable due to extreme hypothermia of a bad chute to deploy the
chute and came down like a xxkx rock with no drift factter to speak of.
Also, they normally stray ½ to one mile of an electronic course either right
or left and thats not out of the ordinary. They could not be 8 or nine miles
off to the east he agreed so his depaoyed chute explanation is the only
way COOPER could have come down on ths or ne either the Washougle R or as he
a small stream leading into that river.xhxx He thinks COOPER may have been
hurt in landing and made his way to a tributary stream or the Waushougle R
for water. This is his explanation for the money appearing as far away as
TINA"S BAR. This would be 24 miles from where the monmey was found to the
entrance of the Washougal enters the Columbia R, 4 miles more up to where the
Washougal makes a turn from the east plus whatever mileage on a tributary
stream. It exceeds 28 miles for the money to tavel to XXX TINA'S BAR. Its
hard for me to buy this although I suppose it is possible. M agrees he is only
guessing as to where COOPER came down and believes as we do the he did not
make it alive. I agreed we would let him and/   know if we founf anything
M said he would like to see us some time. He still flies his own plane.
All in all I dont think we learned much more than what was in his book.
He seems straight foreward and easy to talk to. I didn't get his home address
and he didn't offer it. Howevr his daughter xitx will forward any mail to him

See you soon, regards

[TEN]

Beating the Bushes

Cooper Crashed to His Death

H IMMELSBACH PHONED ME AT my home in the early evening of June 13, 1994, the night before I flew up to Washington. After a very congenial greeting, the first thing he said was he had classified Cooper's clothing as a service uniform. I then told him I had come to the same conclusion. He then said the $5,800 of Cooper's ransom money that was found by Brian Ingraham had been sent to the FBI laboratory, and it was determined to have been the middle part of $14,000 stuck together. That convinced me it had been under water for a long time and supported Harry's theory that it had been dredged onto Tina's Bar by the Army Corps of Engineers in October 1974. Among other information he imparted to me was that Cooper had been very profane in his dealings with the airlines stewardesses. That surprised me, because it wasn't reported in any of the three books I had studied in my research. And he had stated in his book that the flight crew had reported Cooper had appeared to be "rational and calm." Also, Tosaw mentioned that Cooper used foul or profane language only one time, and that was when there were delays in refueling Flight 305 at the Seattle Airport, when he said "dammit" two times. Tosaw also reported that Cooper offered Alice Hancock and Florence Shaffner $4,000 as they were deplaning at the Seattle Airport. Tosaw also wrote that just before turning out the lights between the first class and coach sections, as Cooper had told her to do, Tina looked back at Cooper, and he waved her a friendly farewell salute. From these reports, I couldn't visualize Cooper using profane language in his dealings with the three airline stewardesses. Himmelsbach and I concluded our congenial, informative conversation, and that was the only time I had any contact with him. The only valuable information I received from him was his classification of Cooper's clothing as being a service uniform. It supported my opinion and gave me confidence that my profile of Cooper's being from Las Vegas was most likely correct.

The first location Harry took me to was the Washougal River watershed area for me to see for myself that it was not realistic to believe that Cooper landed there, and that the money bag had traveled about twenty-four miles to Tina's Bar. I quickly took note that both the main Washougal River and the Little Washougal River are white-water rivers at numerous locations, and converge about two-and-a-quarter miles north of the Columbia River. Then at the foot of the Washougal River, there is a calm-water pond

Big Washougal River White Water Rapids

Little Washougal River White Water Rapids

Calm Water Basin at the Foot of the Washougal River

Extension of Calm Water Basin at the Columbia River

about two-tenths of a mile long and about one-tenth of a mile wide, with inlets on both sides at the shores, and islets in the middle. I took photos of all of the obstacles, hazards, and other conditions that convinced me that the money bag could not have made it to the Columbia River without being torn apart or having settled to the bed of the pond or being forced into an inlet.

That was enough to convince me that Harry was correct in discounting the theory that Cooper had landed in the Washougal River watershed area.

Also, in order to reach that far after bailing out, he would have had to deploy his chute to carry him at least five miles to the very west edge of the Washougal River watershed where the Little Washougal River arcs to the west for less than a mile.

The next two days, Harry and I searched a peninsula, which was the least likely area to find anything related to Cooper, but it was Harry's systematic method of covering the easiest search areas before the islands. When we started each strip of forest, Harry marked a tree with a small spot of orange spray paint, then when we cleared the strip at a wide opening, he sprayed another tree to mark where we had searched.

One time when we reached a wide opening where there was a pedestrian path, a middle-aged woman saw us and asked what we were doing. Without batting an eye, Harry told her that we were engineers and were surveying the area. She appeared to believe him, was satisfied, thanked him and went on her merry way down the path.

As soon as she was out of earshot, Harry told me he did

not want to broadcast what we were doing because of the many D.B. Cooper glorifiers in the area who might not want anybody to find their idol who beat the system, and especially not find him dead.

The only ones we had told about our investigation of the Cooper case were Himmelsbach, who told J.T., the elderly couple that lived near Tina's Bar, the flight crew, FAA, Northwest Airlines, Earl Cossey and the Port of Portland employees.

In our easy search through the puny blackberry vines, we did not find anything other than soda and beer cans, although I did see a small bird's nest on the ground with two fuzzy baby birds in it. They were obviously easy prey for any predator. But when I told Harry, it did not dispel his belief that Cooper's remains would be scattered by wildlife and easy to find. He was also pretty much of a wildlife naturalist, and was recognized by one retired San Diego P.D. officer as a bird expert, who told me as much. When I asked Harry about his being a bird expert, he said he wouldn't swear to it in court, but he had read every book he could find about birds.

He wasn't disturbed about the birds on the ground, because as he explained to me, that peninsula was visited by many people on weekends, and for that reason, the predator wildlife avoided it and preyed in unpopulated areas, of which there were many in that vast wild country. He then again explained to me that the Columbia River islands were public access only by permit, there were few trespassers, if any, therefore, the predators thrived on the islands.

As I recall, it was after our first day of searching the peninsula when we returned to Harry's home, sat down in his
family room, and he turned on the TV news. We got there
just in time to see the great O.J. Simpson white Bronco
chase. It was announced that the chase had started at what
is called the "El Toro 'Y'," because it is where the I-5 and
I-405 converge southbound, and the I-405 ends. And it was
only a few miles from my home at that time. As Harry com-
mented that the chase was going northbound, because the
car shadows were to the east of the cars, and the sun was in
the west, I counted twenty-five black-and-white police cars
in the parade of pursuers in all lanes of the freeway. When
I told Harry the number, we both laughed, because it was
obvious to us that every cop along the way got into the act,
and, if lucky, just might get on TV somewhere along the
way on the parade route. Then when the Bronco drove in
the gate at O.J.'s mansion, and the gate was locked as soon
as it entered the mansion grounds, the TV-hopeful cops
were out of luck.

I then told Harry that for years before I retired from
the CHP, the strictly enforced CHP policy was that no
more than two officer units and one supervisor could be
involved in a pursuit. And if a motorcycle officer initiated
a pursuit, it was required to drop out as soon as a car unit
could take over the pursuit. Then I said, but those days
must be gone forever. Then, on Saturday, June 18, 1994,
Harry drove us to parachute rigger Earl Cossey's home to
interview him in his home in a beautiful area east of
Seattle. As I have earlier related, Cossey's first comment
to Harry and me was that we were crazy to get involved

in the Cooper case. He then humorously told us of the mass law enforcement chaos that persisted for days and weeks after Cooper's skjacking. The way he described the confusion, it reminded me of the movie *The Russians Are Coming, The Russians Are Coming*, with Jonathan Winters as a policeman running around repeatedly yelling, "We've got to get organized."

Cossey then started explaining the facts of parachuting. He stood up from the sofa, leaned forward, and said that was the face-down position a chutist had to be in to avoid getting tangled up in the shroud lines when the chute was deployed.

He then said that when Cooper stepped off of the stairway, he would have "spun ass over teakettle," and with his raincoat flapping and the money bag bouncing around, he would have had great difficulty getting in the face-down position and to find and pull the ripcord handle. He then said that the ripcord handle on the NB-8 military chute that he used was in a pocket, and that chute was difficult to deploy under the best of conditions. He then said that in the severe sub-freezing temperature, his fingers would have become too numb in just seconds for him to grab the ripcord handle and deploy the chute.

With all of his expert demonstrations and explanations, he expressed his opinion that Cooper would have fallen at 120 to 150 miles per hour, and most likely plunged to his death.

Harry and I openly agreed with him. And it cleared up that critical issue in the case, and despite the many expert opinions otherwise, including that the theory Cooper survived his jump, was actually Richard Floyd McCoy, Jr., and repeated his performance on April 7, 1972.

Most of all, that logical, expert conclusion affirmed the part of Harry's theory that Cooper's remains are on one of the Columbia River islands.

Cossey then told us that all parachutes are unique to the rigger, and if we found any parts of a chute, he could identify them as his work. He then took us into his garage and showed us some of his buckles and other hardware that he used.

As Harry and I departed, I gave Cossey a California Highway Patrol baseball cap as a token of appreciation, and a reminder of the two "Cooper crazies."

On the way back to Harry's, I told Harry I was convinced his Columbia River island theory was the only answer to Cooper's fate and location. In discussing all of the details, Harry explained that Cooper probably crashed into a tall tree at over 120 miles per hour, the money bag broke loose from him, and was launched into the main channel of the Columbia River. And that Cooper had to be within two hundred feet of the river, so that limited the area he would have to search on the islands.

We then took the next day, Sunday, June 19, off, as Harry and his wife, Ruth, were devout Catholics, and they went to morning Mass. That afternoon, Harry and I discussed all of the details of the Cooper case as we knew them, and I again agreed with him that the only place where Cooper's remains could be located would be on a Columbia River island. We also agreed that if Cooper had landed on a shore of the river, his remains would have been found years ago, because the mainland was open to public access and the area was fairly well populated. But the islands could be legally accessed only by permits issued by the Port of Portland.

In considering all of the islands, we agreed that the most likely of all of them was Government island, and it should be the primary target. Being about six miles long and about one mile wide in the middle, it was the largest. Although cattle grazed on that island, they grazed in open pastures; most of that island was forested and much of it was concealed by dense, tall, thorny blackberry vines where exposed to sunlight. There was also a caretaker on that island, but he rode a tractor much of the time, and most likely never ventured into the massive vine-concealed areas.

Harry was eagerly looking forward to searching Government Island, even though he would have to buy a small boat with an outboard motor and a cell phone to do it. He also had a heart condition. So, every day when Harry searched, he gave Ruth a written itinerary and a map of where he was going to search, a time that he would return, and with instructions to notify the sheriff's department if he did not return by the given time. He also wore a red sweatshirt and red baseball cap, and he carried a couple of smoke bombs that emitted a bright color. He told me that if he was able to do so, he would set off a bomb if he heard a helicopter approaching or overhead. In very plain words, finding Cooper's remains or any other evidence of his whereabouts or fate was a do-or-die dream of Harry's to finalize his near-lifetime of seeking criminals and justice. And one way or another, he was going to give it his usual best shot, bad heart or not. And at seventy-three years of age.

The next day, Monday, Harry first took me to Tina's Bar, where eight-year-old Brian Ingraham had found the $5,800 on February 10, 1980. Harry and I both took photos of the sandy river bank and of the Columbia River. Although the banks are frequented by old fishermen that fish from the shores, it was quite easy to see how the money could be partially buried there for over eight years without being noticed. Like Harry's being solely focused on finding Cooper's remains, the old fishermen's sole goal was to catch fish, and one of them could have stepped directly on top of the money and never given it any notice.

Harry and I then continued searching the same peninsula for two more days, then I flew home, leaving him with my best wishes for a speedy discovery of Cooper's remains, and my total agreement with him and his theory of where they were located.

As we parted at the Portland International Airport, Harry reminded me to be ready and packed to catch the first flight back to "Cooper Country," even if I had to take a "redeye" special, to cover for him in front of the TV cameras, as he hid way out of sight.

Harry L. Grady at Tina's Bar

Vector–23 control facility near Battle Ground

*Harry L. Grady at
Kelly Point Peninsula
with grappling pole*

*George C. Nuttall at
Kelly Point Peninsula*

ELEVEN

The Iron Curtain

Government Island Bomb

A S HE HAD DONE before I went up to Washington to confirm his Columbia River island theory, Harry continued to send me every news article related in any way to the Cooper case.

Then two months after I returned home to Orange County, Harry sent me a newsclipping dated August 16, 1994. It reported that the caretaker of Government Island had run over an explosive while riding on his tractor, and the explosion had lifted his tractor off of the ground. He reported it to the Multnomah County Sheriff's Department, and they responded by searching the island for marijuana plants, and feared that the explosive may have been a booby-trap. The deputy sheriffs and Oregon State Police officers hacked their way through twelve-foot-high walls of blackberry vines into a marijuana patch, but did not find any more explosives. The article also reported they found eighty marijuana plants, which was not a sizeable seizure; the sheriff's department routinely raided Government Island every year to search for marijuana plantings.

When I read the article, I immediately thought of J.T. and his scare story about marijuana growers shooting strangers in the Washougal River watershed area. Of course, booby-trapping is a much better way to eliminate threats of discovery, because the ones who plant the bomb can be miles away when it automatically detonates when disturbed. And unlike having to be on the alert for intruders around the clock, and trying to snipe-shoot them with a high-powered rifle and scope from a distance of a hundred yards or more.

This report caused me to have concern for Harry's safety, so I quickly phoned him. He calmed my fears when he casually told me that Government Island had been a military practice base during World War II, and he was certain that the explosive devise that the caretaker ran over was an old explosive that the military had carelessly lost and abandoned in the confusion of maneuvers during the war, and the wartime in general.

Knowing that Harry was aware of just about everything of importance in his environment that could affect him and his wife, Ruth, it relieved me to know that he was on top of the situation. Also, I already knew from a report a few years earlier that the military had lost and abandoned explosives on temporary bases during World War II. One tragic incident reported in the news had occurred on Kearny Mesa in San Diego County at what had been the Navy's

Camp Elliot during the war. Some young boys were exploring or playing on the abandoned Navy base when they stumbled across an old World War II explosive. It exploded, and as I recall, it killed one or more of them. Regardless of the extent of their injuries, I clearly recalled that incident that I could relate to Harry's explanation of the probability of the Government Island explosion.

Even the possibility of another abandoned military bomb on Government Island couldn't stop Harry from searching that island, but some mysterious somebody did.

In a letter dated February 7, 1995, Harry angrily wrote that the Port of Portland had a new legal counsel, and he would not issue him any more permits to access the islands, and specifically Government Island, unless he would sign over his million-dollar umbrella liability insurance policy to the Port of Portland. (WHY?)

And enclosed with Harry's letter were copies of his two letters to the "Office Facility Administrator" asking for the permits, and a copy of his issued permit to access Hayden Island. Another suspicious part of their permit issuance process was that Harry's permit to access Hayden island did not expire until May 31, 1995, but they did not cancel it, even though it was valid for seven months after he was denied additional access permits. (WHY?)

Knowing Harry had to be greatly disappointed in this latest roadblock of his trying to do what was just and to again serve public interests, I immediately phoned him. He was still angry when he answered the phone, which was out of character for him, as I had always known him to be. When I asked him what had happened, he just replied, "It's

TO   Mr. ████████████
     Office Facility Administrator
     Port of Portland
     Box 3529,Portland,OR 97208

DATE 10-27-94

Vancouver,WA 98███

Dear ██████████

May I respectfully again request access to Port of Portland property
to conduct a walking search for the remains of one "D.B.Cooper" on
Government Island and adjacent islands of Sand (AKA: Tri-Club),
Lemon, McGuire and the western halfSand (AKA: Ackerman-near east end
of Government Island) from 2-1-95 to 12-1-95. Inasmuch as this search
may take more than one year I would appreciate the option of
renewing the search on 2-1-96.
My personal liability insurance (Exhibit "B") is in force subject to
renewal 7-25-95. I will forward verification of renewal then as before
to ████████████. I condier this search area as prime with the
greatist probability of it being "Coopers" landing area.
I would expect to effect continuing contact with the caretaker of
Government Island during this search subject to your approval.
I assure you that I will abide by the Ports requirements agreed to
as set forth in Exhibit "A" and my longhand request for access to
western Hayden Island in June of this year. Additionally, I will
follow any additional requirements the Port of Portland may see
fit to impose.
Thanks again for your kind consideration in the past, I remain,

                                   Sincerely yours

                                   Harry L. Grady

2-7-9ɔ

Dear George:

I am sorry to report that I wont be searching anymore for Dan
COOPER as you can see by the attached letter to the Port of Portland.
There is a new young lawyer that put unreasonable requirements in my
mind on my insurence carrier. Plus stalling tactics in the last week
aND A HALF LED ME TO BELIEVE that they would prefer I not bother them.
First, a new gal filling in for [   ] who was on leave made up
and had approved a Port permit last week allowing me to search HAYDeн
ISLAND (again). I pointed out this error and tha gal [   ] said she
would redo it for Government Island. The young (new) lawyer approved
this latter mistaken permit without adding additional commitments by
my insurance carrier. This commitment in my mind wasunreasonable that
was added yesturday in the corrected permit for Government Island.
In my opiőn they did this probably hoping I would just go away. If
that was the message they accomplished their (his) goal. I'm too old
to play these buracratice games.

        I'm sorry George this turned out this way but so be it. I hope
all is going well with you. Were doing OK.

                                        Regards

                                        Harry

all yours now, so do whatever you want to do with it." Early in my joint venture with Harry to try to find Cooper's remains, or other evidence of his fate, I told Harry that if he or we discovered anything conclusive about Cooper, I would author a book about it. But the only conclusions we had arrived at were where we were certain Cooper's remains were located, and my theory that Cooper was a former Green Beret, a compulsive Las Vegas gambler over his head in debt to Mafia loan sharks, who had given him his very last warning to pay up—or else!

But being as naive as I was about getting a book published by a major publisher, I soon learned it was like trying to break into Fort Knox. And it didn't take long for me to amass a sizeable pile of form-letter rejection notices.

Despite the many strange events and obstacles that Harry and I had experienced in our efforts to conduct a professional investigation of the elusive case, I decided the only honorable action I could take would be to pass our conclusions on to FBI Director Louis Freeh. I had learned during my twenty-nine years on the California Highway Patrol that if one wanted action on a matter, they had to go straight to the top.

So, I typed a letter to Director Freeh and mailed it to him on May 24, 1995, explaining our conclusions. And I enclosed photocopies of my driver's license; Social Security card; FBI National Academy I.D. badge, which we were allowed to keep; and California Highway Patrol retiree ID card with concealed weapons permit endorsement. Then, two months later, on a Saturday I received a reply from Inspector-in-Charge John E. Collingwood, Office of Public and Congressional Affairs, dated July 25, 1995. Therein, he wrote that FBI Headquarters personnel had reviewed the information I had provided, and a copy of my letter was being forwarded to their field office in Seattle. It went on to say that I would be contacted by that office should further information be needed, and if I had more details to be provided, please contact a representative at that office. It then listed the address and phone number of the Seattle FBI field office.

With no more information to provide, I figured that was the end of it. Then, the following Thursday morning, I received a call from the then-chief Cooper case special agent, whom I will call Agent "A" (name on file with my attorney). After we exchanged congenial greetings, he somewhat spontaneously blurted out that they had received a call from Las Vegas and the caller told of a person who reportedly planned to commit a major crime in the Pacific Northwest.

The report from Las Vegas was exciting to me, because it fit perfectly with my profile of Cooper coming from that Mafia-infested gambling mecca. I then wanted to know more about what the caller had revealed about the major crime planner.

But before I could attempt to delve into that warning phone call, Agent "A" quickly revealed to me that the original chief Cooper case agent was of superior intelligence, and had graduated number two in his Naval Academy class. He told me his name, but I will not disclose it herein (name on file with my attorney). Agent "A" then told me that the superior agent had been harassed by his supervisors who gave by him crappy details, and he finally resigned and was hired by the CEO of a top corporation. When I asked Agent "A" if he intimidated his supervisors, he replied "Yes." And it made me wonder why the FBI would not want an agent of superior intelligence to serve indefinitely as the chief Cooper case agent. (WHY?)

Agent "A" and I had an enjoyable exchange of humor about some of the FBI special agents that I knew from my days at the FBI National Academy in 1975, and he had known for years. Then when I got around to asking him if the FBI would conduct a search of the Columbia River islands, where Harry and I are certain Cooper's remains are scattered, he said that they didn't have the manpower, because they were all too busy trying to track down the Unabomber.

That almost made me laugh, because the Unabomber had been mailing or planting bombs for seventeen years since 1978. This made it clear to me that the FBI had no desire to search, and with no more than ten agents spaced no more than twenty feet apart for no more than ten days. And after they had searched the wrong area for weeks in 1971 and 1972 with dozens of FBI agents, law enforcement officers and four hundred Fort Lewis soldiers, or some two hundred soldiers as reported by Himmelsbach. (WHY?) What also surprised me was that Agent "A" did not question me about how Harry had concluded that Cooper's remains were on a Columbia River island, nor my investigation to confirm Harry's well-based theory. I had to conclude that the FBI was not interested in finding Cooper's remains, and that added to my curiosity of why Harry and

I were unable to get in contact with the flight crew of
Cooper's skyjacked Flight 305, and why the Port of Portland legal counsel refused to issue Harry any more permits
unless he signed over his million-dollar umbrella personal
liability policy to them. (WHY?)

What made it more interesting to me was that Himmelsbach
wrote in his 1986 copyrighted book that the D.B. Cooper
case had been most thoroughly investigated by the world's
best investigative organization. That statement sounded to
me like past tense, and it was over, done and dead. He also
wrote of the FBI's enormous capacity to investigate and
solve crimes. But according to Agent "A," they didn't have
the manpower to spare to solve the crime that Himmelsbach
reported resulted in one of the largest manhunts in the history of the FBI. And only ten special agents spaced twenty
feet apart were needed to search for no more than ten days.
Not two hundred or four hundred soldiers.

Despite those omissions and diversions in our conversation, we had a very pleasant and informative exchange.
Mostly, the parts about the phone call from Las Vegas and
the first chief Cooper case agent who had resigned because
of harassment. Needless to say, the only critical information he divulged to me was the phone call from Las Vegas
that there was going to be a major crime committed in the
Pacific Northwest. And Cooper's skyjacking was the only
truly major crime committed in the Pacific Northwest any
time before or after his highly-publicized skyjacking. There
may have been any number of bank robberies, but they are
common crimes routinely committed throughout the U.S.,
including in the Pacific Northwest.

I was overjoyed to hear that bit of unreported information, because it fit right in with my profile of Cooper, and three years later, it tied in with more critical reports that I discovered that proved to me beyond any doubt whatsoever why the FBI has never reportedly solved the D.B. Cooper case.

May 24, 1995

Director Louis Freeh
Federal Bureau of Investigation
9th & Pennsylvania Avenue N.W.
Washington, D.C. 20535

Subject: D.B. Cooper Skyjacking Case - Most Probable
           Location of Cooper's Remains.

Honorable Director Freeh:

     This no doubt sounds somewhat unusual, but my ex-San Diego
P.D. partner and I collected and comprehensively analyzed all
of the available information on the Cooper case as a hobby and
professional challenge. In doing so, using our over 70 years
of combined law enforcement and investigative experience, we
concluded with at least ninety-percent certainty that D.B.
Cooper's remains were scattered by wildlife on one of the islands
shown on the enclosed maps, after he free-fell to his death.
     Our investigation included interviews with retired FBI
Special Agent Ralph Himmelsbach, the case agent; and Earl
Cossey, the parachute packer and expert parachutist. They both
agreed that Cooper's chances of a survival landing were next
to impossible under the conditions that existed, and Cossey
estimated Cooper's free-fall drift to be about one mile to the
northeast of where he jumped. From this information and other
data, we believe he most likely landed on Government Island.
     We further concluded that all of the money went into the
Columbia River and decomposed, except for the partially
decomposed $5,800 found on a bank of the Columbia in February
1980.
     Himmelsbach readily admitted in his book, "Norjak", and
in telephone conversation with me, that that find was proof
that they had searched the wrong areas near the Lewis River
in 1971 and 1972. Although the Fort Lewis Army troops did find
two other unrelated bodies during those searches.
     My partner lives in the Vancouver, Washington, area, which
prompted our review and analysis of this case. He had planned
to search Government Island, as he had done on other islands,
but discontinued his efforts for several valid reasons. One
being the marijuana growers who protect their illegal crops
with booby-traps, as explained in the enclosed newsclipping,
in addition to maps of the target search areas.
     In that he decided his searching could be too hazardous,
we decided to apprise the Bureau of our comprehensive conclusions
for whatever value they might be to solve this case.
     We also believe that a law enforcement search may reveal
other crimes, evidence, or bodies like found in 1971 and 1972
in the Lewis River areas, in addition to the well-publicized

-1-

marijuana crops and booby traps. And with the Oklahoma City
bombing revealing the explosives threat in our nation, the booby-
traps might be of more than casual interest.

My partner wishes to remain anonymous at this time to
protect his privacy and serene life-style at age 74. Also, during
his over 41-year career, his life was threatened by Mafia members
who he succesfully investigated and prosecuted in San Diego.
But if his identity were to be protected with certainty, I'm
sure he would agree to an interview to corroborate what I have
presented, and possibly more.

As a point of interest, Himmelsbach and I came to our own
independent opinions that Cooper's dark, or black, attire
indicated that it was a service uniform, such as worn by
bartenders, limousine drivers, et al. In addition, from all
of the data, and the entire event, my own assessment of Cooper
is that he was a loner casino worker from Las Vegas, a compulsive
gambler, and hopelessly in debt to loan sharks who had given
him a time-period ultimatum to pay up or else. Of course, we
will never know unless his remains are found and identified.

If any of this is of interest, please do not hesitate to
have one or more of your agents contact me at any time for all
of the pertinent details. I have volumes of documentation, but
the critical data can be fully explained in less than two hours.

I have also enclosed copies of some of my identification
cards as evidence of my past activities, positions and status.

Wishing you and the Bureau the best of success in your
investigation and prosecution of those responsible for the tragic
Oklahoma City bombing.

Most sincerely,

George C. Nuttall, Captain, California Highway Patrol, Retired
██████████████████████████

Telephone: ████████████████████

enclosures
cc: file

-2-

U.S. Department of Justice

Federal Bureau of Investigation

Washington, D.C. 20535

July 25, 1995

Mr. George C. Nuttall

Dear Mr. Nuttall:

Your May 24th letter to Director Freeh regarding the D.B. Cooper case was referred to me for response.

Appropriate personnel at FBI Headquarters have reviewed the information you provided, and a copy of your letter is being forwarded to our field office in Seattle. You will be contacted by that office should additional information be needed. In the interim, if you have more details to provide, please contact a representative of that office directly which is located in Room 710, 915 Second Avenue, Seattle, Washington 98174, telephone (206) 622-0460.

Your interest in writing is appreciated.

Sincerely yours,

John E. Collingwood
Inspector in Charge
Office of Public and
    Congressional Affairs

CONFIDENTIAL

July 30, 1995

Federal Bureau of Investigation
915 Second Avenue
Room 710
Seattle, Washington 98174

Reference: D.B. Cooper Case - Attached Letter of Response
              from FBI Inspector in Charge John E. Collingwood,
              Washington, D.C.

To Whom It May Concern:

It was most encouraging and gratifying to receive the
Reference response, and my partner and I hope we can be of some
assistance with our D.B. Cooper case findings.
      Due to this positive response from your FBI Headquarters,
my previously mentioned anonymous D.B. Cooper case partner
consented to my revealing his identity, address and phone number.
However, only with the promise that it would remain strictly
confidential, as he does not want any publicity that would
involve or identify him, for reasons previously mentioned in
my letter of May 24, 1995.
      He is: Harry L. Grady, DOB: 3-17-21

It was Harry's over 43 year career as a San Diego City
Lifeguard, San Diego P.D. Officer, Naval Intelligence Special
Agent, and San Diego County District Attorney Organized Crime
Investigator that prompted him to review and analyze the Cooper
case. I then joined him in July 1993, at his prompting. One
of Harry's many successes during his long and distinguished
career is illustrated in the attached newsclipping. And we both
feel that Cooper's remains are out there on a Columbia River
Island, much like those of the "missing" naval officer's that
were finally found, due to Harry's similar "hunch." But in
Cooper's case, we base it on facts and logic, not just a hunch.
      We both hope that we can be of some assistance, so please
contact us if we can help in any way. In closing, I must clarify
that we do not agree with Himmelsbach's "Washougal Drainage
Theory", and we can factually and logically explain why.

Most sincerely,

George C. Nuttall, Captain, California Highway Patrol, Retired

                          attachments
                          cc: Harry L. Grady
                              file

TWELVE

The Ongoing Whodunit

The Almost Dead and Done Case

A S WE HAD DONE from the beginning of our joint investigation, Harry and I sent copies of all of our written correspondence to persons of interest to each other for our dual files.

After talking to Agent "A," I phoned Harry to tell him the good news and the bad news. The good news being the reported telephone call from Las Vegas that supported my profile of Cooper, and the bad news that the FBI was not interested in his Columbia River island theory or searching the islands.

As he had been after being denied any more access permits by the Port of Portland to continue his search of the islands, Harry was not pleased with the entire series of mysterious events we had experienced. Most of all, with his years of donating his efforts and expertise to determine where Cooper's remains were located and my handing that vital information to the FBI on a silver platter, and they weren't interested, because they were all trying to catch the Unabomber. Hell, by that time in 1995, they hadn't been able to catch him in seventeen years. With that, Harry was even more angry with the FBI for using that lame excuse. We then agreed that with that and all of the other strange events that we had experienced in this confused case, something was suspiciously amiss. Then, after brainstorming for about a half hour to come up with some plausible reason why the FBI was not interested in even a simple ten-or-twenty-man search for Cooper's remains, we drew a blank. In 1971 and 1972, they had searched the wrong area about twenty miles north of where he had to have jumped, and with dozens of FBI special agents and local law enforcement and four hundred or two hundred Fort Lewis soldiers, and now they weren't at all interested. (WHY?)

After we completed our disgruntled conversation and hung up, I thought of when I was at the FBI National Academy at the FBI Academy in Quantico, Virginia, in the summer of 1975. Some of the FBI agent instructors joked for weeks about their not being able to find Patty Hearst for about eighteen months. Then just before we graduated on September 30, 1975, they found and arrested her. It was such an embarrassment to the FBI that they made light of it. And, so much so, that FBI Director Clarence Kelley joked about it during his speech at our graduation ceremony.

However, the D.B. Cooper and Patty Hearst cases were very different. Patty Hearst was running with William and

Emily Harris in the Symbionese Liberation Army (SLA) and
had many sympathizers and supporters in that era of revo-
lution and anarchy who could harbor them. Conversely,
Cooper's remains were by all logical reasoning laying out
there in one exposed area to be discovered. And the Cooper
case is still the only reportedly unsolved skyjacking case of
over 2,111 during the 1960s and 1970s. (WHY?)

With the many questions in my mind about the case, I
phoned Seattle FBI Agent "A" two times to try to tactfully
pry some more meaningful information out of him. During
our first conversation, he said that there were four composite drawings of Cooper. Although that was not critical
news, I took note of it because Himmelsbach had reported
that FBI artists had developed three "impressions" of
Cooper, and they had been widely distributed, including to
the press. That disparity was not of great significance, but
it made me wonder if the Portland and Seattle FBI special
agents were coordinating and communicating with each
other. Other than that minor bit of information, Agent "A"
didn't say anything else of importance, and we had a very
pleasant conversation.

The second time I phoned Agent "A," he was not in the
office, and returned my call a few hours later. The first
thing he said was that he was no longer the chief Cooper
case agent, and that the case had been reassigned to a
younger, newer agent. When I replied that I preferred to
talk to him, not a new Cooper case agent, he expressed his
appreciation for my interest in him and his efforts and
knowledge of the case.

Above all in my mind was, why does the FBI keep

bouncing the Cooper case around like a football, and especially to a newer, younger special agent. Knowing from my thirty-one years of experience of investigations, continuity can be critical, especially in involved, complex, long-term cases wherein some of the important information is not all documented in written form, and is known only to the initial investigator(s).

Also, with the case being dumped on a younger, newer special agent, it appeared to me that the Cooper case had been buried in an elephants' graveyard to get it to go away forever.

The disparity in the number of composite drawings as reported by Himmelsbach and told to me by Agent "A" reminded me of some of the conflicting and contradictory reports by Tosaw and Himmelsbach. One was that Himmelsbach wrote that when Flight 305 landed in Reno, there were only two chutes on the plane. Conversely, Tosaw wrote that Cooper used only the NB-8 military chute, and when Harry and I interviewed Earl Cossey, the parachute rigger who owned the four chutes, he told us that three chutes were returned to him, and the only one not returned to him was the NB-8 military chute. And Himmelsbach wrote that he was the Portland FBI Division Cooper case agent. As such, one should be able to assume that he knew all of the details of the case.

With all of the mishmash reported in the case, I was more determined than ever to keep digging for any missing connections that might just pop up in the future, one way or another. Then they did, starting three years later, in 1998, and like a great big bomb.

And what I discovered strongly indicated that the bomb originated before the fact in Washington, D.C. And Agent "A"'s disclosure to me that they had received a call from Las Vegas that there was going to be a major crime committed in the Pacific Northwest fit perfectly and answered the multitude of questions Harry and I had about the mysterious, and suspicious, case.

Artist's rendition (composite drawing) of
Cooper with sunglasses

WANTED BY THE FBI

NATIONAL FIREARMS ACT; MATERIAL WITNESS

William Taylor Harris

FBI No. 308,668 L5 — Date photograph taken unknown
Aliases: Richard Frank Dennis, William Kinder, Jonathan Mark Salamone
Age: 29, born January 22, 1945, Fort Sill, Oklahoma (not supported by birth records)

Height: 5'7"	**Eyes:** Hazel
Weight: 145 pounds	**Complexion:** Medium
Build: Medium	**Race:** White
Hair: Brown, short	**Nationality:** American

Occupation: Postal clerk
Remarks: Reportedly wears Fu Manchu type mustache, may wear glasses, upper right center tooth may be chipped, reportedly jogs, swims and rides bicycle for exercise, was last seen wearing army type boots and dark jacket.
Social Security Numbers Used: 315-46-2467, 551-27-8800, 359-48-5467
Fingerprint Classification: 20 L 1 At 13
S 1 10

Emily Montague Harris

FBI No. 325,804 L2 — Date photographs taken unknown
Aliases: Mrs. William Taylor Harris, Anna Lindenberg, Cynthia Sue Mankins, Emily Montague Schwartz
Age: 27, born February 11, 1947, Baltimore, Maryland (not supported by birth records)

Height: 5'3"	**Eyes:** Blue
Weight: 115 pounds	**Complexion:** Fair
Build: Small	**Race:** White
Hair: Blonde	**Nationality:** American

Occupations: Secretary, teacher
Remarks: Hair may be worn one inch below ear level, may wear glasses or contact lenses; reportedly has partial upper plate, pierced ears, is a natural food faddist, exercises by jogging, swimming and bicycle riding, usually wears slacks or street length dresses, was last seen wearing jeans and waist length shiny black leather coat.
Social Security Numbers Used: 527-12-2456; 429-42-8003

Patricia Campbell Hearst

FBI No. 325,805 L10 — Date photograph taken unknown
Alias: Tania
Age: 20, born February 20, 1954, San Francisco, California

Height: 5'3"	**Eyes:** Brown
Weight: 110 pounds	**Complexion:** Fair
Build: Small	**Race:** White
Hair: Light brown	**Nationality:** American

Scars and Marks: Mole on lower right corner of mouth, scar near right ankle
Remarks: Hair naturally light brown, straight and worn below shoulders in length, however, may wear wigs, including Afro style, dark brown of medium length, was last seen wearing black sweater, plaid slacks, brown hiking boots and carrying a knife in her belt.

CAUTION

THE ABOVE INDIVIDUALS ARE SELF-PROCLAIMED MEMBERS OF THE SYMBIONESE LIBERATION ARMY AND REPORTEDLY HAVE BEEN IN POSSESSION OF NUMEROUS FIREARMS INCLUDING AUTOMATIC WEAPONS. WILLIAM HARRIS AND PATRICIA HEARST ALLEGEDLY HAVE RECENTLY USED GUNS TO AVOID ARREST. ALL THREE SHOULD BE CONSIDERED ARMED AND VERY DANGEROUS.

Federal warrants were issued on May 20, 1974, at Los Angeles, California, charging the Harris' and Hearst with violation of the National Firearms Act. Hearst was also charged in a Federal complaint on April 15, 1974, at San Francisco, California, as a material witness to a bank robbery which occurred April 15, 1974.

IF YOU HAVE ANY INFORMATION CONCERNING THESE PERSONS, PLEASE NOTIFY ME OR CONTACT YOUR LOCAL FBI OFFICE. TELEPHONE NUMBERS AND ADDRESSES OF ALL FBI OFFICES LISTED ON BACK.

AREA CODE 213   477-6565

11000 WILSHIRE BLVD.
LOS ANGELES, CALIF.

C M Kelley

DIRECTOR
FEDERAL BUREAU OF INVESTIGATION
UNITED STATES DEPARTMENT OF JUSTICE
WASHINGTON, D. C. 20535
TELEPHONE, NATIONAL 8-7117

Entered NCIC
Wanted Flyer 475
May 20, 1974

[THIRTEEN]

The Paper Trail

The Iron Fist Key Link

ALTHOUGH HARRY AND I had been shut out and were at an impasse in our Cooper investigation, he continued to send me all of the newspaper articles related to Cooper's skyjacking. None shed any new light on the case, and some were so absurd, even bordering on fantasy, that we had to laugh, because we knew the true case details. And the several TV versions I viewed were just as misleading, including the one featuring J.T.

In our numerous phone conversations after Harry had to give up his searching, we continued to discuss all we had learned about the case in our somewhat short-lived investigation. And the primary issue that always arose was about there not being any report of Cooper's skyjacked Flight 305 being tracked on radar by the Portland International Airport air traffic controllers. Or, if they had, and we had every reason to believe that they had tracked the plane, then why didn't they know and tell the FBI where Flight 305 was located when Cooper jumped at 8:13 P.M., or within a mile or so of that location.

With the southwest wind pushing Cooper to the northeast and the money found on Tina's Bar, Cooper had to have crashed to his death on a Columbia River island after jumping from south of the river, and within ten miles of the airport.

Considering all of that, along with all of the other details of Cooper's jump that we had uncovered, Harry and I completely agreed that this case was as simple as one could hope for, and Cooper's remains should have been discovered and the case solved within a week of his now most-publicized skyjacking in U.S. history.

Being addicted to true crime, cop, and criminal stories since childhood, just like Harry, I watch all of those types of TV shows that I can find by surfing the channels with my handy remote control. And with all of the useless TV shows being broadcast for decades, there's nothing else worth watching, anyway.

So, in 1998, I just happened to flip onto a biography about the scandalous life and dictatorial reign of the FBI by J. Edgar Hoover. I was glued to the TV as I viewed an episode based on a book by Anthony Summers, entitled, *Official and Confidential: The Secret Life of J. Edgar Hoover*, and copyrighted by Anthony Summers in 1993.

The episode revealed Hoover's addiction to horserace gambling; betting with Mafia bookies, who forgave his losses; homosexuality; and his being blackmailed by the Mafia with a photo of him in a homosexual act.

The title of Summers's book sparked my memory, because my daughter had given Summers's book to me as a gift just a few months earlier. But not being an addicted, avid book reader, and with other pressing matters at that time, I had put it in my office library to maybe read at my leisure.

After the TV episode had concluded, I rushed up to my upstairs office and pulled Summers's book from the shelf. To my surprise, I also noticed another book next to it entitled, *Double Cross*, by Sam and Chuck Giancana, and copyrighted in 1992. Chuck is the younger half-brother, and Samuel M. Giancana is Chuck's son, and nephew, namesake and godson of Chicago Mafia Outfit boss Sam "Mooney" Giancana, who was assassinated, Mafia-style on June 19, 1975.

As I initially thumbed through the two books, I quickly realized that I had hit the mother lode of published information and discovered the golden keys to the missing link of the D.B. Cooper case, and why the FBI had never reportedly solved the case.

Then in Summers's book, he briefly wrote about retired FBI Special Agent Wesley Swearingen. I then learned that Swearingen had authored a book entitled, *FBI Secrets: An Agent's Exposé*. I knew Swearingen was an honest FBI agent from a TV episode I viewed about Elmer "Geronimo" Pratt, so I bought a copy.

With those books in my hot, sweaty little hands, I pushed all of my then-very-minor pressing matters aside and started reading and highlighting all of the critical Cooper-related information as I had done with the three Cooper case books.

Summers wrote about Hoover and Assistant Director Clyde Tolson, an exceptionally handsome young man whom Hoover had promoted to assistant director after only three years on the FBI, and with no field experience, who stayed free of charge at the Del Charro Hotel in La Jolla and the Ambassador Hotel in Los Angeles, in addition to hotels in other upscale cities.

In the Introduction of this book, I wrote that Harry and I knew one integral fact in the 1940s and 1950s, but it was of no consequence at the time, until I discovered a key connection in 1998. That fact was that Hoover went to the Scripps Clinic in La Jolla every year for his annual physical examination, when even the U.S. Presidents went to Bethesda Naval Hospital in Maryland, in a suburb of Washington, DC.

I learned of Hoover's trips to Scripps when I was a teenager growing up in San Diego. A close friend of my mother's had an old maid friend who was a nurse at Scripps, and had served as Hoover's exclusive nurse for years when he was there for his annual physical exam. Then, during his visit one year in the late 1940s, Hoover invited her to fly to Washington, D.C. as his guest. She was certain he had romance in his heart for her, so she bought an expensive wardrobe for the romantic occasion, then on the prearranged date, she gleefully boarded a plane and flew to Washington, D.C. She was graciously met at the airport by two FBI agents, who acted as her escorts, toured her to all of the highlights in the Capitol for days and to her hotel room, then returned her to the airport. Not once did she see or hear from Hoover, and she had presumed that the expensive trip would be at his own personal expense, and for romance.

But after studying and highlighting Summers' excellent exposé of Hoover, I had to conclude that the old maid's expensive, disappointing trip was paid for by U.S. taxpayers. Then in July 1954, when I was a San Diego Police Department motorcycle officer, I was assigned to the 2:00 to 10:00 P.M. shift for the first time, after twelve weeks of day shift to get the hang of enforcement riding without killing myself. And the 2:00 P.M. shift motorcycle officers worked a drunk driver watch from 7:00 P.M. to 3:00 A.M. on Friday and Saturday nights. On that later shift, we doubled up with a partner, which we did not do on the day or 2:00 P.M. shifts. I was partnered with Bob Cooper, and we were assigned to Beat 232, which included Mission Beach, Pacific Beach and La Jolla.

As soon as we were dismissed by the sergeant after line-up for beat assignments and any important information, a veteran motor officer asked me if I knew the unwritten policy about Beat 232. I responded that there were so many unwritten policies, and I asked him which one he was talking about. He solemnly said, "Motors don't go into La Jolla unless they get a call to go there."

I couldn't wait to tell Cooper, because I knew he was always ready and willing to stir the pot whenever he saw an opening. When I caught up with him in the garage and told him about the Beat 232 unwritten policy, he smiled and said, "Is that so?" because La Jolla was a sore subject with most P.D. officers, including the two of us.

That was because soon after Chief Adam Elmer Jansen was promoted to chief in 1947, he closed the East San Diego and Ocean Beach substations, but retained the La

Jolla substation. Although the La Jolla substation was farthest from the police headquarters at Market Street and Pacific Coast Highway, the traffic division officers provided one-hour overlap beat coverage. Despite that already in-place scheduling, the La Jolla substation remained in operation to placate the better-than-thou residents of the "Crown Jewel" of San Diego City. And the captain commander of that substation lived in La Jolla and catered to the elitists of that Utopia.

Conversely, at the other end of the City of San Diego was Logan Heights, which was populated mostly with African-Americans and Mexican-Americans, and was patrolled by many racist, hard-nosed, overly-aggressive officers. And it was not a well-kept secret that Chief Jansen was a racist and an empire-building politician.

So, as soon as Cooper and I departed from the police garage, we headed straight for the La Jolla substation. We knew Officer Jack Fowler was the evening shift desk officer, and he was always good for many laughs. So, we couldn't wait to see what would happen when we crossed the border into the sovereign "State of La Jolla."

Jack was pleased to see us, and immediately asked if we wanted some coffee. I only drank coffee with breakfast, so Cooper had coffee and Jack made cocoa for me. We had a fine time, said our goodbyes to Jack, and rode south to Pacific Beach.

On the Saturday of the next weekend, Cooper and I again tried our luck and went to see Jack at the La Jolla substation in about the middle of our shift. After we had some more coffee and cocoa, Jack asked where we were going to have dinner. When we told him we were going to go to Sheldon's, where we ate in the kitchen, ordered our hot sandwiches directly from the cook, and paid half price, Jack said we could order from the menu and eat for free at the Del Charro Hotel.

When we told Jack we would like to give it a try, he told us to go to the kitchen screen door, let the chef know we were there, then go to the first door to the left into a banquet room, sit down at a table, and wait for a waiter.

Cooper and I left Jack and went directly to the Del Charro Hotel, which was only a few blocks away, and did as he told us to do. It worked like a charm, and a waiter soon arrived with silverware, white cotton napkins, a silver coffee pot full of hot coffee, and menus, and placed them on our table, covered with a white, crisp, spotless tablecloth.

Cooper and I pondered the menu, looked at each other, then decided what the hell, and ordered filet mignon steaks when the waiter returned with our fresh salads.

When we completed our delicious dinners, we each left a fifty-cent tip for the waiter, which was about ten percent of the total price of the two steak dinners, and we left and headed back south to Pacific Beach.

When we arrived at "P.B.," as Pacific Beach was called by most San Diegans, we sat in just west of Mission Boulevard and Grand Avenue, the intersection of the two busiest streets in P.B., and watched for violators. We were there for only a few minutes, when I looked at Cooper and said, "You know, I don't feel right about the free dinners at the Del Charro. There's something about it that doesn't seem right to me."

Cooper looked back at me, and said, "I know. I feel the same way."

Probably what made us feel that way at the time was that nearly all of the restaurants that charged us only half price did so because it was cheap extra police protection against robbers, loud drunk hell raisers, or other undesirable customers. And in most of those half-price restaurants, we ate in the kitchen and ordered from the cook, and without waitress service.

In our following discussion about free Del Charro dinners, Cooper and I agreed that there was probably no need for extra police protection at that exclusive, first-class hotel, because there were probably enough armed house detectives there to fill a large Cadillac sedan. And that was with good basis, because President Eisenhower had stayed there the year before in 1953, the year it was completed and opened. So, we never went back.

The next day after I connected Hoover to my profile of Cooper, I phoned Harry to break the news to him. When I told him, he was quite reluctant to accept the possibility that the Cooper case had never been reportedly solved by the FBI because it had been a J. Edgar Hoover cover-up from before it even happened.

Harry then told me that one summer when he was assigned to the La Jolla substation on the San Diego P.D., he had served as a courtesy escort for Hoover and Tolson while they were there for Hoover's annual physical examination at Scripps. He said whenever the three of them went to the beach in swim trunks in front of the La Jolla Beach & Tennis Club, Tolson always carried a loaded revolver hidden in a folded newspaper.

What made it difficult for Harry to accept my theory that

Hoover had covered up the Cooper skyjacking case was that Harry was very fond of Hoover, because the powerful FBI director had treated him with the greatest kindness, courtesy, and respect.

A few months after I discovered Summers's, the Giancanas' and Swearingen's books that connected Hoover and my profile of Cooper, I started attending a weekly breakfast with other retired California Highway Patrol officers at a family restaurant in San Juan Capistrano. I had known one of the retired officers who attended every week since the late 1950s when we were both assigned to the San Bernardino squad. His brother-in-law was a retired FBI special agent, and when I told the retired CHP officer of my Cooper case Hoover cover-up theory, he wasn't convinced of it, and said he would discuss it with his brother-in-law. I thought that might be interesting, so I said, "Good."

That same CHP retiree hosted a potluck Christmas dinner at his condominium complex recreation room for a few years, and at the next one I attended, his retired FBI special agent brother-in-law also attended for the first and only time. He made it a point to sit next to me at the same table, and the subject of the Cooper case quickly arose. The first issue I mentioned was that there was no report of the FBI having the Portland International Airport traffic controllers track Cooper's skyjacked plane to determine where it was located when he jumped at 8:13 P.M. The brother-in-law immediately snapped back, "If you're going to get mad about it, I don't want to talk about it anymore." I said, "I'm not mad about anything, I just mentioned a critical issue in the case."

The retired FBI special agent brother-in-law turned his back to me for about two very long minutes. I could tell his "Hooverite" FBI agent head was spinning with ideas of how to divert the subject away from the sensitive Cooper case. So, I just patiently waited to hear what he had to say next, and if anything about the FBI.

He then turned back facing me and started telling me about his personal contacts with Director Hoover. He told me about the times he and another agent met Director Hoover and Clyde Tolson at the airport and drove them to the Los Angeles FBI office for an inspection. When the inspection was completed, they drove the two of them to the Ambassador Hotel for their overnight stay. Then the next morning, they drove them to the San Diego FBI office for an inspection, then to La Jolla, where they dropped them off at the Del Charro Hotel.

Like so many of the old Hoover FBI special agents, he enjoyed telling me about his personal contacts with the "FBI God." So, as soon as he had finished his very interesting experiences with Hoover, I asked him if they dropped Hoover and Tolson off at the Del Charro Hotel just the day before the Del Mar race track season opened. Without hesitation, he replied, "Yes, in fact we did."

He was so proud of his knowledge of Hoover's habits and precisely scheduled inspection trips, he had no idea that he had just confirmed Summers' writings of Hoover's well-planned so-called "inspection" trips at government expense to go to the Del Mar race track.

The retired CHP officer brother-in-law of the retired FBI agent then told some other CHP retirees of my Cooper case

Hoover cover-up theory, and some made fun of it. At a later breakfast of retired CHP officers, one officer who had worked under my supervision when I was a lieutenant in the Westminster CHP office said in my presence and that of others, "D.B. Cooper," then laughed.

It amused me, because it strongly indicated to me that the retired FBI agent had convinced his retired CHP brother-in-law that my Hoover cover-up theory was a bunch of nothing, as any good old Hooverite FBI agent would do to save face. I had known for decades how FBI special agents stick together like U.S. Marines, and would do anything to protect the mythical name of the FBI that Hoover had sanctified with propaganda during his forty-eight years of iron-fisted reign over that elitist organization. And Hoover protected that image from outsiders with his well-known secret "Dirt" files on anyone he thought or knew he had to control.

Even when I attended the FBI National Academy in the summer of 1975, over three years after Hoover's mysterious "heart attack" death on May 2, 1972, I could sense Hoover's ghost in the FBI Academy on the grounds of the Quantico, Virginia Marine Base. Whenever an FBI special agent section counselor or classroom instructor spoke of another agent, they praised them to the high heavens as though they walked on water.

That was, except for the FBI special agent of an eight-hour class on employee evaluations, which all 250 in my N.A. 102nd Session had to attend. The instructor, who was obviously bored with teaching that subject, was a very good magician and entertained us with his slight-of-hand tricks for about two hours of the eight hours. Of course, any

police supervisor who has had to prepare employee evaluations knows how subjective they can be because too much
truly objective criticism of a subordinate can permanently
destroy the supervisor-employee relationship. Then near
the end of the eight hours course, the obviously bored
instructor told us that ninety percent of the FBI special
agents that passed their one-year probationary period were
rated above average. That doesn't really balance out very
well mathematically using a scale of one to ten, but
according to all other special agents, they were all "tens."
This was much like President Reagan's "Eleventh Com-
mandment" that a Republican shall never criticize another
Republican.

However, I did not respond in any way to the intended
insult and ridicule, because I considered the source, and
knowing that it would take the best part of eight hours to
orally explain all of the critical relative evidence Harry and
I had uncovered. And I did not want to waste one minute of
my time explaining to them how master blackmailer Hoover
was being blackmailed by the Mafia.

So, despite how any active or retired FBI special agent
attempts to discredit my Hoover cover-up theory, they can
buy a copy of this book, and read the truth, the whole truth,
and nothing but the truth, so help me God.

[FOURTEEN]

First Critical Link Discovery

Johnny and Clyde

SUMMERS' 1993 COPYRIGHTED BOOK, *Official and Confidential: The Secret Life of J. Edgar Hoover*, was the most extensive and revealing of the three books I discovered about Hoover's connections to the Mafia. Summers wrote that he had 850 people personally interviewed by fourteen qualified professionals in their respective fields to collect the details of Hoover's secret life, and it took four years to complete and publish his masterful 499-page hardback book, including the epilogue and sources. With those credits, I had to place my utmost confidence in every word that he wrote about J. Edgar Hoover's clandestine, criminal, scandalous, perverted life from birth to death.

As Summers wrote, John Edgar Hoover was born on Sunday, January 1, 1895 at 413 Seward Square S.E., Washington, DC, and maintained a dossier on himself as a child.

His father worked for the government as a printmaker in the mapmaking department, and during World War I, doctors sent him to an asylum when he had a nervous breakdown. He was described as a pitiful sight. He repeatedly returned to the asylum, but his health continued to decline, and he died in 1921, when J. Edgar Hoover was twenty-six years old.

Hoover's mother was the dominant parent in the family, and Hoover lived mostly alone with her after his father's death, until she died in 1938. During that time, one of Hoover's nieces lived with them in the 1920s, and she described adult Hoover as behaving like a spoiled child. Shortly after his mother's death, he distanced himself from Tolson and started dating women. Hoover was also reported to be like Howard Hughes, in that he constantly worried about germs, and to ward them off, he insisted that his office be kept cold, and later had an ultraviolet light installed because it was reported to eliminate viruses.

Rumors of Hoover's homosexuality flourished, and so much so, that in the 1960s, FBI agents amused themselves by referring to "J. Edna" and "Mother Tolson." And one homosexual author considered writing a magazine article about Hoover and Tolson and entitle it, "Johnny and Clyde," but he never wrote it. There were also reports of Hoover having sex parties with boys at his home, and that he was arrested in New Orleans in the late 1920s when caught having sex with a young man. But he was not prosecuted, because a former FBI Inspector, and close associate of Hoover's, interceded and successfully had the case dropped. Another report of Hoover's homosexual activities was from a veteran movie producer. He frequented the Del Mar race track, as many Hollywood celebrities did at that time, and he reported that Hoover went to the Del Mar race track every year with a different boy, and was caught in a restroom by a newspaperman. But Hoover was so powerful, nobody said anything.

Not reporting Hoover's sexual and other illegal or immoral activities, and his forty-eight-year iron-fisted reign of the FBI were perpetuated by the well-known dossiers he amassed on everyone he thought could harm him or his illustrious career, and many more. He even had a file on Lucille Ball, because she registered to vote as a Communist in 1936 at her grandfather's insistence. And even though we all vote by secret ballot, and she could have voted as a Democrat or Republican, then lied to grandpa.

Summers reported numerous occasions about Hoover's homosexuality, including his going to a psychiatrist in about 1946 because of continuing rumors about his homosexuality. But Hoover's visits to the psychiatrist were short-lived, because he was even afraid to trust the therapist, despite the doctor/patient privileged communication. Thereafter, Hoover used FBI agents to intimidate the press to supress rumors of homosexuality whenever possible.

The hypocrisy of Hoover's homosexuality was that he would fire any homosexual, and even sexually promis-cuous, agents, because they could be prime targets for blackmail by enemy agents. And the U.S. had been under potential enemy attack starting in the 1930s and until the end of the Cold War with the USSR up until the late 1980s when President Reagan persuaded the Russian prime minister to "tear down this wall," over a decade after Hoover's mysterious death. My first insight into Director Hoover's file-collecting methods and his ruthlessness was when I was in my second year on the San Diego Police Department in 1953. On the 3:00 P.M. to 11:00 P.M. shift, my partner I and were on Beat 19 in East San Diego when we received an unusual radio call. It was unusual because nearly all radio calls were in the 10–11 code and very brief. But this call was in narrative form directing us to meet the owner of an upscale steakhouse and bar at the kitchen door next to the alley.

My partner was driving, and he drove north up the alley that intersected with El Cajon Boulvard. When he parked near the kitchen door, the middle-aged, impeccably dressed owner in an expensive suit stepped out of the kitchen screen door to meet us. He quickly told us that the two men sitting at the bar had flashed government IDs at the bartender, said they were FBI agents, and wanted to check every bill he took in to check them to determine if they were counterfeit.

My partner, the owner and I all knew that the Secret Service investigated counterfeiting, not the FBI, so we all three suspected that the two imposters might be trying to determine how much money was in the bar till before robbing the place. The two imposters were facing to the east at the bar, and the kitchen door was to the north and behind them, so we could watch them without them seeing us. My partner and I decided he would watch them while I radioed for FBI agents to meet us there. After I radioed for the FBI agents to meet us, I waited on the sidewalk to the west of the steakhouse on El Cajon Boulevard so they could more easily find our location.

When they pulled up to the curb, the passenger special agent wearing a bow tie stepped out and asked me what we had. As soon as I explained the situation to him, he and the other special agent went directly in the front door of the steakhouse, walked over to the two imposters at the bar and demanded to see their IDs. They produced their U.S. Army IDs, and the two FBI special agents immediately arrested them for impersonating FBI agents. One was an Army corporal and the other was a private. But, maybe, not for much longer.

After the two arrestees were secured in the rear seat of the FBI car, the special agent wearing the bow tie told me he wasn't sure that the U.S. Attorney would prosecute them, but he thought a night in the county jail just might be a lasting lesson to them, or, if not, maybe dishonorable discharges would.

We all then departed, after the steakhouse owner thanked my partner and me for such quick action, which had relieved him of his fear of being robbed.

After darkness had fallen, about two weeks later, my partner was driving westbound on Montezuma Road in the College Park area when we fell in behind a station wagon pulling a wooden box trailer with no tail lights. I told my partner to pull it over and I would advise the driver that the trailer tail lights were out, and give him a verbal warning.

As soon as we had the vehicles pulled over, I got only as far as the rear of the trailer when the driver met me, and he looked like he had been put through a wringer, but was still dripping wet. Even in that condition, he looked very familiar to me. Then when I looked closer at his face, I recognized him as being the FBI special agent who had been wearing the bow tie at the steakhouse arrests.

Without hesitation, he started telling me his very sad story. He said he had been directed personally by FBI Director J. Edgar Hoover to investigate a prominent San Diego resident, and when he had completed the investigation, to personally deliver the report to Hoover at his Washington, D.C. office on his way to his new assignment in an East Coast field office.

With that, he and his family were to be moved to his new location on the East Coast at government expense. He had sold his home and made arrangements for the movers to start loading his family's entire household belongings that morning. But in late afternoon of the prior day, he received a phone call from Hoover that he no longer needed his report, and his transfer to the East Coast field office had been cancelled.

As the beaten FBI special agent then explained to me, he had only fourteen hours so far that day to locate and rent another home, and move all of his family's household belongings to that home in that trailer that he had to borrow from a friend. Before he had finished his nightmarish horror story, I could easily understand why two of the three San Diego boys who had joined the FBI in the late 1940s had resigned in less than two years.

Above all, I had first-hand confirmation of Hoover's "Dirt" files, which had been rumored for years, and more importantly, how ruthless and indifferent he was with respect to the welfare of his own loyal special agents and their families.

I learned my second lesson in Hoover's "Special Investigations" when I was a duty officer and instructor at the California Highway Patrol Academy in the early 1960s. There was an FBI special agent who had instructed a class at the academy for over a decade, and loved to tell amusing inside FBI stories, which was a rarity and risky for any FBI special agent to dare to do. One evening at supper in the dining room, he told a small group of us about one of his fellow San Francisco field office special agent's harrowing experiences with Hoover's "Special Investigations." And as Hoover had done with the San Diego FBI special agent who wore a bow tie, Hoover had bypassed all levels of administration and supervision, and had personally contacted this special agent and given him directions on whom to investigate. And when he had completed the investigation, to personally deliver the report to him in his Washington, D.C. office. But in this case, this veteran special agent, who was within a couple of years of retirement, was not told that he would be transferred upon the completion of his investigation. Of course, as in the case of the San Diego FBI special agent who wore bow ties, transfers could be made or cancelled with one stroke of Director Hoover's pen. And every FBI special agent was well aware of the absolute power of that pen. As they say, "Power corrupts, and absolute power corrupts, absolutely." And Director Hoover had proven that for decades.

When the stressed-out veteran San Francisco special agent arrived at Hoover's D.C. office, he did not have to wait very long to be admitted to the inner sanctum. He was greeted by Director Hoover, who was sitting at his immense desk, and the reporting special agent choked out a responsive greeting as Hoover shook his hand. Director Hoover then received the report from the shaking special agent, sat down, and started scanning through the report.

After about a minute of thumbing through the numerous pages, Director Hoover thanked the the still stressed out special agent and dismissed him. As the special agent turned to quickly leave, he was shocked to see that there were two identical doors side by side, and he had no idea which one was the door to the escape route. He had a fifty-fifty chance to open the right door, but he lost. When he opened the closet door, he was so flustered that he stepped into the closet and closed the door behind him. The last time he had seen Hoover face to face, he was still thumbing and scanning the report, so in his panic state, he assumed that Hoover hadn't seen him go into the closet. With that great hope, he decided to remain in the closet until after Hoover departed from the office at the end of the work day, then sneak out.

Then after several minutes of sweating in the closet, he heard Director Hoover say something to the effect of, Agent So-and-So, you are in the closet. With that, the special agent opened the door, thanked Director Hoover, and quickly departed out the hallway door.

Then on his six-hour trip to the Washington National Airport and flight home to San Francisco, he fretted over going to his field office in fear that his transfer orders to some Godforsaken hell hole would be waiting for him. But it did not happen.

When we all stopped laughing, we all agreed that Hoover probably had those twin doors installed that way to test his special agents' stress tolerance levels.

With that second inside exposer to FBI Director Hoover's "Special Investigation" tactics, I became well aware of his unleashed blackmail and control of all who could get in his way and cut his absolute power reign short.

But two can play the same blackmail game, and Summers wrote about Hoover being blackmailed by Mafia gambling boss Meyer Lansky for decades with proof of Hoover's homosexuality, and probably with photographs. And this report was what I discovered that connected my Cooper profile with Hoover and conclusively convinced me forever that the so-called unsolved Cooper case has never been reportedly solved by the FBI because it was a J. Edgar Hoover cover-up from the very beginning. If it wasn't, why was the list of 10,000 $20 ransom bills not released to the press even before Cooper's skyjacked Flight 305 took off from the Seattle Airport, and why has there never been any report of his skyjacked plane being tracked by the Portland International Airport air traffic controllers, as mandated by FAA rules?

And Summers' report of Hoover being blackmailed by Mafia gambling genius Meyer Lansky, is corroborated by retired FBI Special Agent M. Wesley Swearingen in his book, *FBI Secrets*, which I will cover later herein.

Summers also wrote that FBI Assistant Director William Sullivan divulged that an FBI senior aide with a passkey had rummaged through Hoover's desk after hours and discovered lewd, filthy magazines of the most lurid nature about abnormal and perverted sexual activities.

Also, that Hoover had become so paranoid about the ongoing rumors about his homosexuality that he went to a psychiatrist in 1946. Then Hoover became more paranoid about his homosexuality and didn't even trust psychiatrists, so he refrained from seeing any for a while. Then in late 1971, he saw one just the year before his mysterious death on May 2, 1972.

I say "mysterious," because Summers wrote that President Nixon's White House aides G. Gordon Liddy and E. Howard Hunt met with a former CIA poison specialist physician on March 24, 1972, just a little over five weeks before Hoover's death on May 2, 1972. Liddy and Hunt met with the doctor to find out how they could kill *Washington Post* columnist Jack Anderson, who had published numerous articles about White House leaks of corruption and FBI dossiers on the private lives of public figures, black leaders, newsmen, and show business people.

It was apparently during that meeting that the subject of thiophosphate was discussed. Thiophosphate is an element in insecticides, is highly toxic to human beings, and if ingested, can cause a fatal heart attack within minutes, and cannot be detected by autopsy if it is not conducted within hours of death. And if placed on a toothbrush, a person can suffer a fatal heart attack within seconds after brushing their teeth with that toothbrush.

Then, after Hoover's residence had been burglarized two times in the two weeks before his death by thieves searching for files, he was found dead next to his bed by his black housekeeper, Annie Fields, at about 8:30 A.M.

Hoover's personal physician arrived at the house within

an hour, and rigor mortis had already set in. He estimated that Hoover had been dead for hours, and had probably died at about 2:00 or 3:00 A.M. He was surprised, because he knew that Hoover had been in good health, and he did not recall ever prescribing Hoover any medication for high blood pressure or any other heart condition.

Two medical examiners then arrived at the Hoover residence shortly after 11:00 A.M. And despite Hoover's personal physician telling them that Hoover had been in good health, after some discussion between the two medical examiners about the possibility of poisoning, they decided not to perform an autopsy. That was quite irregular, because if an attending physician cannot sign a death certificate, state laws generally mandate that an autopsy be performed. However, if Hoover had been poisoned with thiophosphate, an autopsy would not have detected it that many hours after his death. But it was still suspicious.

Washington Post columnist Jack Anderson had also published articles about Hoover's denial of the existence of the Mafia. And Hoover had denied the existence of organized crime syndicates for decades, despite all of the following:

1. The U.S. Navy's World War II deal with imprisoned "Lucky" Luciano to help with securing the New York Harbor after the suspicious destructive burning of the *Normandie* in that harbor.
2. The 1951 Senator Estes Kefauver Select Senate Committee's report that there were at least two organized crime syndicates in the U.S.

3. The 1957 New York State Police raid on the Appalachian summit meeting of Mafia bosses.

4. The 1957-1959, three session, 30-month Senator McClellan Select Senate Committee investigation of organized crime syndicates in the U.S. after the highly-publicized Apalachin summit raid by the New York State Police. And when the findings of that committee exposed the existence of organized crime, Hoover was greatly embarrassed. But even that report did not alter his stance on the existence of the Mafia.

5. The 1963 testimony of Mafia underling Joseph Valachi before a senate committee revealing all of the inner workings of the Mafia, or "La Cosa Nostra,"- "Our thing." But Hoover still held back on any actual pursuit of the Mafia.

In addition to Meyer Lansky's blackmailing Hoover with photos of him in a homosexual act of orally copulating an unidentified man, and reportedly confirmed by others, Hoover's addiction to horse race gambling was his other cozy connection to Mafia bosses. Hoover met national radio news reporter Walter Winchell at the Mafia-infested Stork Club in New York, and Winchell introduced Hoover to New York Mafia godfather Frank Costello. Costello then gave Hoover tips on fixed horse races, and in addition to making bets at the tracks on those sure winners, Hoover at times made bets on other horses with Mafia bookies. When Hoover won, they would pay him his winnings, and when he lost, they forgave his losses and wrote it off.

Summers wrote extensively about Hoover meeting and socially associating with numerous Mafia mobsters in upscale restaurants in New York, Florida, Del Mar, and other Mafia haunts. Summers also wrote that Hoover served under eight presidents, and many feared him, including Nixon. And I can personally recall that when Hoover reached the FBI mandatory retirement age of seventy years, President Johnson waived that mandate indefinitely for Hoover. With that questionable act, Hoover served as FBI director for another seven years until his mysterious death at age seventy-seven on May 2, 1972.

Upon hearing that news report, from what I had learned about President Johnson on the California Highway Patrol, I concluded that Hoover probably had a dossier file on LBJ about a foot thick.

The extent of Hoover's corruption is well documented in Summers' nearly five-hundred-page book. And if anyone has any doubts about my connecting him and his methods with my profile of D.B. Cooper and why the FBI has never reportedly solved the D.B. Cooper case, just read *Official and Confidential: The Secret Life of J. Edgar Hoover.* And if that doesn't convince you, then read *Double Cross* by Chuck and Samuel M. Giancana and *FBI Secrets* by M. Wesley Swearingen.

In addition to what I learned in my seventeen years collecting information related to the D.B. Cooper case, I had a few personal learning experiences about the FBI and Director Hoover during my twenty-nine years on the California Highway Patrol. Or "California Haywire Patrol," as CHP Academy instructor Sergeant Jim Booth called it when

I was a CHP cadet in 1954. The first was when I was a sergeant in the Sacramento CHP squad. An officer discovered a Corvette with switched Washington State plates on a Sunday. Certain it was a federal Dyer Act car stolen from out of state, I radioed for an FBI agent to meet us there. The FBI's response was that they didn't investigate Dyer Act cases unless there were other crimes involved. I then radioed for an NATB investigator, and one responded. Within thirty minutes, he determined it was a Dyer Act stolen from Alabama. And we later found a revolver and numerous IDs in the thief's apartment.

Then when I was a lieutenant in the Yreka CHP office, about twenty-five miles south of the Oregon border, two Redding FBI resident special agents frequently visited our office and directed me to immediately notify them of Dyer Act recoveries and arrests. The CHP took credit for the recoveries and arrests. I knew it would be double reporting, so I never notified them.

Then in an April 1976 edition of the *Orange County Register*, almost five years after Hoover's death, it reported that Congress discovered that Hoover had been falsely reporting FBI Dyer Act recoveries and arrests made by local and state law enforcement agencies to pad his annual budget requests.

Summers also reported about the decades-old corrupt FBI Recreation Fund. The first day I was at the FBI National Academy, on July 14, 1975, on the Quantico Marine Base in Virginia, our session of 250 law enforcement officers from within the free world were required to donate $37.50 for three separate funds. One was $17.50 for our sectional social dinners, and there were five sections of fifty each, another was $10.00 for a legacy to commemorate our session at the Academy, and the third was to the FBI Recreation Fund.

My annual salary at that time as a CHP lieutenant was about $22,000, so ten dollars to an FBI fund did not cause me any concern. But my wonderful roommate was the chief of police in a small Pennsylvania city, and his wife told me that his gross income the year before in 1974 was less than $10,000.

In one of our classes, the FBI special agent instructor told us that after Hoover died, Congress lowered the mandatory FBI retirement age from seventy years to fifty-five years to rid the FBI of all of Hoover's top executive cronies.

Then on my way to dinner shortly before 5:00 P.M. on the day I was elected Class Spokesman (president) of our session, a member from another section stopped me and asked me about the FBI Recreation Fund and what it was for. I hadn't given it any thought, so I told him I would sure find out.

I then went straight to the National Academy FBI inspector commander's office and asked him. He immediately picked up his phone, punched some numbers, said he was sorry he as running late, hung up and rushed out of the office.

It was crystal clear to me that his only answer was no answer, even though it was obvious to me that he knew exactly who was getting the $10,000 a year or more. And his career would be over if he so much as told one person outside the exclusive insider FBI loop who that money was going to. That was my first personal experience with the FBI code of silence, until I got involved in investigating the D.B. Cooper case.

Then in the same April 1976 the *Orange County Register* article about Hoover padding his budget requests with Dyer Act recoveries and arrests made by other law enforcement agancies, it reported that Congress had discovered that all of the FBI Recreational Fund monies had been for the benefit of the top FBI executives.

And I earlier estimated "$10,000 or more," because all of the hundreds of FBI Academy special agent cadets every year probably also had to pay into that fraudulent fund for the "Recreation" of high-paid FBI executives. And 1,000 officers a year attended the FBI National Academy.

The worst part of this Hoover scam was that he had died over three years prior to my attending the FBI National Academy, and it had taken Congress that many years to discover and report the fraud and hadn't put a stop to it before my July-to-September 1975 session. And my roommate was not the only member of my session that I learned of that made meager salaries. It was like robbing the poor to pay the rich.

In regards to Hoover denying the existence of the Mafia right up to his demise, our session received a two-hour class on organized crime by the FBI's only so-called Mafia expert. When he told us that it had taken the FBI years to discover why Mafia boss Albert Anastasia and past hit man of "Murder, Inc." had been assassinated in 1957, I nearly laughed. Hoover's FBI was well known to illegally bug phones and perform their unlawful "Black Bag" burglaries of homes on Hoover's orders. But years of not knowing why Anastasia was assassinated made it clear to me that no Mafia phones had been bugged nor were there any "Black Bag" jobs conducted on Mafia homes.

In fact, when I first met FBI Special Agent Dexter Maddox, who screened me and the others in the Los Angeles area to clear us to go to the National Academy, we hit it right off because he was also from my hometown of San Diego, and he had lived only a few blocks from where I grew up. So, he opened up to me and told me about the FBI's "Black Bag" jobs, and how many he had conducted with other special agents. And he laughed when he told me about the times when they almost got caught when the home owner and target of their illegal activity returned while they were still inside the house. He said that at least once, they had to rough the target home owner up as they rushed out the front door to make it look like a common street thug burglary; then they ran like hell.

Hoover's claim during his forty-eight years as FBI director was that organized crime, and more specifically the Mafia, was a local problem, despite it being well known that the Mafia operated interstate in New York, Chicago, New Orleans, Miami, Los Angeles, Las Vegas, San Diego, and any number of other major cities.

I had been on the San Diego Police Department for only three months when I was assigned to a downtown skid row beat in a two-officer patrol division beat car. Within days on that beat, I was told about some of the Mafia hoods in San Diego. The most prominent were Tony Mirable, Frank "Bompo" Bompensiero, and Frank Matranga. And on one of my first days back to work after two days off, my partner that shift told me that the son of Los Angeles Mafia Godfather Jack Dragna had been to town, and had openly boasted to every listener about who he was.

Then in the late 1990s, I viewed a TV documentary about the FBI's first all-out effort to investigate and bring down the New York Mafia. The head of that FBI Task Force was FBI Special Agent Bruce Mouw (pronounced "Mow"). Mouw stated that when they started their investigation in 1980, they had absolutely no information or intelligence on the Mafia. They had to start by trying to determine where the Mafia hoods met, then take telescopic photos of them hanging out in front of or entering and leaving the restaurants and bars.

As a result of that investigation, after years of painstaking efforts, including photos and finally bugging homes and other meeting places, the FBI was finally able to identify, prosecute and convict Mafia Godfather John Gotti and many others.

Based on all of the documented and otherwise incriminating circumstantial evidence, there should be no doubt whatsoever that J. Edgar Hoover used the almost unlimited powers of his office to protect the Mafia. In doing so, he aided and abetted in the Mafia murders of thousands of human beings in gangland wars, and many innocent people. And based on my extensive investigation of the D.B. Cooper skyjacking case, and most of all, my profile of Cooper, I believe Hoover was responsible for Cooper's near-certain suicide jump to avoid a slow, sadistic, tortuous death at the hands of Tony Spilotro.

Summers' 1993 copyrighted book was based on 850 interviews, including references to Chuck Giancana, half-brother of Mafia godfather Sam Giancana, and Samuel M. Giancana, son of Chuck and godson of Sam Giancana, authors of their 1992 copyrighted book, *Double Cross*. Although Summers' book is just as well documented and believable as the Giancanas' book, theirs' is based on what could be best classified as an inside story of mobster Sam Giancana's criminal life. And it corroborates all that Summers reported about J. Edgar Hoover being blackmailed and controlled by the Mafia.

If there is any humor in this tragic, scandalous history of our great nation, it is that "Master Blackmailer" J. Edgar Hoover was being blackmailed by the most notorious extortionists of all time in the U.S.—the Mafia.

FIFTEEN

Harry Grady's Biggest Bust

B of E Extortion Racket

S UMMERS ALSO WROTE ABOUT notorious San Diego Mafioso Frank "Bompo" Bompensiero seeing Hoover at the Del Mar race track when Mafioso Jimmy "The Weasel" Fratianno pointed Hoover out to him. And Bompensiero blurted out so everybody could hear, "Ah, that J. Edgar's a punk, he's a fuckin' degenerate queer." When Hoover and Bompensiero happened to later meet in the men's restroom, Hoover said "Frank, that's not a nice way to talk about me, especially when I have people with me." Fratianno then knew Bompensiero and Hoover had met before, and Bompensiero had no fear of Hoover.

Harry Grady was very familiar with Frank "Bompo" Bompensiero, because he was the key investigator who was instrumental in sending him to prison for being the primary San Diego bagman for elected Board of Equalization Director William G. Bonelli.

In 1946, my brother Ed told me of two of his friends, bar-owner fathers who had been extorted by the Alcoholic Beverage Control enforcement division of the California Board of Equalization. One father owned a beer and wine bar on University Avenue in East San Diego, and only about a block from the San Diego Police Department substation. His bartender was cited for serving beer to a minor. A couple of nights later, the father received an anonymous phone call from a man who told him to put $1,500 in old, small bills in a paper sack and deliver them to a man standing in the recessed doorway of a closed downtown store. The caller told him the man would be standing with his back to him, to not look at his face, say a specific code word, and the man would respond with a given code word. The father did as he was told, then a couple of nights later, he received a second call from the anonymous man who told him the violation had been disposed of.

The other father owned a full liquor license bar on University Avenue in Hillcrest, and one of his bartenders was also cited for serving a minor. He received the same anonymous phone calls and instructions, but because he had a full liquor license, his payoff was $3,000.

And that was when a new Chevrolet or Ford cost less than $2,000, if one could get one in the shortage of new cars for a few years after World War II.

Then, it wasn't until August 1952, when I was in the San Diego Police Department Recruit Training Class that I again heard of the B of E extortion of liquor licensees. That was when a vice bureau detective told my recruit class not to make any ABC arrests, because it would only give the

ABC the opportunity to extort liquor licensees. He said it was being taken care of, and we would learn of it in the news when it was taken care of and cleaned up in the not-too-distant future.

Then, in December 1952, I was assigned to partner with Harry Grady on Beat 8 in Logan Heights, the African-American and Mexican-American section of the city.

Harry was the most qualified officer I ever worked with, but one of the most unhappy for more than one valid reason. In addition to his delayed hiring date shortly after the fire and police system was amended from twenty to twenty-five years of required service, he had not long before just got off of the deputy chief's "Crap List."

As Harry explained to me, he was in the vice bureau when he saw an arrested bookie hand a large roll of money to the sergeant in charge of the vice bureau. Not wanting to be any part of bribery or corruption, he submitted a memorandum request to be transferred back to the uniformed patrol division. But he did not mention his real reason for wanting out of vice. Then for a few years before I worked with him, the deputy chief of field personnel had him assigned to every crappy detail possible, including walking many months of foot beats.

I had experienced my own problems with that deputy chief because he thought I should have joined the fire department instead of the police department, because of my fire department family history, and he obviously thought I would be more of "Good Deed," "Life Saving" Boy Scout than a policeman. It wasn't until a few months after I worked with Harry that I learned from my closest cousin that one of my dozens of San Diego cousins whom I had never seen in my life had been married to the deputy chief's daughter for years. With that, he knew all about my family history.

And he may have heard my fireman grandfather's openly broadcast opinion that "When firemen do their job, they make a friend, but when policemen do their job, they make an enemy." I fully explain that deputy chief's sneaky ways of dogging me to try to get something on me to fire me in my book, *Cops, Crooks and Other Crazies.*

With that, Harry and I had something in common, being fear and hatred for the deputy chief, which helped to cement our lasting friendship of fifty-seven years.

Harry then told me about his part in smashing the Board of Equalization's extortion racket. He said investigators for California Attorney General Pat Brown's office went to San Diego P.D. Chief Elmer Jansen and asked him for one of his officers to help them investigate the Board of Equalization's extortions of liquor licensees. Chief Jansen offered them the head of the vice bureau, the one Harry saw accepting a large roll of money from the bookie. The investigators declined that offer, and said they wanted an officer named Harry Grady. Needless to say, they had done their homework, and it did not sit well with the deputy chief. Regardless, Harry was assigned to work with the A.G.'s investigators, and he told me he gave them more than enough leads, witness/victims' names, and evidence for a grand jury to return indictments. He then said, "If the ones involved are not identified and arrested and prosecuted in the next six months, then Attorney General Pat Brown has to be corrupt."

Then six months later, in June 1953, the arrest of Frank Bompensiero and two others was headline news. But the secret grand jury hearings and indictments were not very secret, because elected Board of Equalization Director William G. Bonelli, who was also indicted, fled to Mexico before he could be arrested. There had obviously been an early leak from somebody long before the indictments were returned, because Bonelli had time to move, and to grease the palms of the right people high in the Mexican government to prevent his extradition back to the U.S. He was never extradited.

At that time, Mexican law enforcement was very happy to extradite U.S. criminals across the border. Just a couple of years before, in 1951, there was a nationwide manhunt for Billy Cook, who had murdered an entire family of four or five and dumped their bodies in an abandoned well in Joplin, Missouri. He was captured in Baja California, Mexico, and without delay, pushed across the border at San Ysidro into the arms of U.S. law enforcement. And the media reported that very swift process was known as "Mexican Extradition."

During the ensuing trial of Bompensiero and the two others, the *San Diego Union Tribune* reported daily on the events and testimony. The most shocking news report to me was that it was learned from victim/witnesses' testimonies that when they delivered the extortion money to Bompensiero, it was in broad daylight in the lobby of the U.S. Grant Hotel, where Bompensiero comfortably sat in a big overstuffed chair smoking a cigar. The extortions had become such business as usual, he no longer had to hide in recessed doorways of closed businesses in the dark of night.

That report made me seriously wonder how those extortions had been allowed to continue for at least six years since I first learned of them in 1946. And made it clear to me why Chief Jansen had tried to pawn his corrupt head of the vice bureau off onto the A.G.'s investigators. To this day, I still wonder how far the corruption extortion racket reached, and who and how many were paid off to look the other way. It is impossible for me to believe that Harry was the only San Diego P.D. officer who had enough knowledge to bring it to an end. But he was definitely the most dedicated and honest officer of all.

It wasn't until August 1955 when I was assigned as a Big Bear Lake California Highway Patrol resident officer that I learned of the very sad part of the Bompensiero saga. A childless couple living two doors from us were of Italian descent and were originally from Los Angeles. The first day I met the wife in our front yard, we introduced ourselves and told each other where we were from. When I told her we were from San Diego, she immediately asked me if I had ever heard of Frank Bompensiero. I told her I knew all about him, and that my old San Diego P.D. partner was the one who was responsible for sending him to prison. She then told me that her family and Bompensiero's wife's family had been close friends for decades and she knew the wife like family. She said the wife did not know what Frank did for a living, and she was emotionally and mentally devastated when she found out, and died of a broken heart less than three years later. She said it had definitely killed her.

In my later research, I learned more about Bompensiero on the Internet. Reports are that he was appointed in 1950 by Los Angeles Mafia boss Jack Dragna to run Mafia affairs in San Diego. And Bompensiero was reported to be the most feared Mafia hitman in Southern California for thirty years. In the mid-1960s, he became an FBI informant to avoid additonal prison time, and he was assassinated Mafia-style on February 10, 1977.

From my own personal recollection of his death, he was shot in the head in Pacific Beach while walking from a phone booth to his home. I can only surmise that he used phone booths to talk to other Mafioso or the FBI, and probably feared his home phone was bugged by one or both.

Very interesting to me is that his death was on the same day of a year that some of Cooper's ransom money was found. My own personal knowledge of Bompensiero began when I was a teenager going to Hoover High School in San Diego. I knew two boys who were close friends, and one married Bompensiero's daughter, his only child, and the other became a San Diego County deputy sheriff. The one who married the daughter suffered a disease that rendered him impotent, so he and Bompensiero's daughter mutually agreed to a compatible divorce, as they were both in their late teens, their lives were ahead of them, and the daughter most likely hoped to have children.

Because Bompensiero and his wife had only the daughter, and no son, Mrs. Bompensiero adored the son-in-law and a loving bond was quickly established between the two. The son-in-law frequently visited Mrs. Bompensiero, and he just happened to do so in 1947, the day after Bugsy Siegel was assassinated in Los Angeles. As I now vaguely recall, the Bompensiero home was on a large lot or acreage, with a parking area in the rear.

The son-in-law went to the rear door, and was met by Bompensiero who told him "Mom" was in the back bedroom sewing. As the son-in-law walked by the kitchen door on the way to the back bedroom, he glanced into the living room and saw several men sitting holding shotguns and other firearms. When he reached the back bedroom, Mrs. Bompensiero said, "I don't like Frank's friends, and I don't know why they are here."

These Bompensiero reports are included herein to illustrate two issues related to the D.B. Cooper skyjacking case. The first and most important is that that supports reports of Hoover being acquainted with and associating with the most feared Mafia hitman in Southern California, and on a first name basis. The other being that Harry Grady had been the only San Diego P.D. officer that the California Attorney General's investigators wanted to assist them in their investigation of the Board of Equalization's extortion of liquor licensees. They had obviously learned of Harry's exceptional investigative expertise, the same expertise he used to develop his theory that Cooper's wildlife-scattered remains are on a Columbia River island.

In addition, the report of Mrs. Bompensiero not liking Bompensiero's friends, and not knowing what they were doing at their home, clearly showed she had no idea that her husband was a Mafia hood. And that supports my Big Bear Lake neighbor's story that she learned it only when Bompensiero was sent to prison for being the B of E extortion racket bagman, and it caused her to die of a broken heart.

SIXTEEN

Second Key Link Discovery

Mexico City

THE SECOND KEY LINK discovery to the D.B. Cooper case that I found in my office library was *Double Cross*, authored by Chuck Giancana, the younger half-brother of Chicago Mafia godfather Sam "Mooney" Giancana, and Chuck's second son, Samuel M. Giancana, nephew, namesake, and godson of Mooney.

The irony of this find was that I had bought the book a few years earlier to read while I was going to have to wait for my daughter at a distance from my home. I had read only about a couple of dozen pages when she arrived, so I just took it home and put it in my office library. Then after seeing the TV show about J. Edgar's Hoover's sordid life based on Anthony Summers's book, I found *Double Cross* next to Summers's masterpiece.

The Giancana book is based on Chuck's life as Mooney's

younger half-brother, and the many experiences he had
with Mooney and the volumes of information about the
Mafia that Mooney imparted to him for over five decades.
To start with, it tells of Mooney's childhood and how
he was given that nickname. Mooney was unruly from an
early age, and in order to discipline him, his brutal father,
Antonio, regularly chained him to an oak tree and beat
him bloody with a razor strop. When he was ten years old,
in the fifth grade, his teachers declared him to be a hope-
less delinquent, and he was sent to a reform school for six
months. Because his brutal father had vowed to take care
of him when he returned, Mooney did not return home
and wandered the streets. He slept in abandoned cars and
under back porches, and stole food from street vendors.
At age twelve, he joined a street gang called the "42." One
of his pleasures was to beat alley cats to death to amuse
himself and the gang members. With that and other bizarre
behavior, he was considered to be the craziest one in the
gang, so he was nicknamed "Mooney." Unlike Benjamin
"Bugsy" Siegel, whom nobody dared to call Bugsy within
his earshot, Mooney was proud of that name, and it
became his lifetime moniker, probably to let everybody
know how crazy he was, and to never cross him. Much
like years later, after he became the Chicago Mafia godfather in 1955, he suspected that one of his underlings had
turned FBI informant. He had other underlings hang him
from a meat hook in a cold meat locker and tortured,
including with a cattle prod in the groin, for two days
until he died in extreme agony. Mooney then had photos
taken of the gruesome sight to show around to warn all of

the others what would happen to them if they dared to cross him in any way.

In about 1950, Mafia gambling boss Meyer Lansky had suggested giving the different Mafia organizations names to improve cooperation and morale, So, the national alliance in New York was named the "Commission" or "Combination" (later TV organized crime shows always called it the "Commission," and it was composed of the five New York Mafia families' godfathers). New York was the "Mob," Chicago was the "Outfit," New Orleans was the "Combine," and so on. And on the many organized crime TV shows, it was reported that the Commission had to approve in advance any hits on Mafia "made men."

In mid-1955, Outfit top bosses Tony Accardo and Paul Ricca were being scrutinized by the IRS, so Accardo stepped aside at a private meeting and passed his godfather position down to Mooney.

Thereafter, Mooney did not have any made men in the Outfit, which allowed him to kill any underling without the approval of the Commission, and he killed at will. A crooked banker was indicted for misappropriation of bank funds, and had a receipt for a $100,000 cash payment made by Mooney on a motel, and kept it in his wallet. The indicted banker attempted to blackmail Mooney in hopes he would use his influence with those he controlled in govermnment to gain an acquittal. And the receipt was the only incriminating evidence the banker had on Mooney.

So, Mooney gave the order to one of his underlings to kill the banker and retrieve the receipt from his wallet. That underling assigned the hit to his own soldier, who was an

SECOND KEY LINK DISCOVERY [173]

ex-cop turned mobster hitman named Sal Moretti. Moretti took three of his Outfit-hopeful goon friends along with him to make the hit, but only for their goulish entertainment, not to help with the hit. Moretti found the crooked banker, shot him in the head, left his body in a vacant lot, then drove away. But he forgot to get the receipt out of the banker's wallet, which the banker had waved in front of some others as being the hiding place of the blackmail receipt.

The receipt was found by the police, and Mooney was taken in for questioning, but released. Four days after the hit on the crooked banker, Moretti's tortured and bloated body was found in the trunk of a car. And along with his messed up clothing and a comb was a warning to every Outfit soldier—Mess up an assignment, and this is what happens to you.

The Giancanas wrote that Mooney was physically brutal in his control of Chuck and the other Giancana family members as an example to the Outfit members that he was always in control of those around him. He believed that if any of the Outfit ever learned that he was easy on anyone, even though they were blood relatives, they might think he was weak. And he knocked Chuck around on many occasions.

He also never let Chuck get into the inner workings of the Outfit, but did buy a couple of businesses that he let Chuck manage.

Repeatedly, in the Giancanas' 495-page book, they wrote about the Outfit controlling every U.S. President since Teddy Roosevelt, and how he and Paul Ricca were welcome guests to the White House. He told Chuck that they always owned the President, no matter who he was, and Ricca had the respect of President Franklin Delano Roosevelt. They also wrote about J. Edgar Hoover being in New York Mob godfather Frank Costello's pocket, and having influence with senators, other politicians and police precinct captains.

Mooney held court at Louie's Service Station, after he asked Louie and his wife to leave for a while. The first time Mooney allowed Chuck to go along with him, Chuck said he couldn't believe what he witnessed. One man who owed Mooney money pleaded with him about how he was unable to pay the debt. He wrote that Mooney gave one of his lieutenants a certain look. Then Chuck later read in the newspaper that the man's body had been found in a ditch, all twisted up like a busted tire.

At a later time, Mooney told Chuck that he had no respect for gamblers and drunks. Chuck and Sam reported that Mooney was in control of Mafia loan sharks for thousands of miles. They also reported that Mooney made numerous trips to Las Vegas and registered in hotels under a variety of false names.

Joe Kennedy had solicited the help of the Mafia to get his son, John Fitzgerald Kennedy, elected president, with the promise that if he got elected, the government would not bother them. It was later reported after the election that thousands of dead people voted, in addition to thousands of union workers in unions controlled by the Outfit, and Illinois swung the vote in favor of JFK to get him elected. Then as soon as he was elected, he appointed Bobby Kennedy as the Attorney General, and Bobby quickly began his war against the Mafia.

That double-cross by Joe Kennedy was the basis for the title of the Giancanas' book, and it infuriated Frank Costello so much that he put out a hit contract on Joe Kennedy. When Joe Kennedy got wind of it, he went to Mooney and pleaded with him to pursuade Costello to take off the hit contract. Mooney succeeded in doing so, and as it played out in the Giancanas' book, Mooney had a better idea of how to rid them of the Bobby Kennedy problem. And that was to assassainate President Kennedy.

Mooney told Chuck that Jack Ruby was his man in Dallas, and he had done a good job of getting Miami Mafia godfather Santo Trafficante out of a Cuban jail and smuggling guns and narcotics across the border.

Within weeks after Bobby Kennedy was appointed Attorney General by his brother, he had New Orleans Mafia godfather Carlos Marcello deported to Guatemala. And other reports I heard of were that Marcello was dumped off in the middle of a Guatemalan jungle to fend for himself. He survived, snuck back into the U.S., and by all reports, was never bothered by the FBI after his return. It was pretty well known in some law enforcement circles that Bobby Kennedy and J. Edgar Hoover were at odds with each other. When I attended the FBI National Academy in the summer of 1975, only a little over three years after Hoover's death, more than one special agent instructor made comments during classes about Bobby and J. Edgar being adversaries. They had been on the FBI long enough to have served under Hoover, and their remarks were obviously slanted toward Hoover's side of the war. However, that was seventeen and eighteen years before Summers's and the Giancanas' books were copyrighted, respectively, and twenty years before Swearingen's book was copyrighted. Since I discovered and studied those books in my D.B. Cooper case investigation, I've often wondered how those special agents now view Mr. Hoover, if they have read any one of those books, and especially Summers's and the Giancanas'.

I do have some idea of how Hoover FBI special agents still revere Hoover, though. My closest cousin married an FBI agent in the 1970s, and she has always quickly shut me up whenever I have started to discuss my Hoover findings in my D.B. Cooper investigation within earshot of her husband.

The Giancanas' wrote that Mooney told Chuck that Lee Harvey Oswald was no more than a "patsy" in the JFK assassination, and Jack Ruby was assigned the task of silencing Oswald after the assassination. And that Oswald's New Orleans uncle was a lieutenant of Carlos Marcello's. I also learned on a TV episode of the JFK assassination a few years ago about Ruby's behavior after he had shot Oswald. And in my mind, it confirmed the Giancanas' report of the Mafia planning and execution of the assassination.

The episode included an account by the Dallas detective who took Ruby to a cell just after he had shot Oswald. The detective said that when he locked Ruby in the cell, Ruby was extremely nervous, and asked him if he had a cigarette. The detective gave him a cigarette and lit it for him. The detective then left Ruby in the cell, and went out to find out how severely Oswald had been injured. He was told that Oswald had died, so he returned to Ruby's cell and told him. He said as soon as he told Ruby that Oswald had died,

Ruby suddenly became calm and relaxed. The detective then asked Ruby if he would like another cigarette, and Ruby replied, "No, I don't smoke."

That account of Ruby's rapid change in demeanor convinced me that the Giancanas' were absolutely right, because Ruby no doubt knew what happened to those who bungled Mafia assignments, just like what had happened to Moretti for failing to retrieve the incriminating blackmail receipt from the dead crooked banker's wallet.

By 1958, Mooney was receiving over $300,000 a month from his share of the Las Vegas gambling profits. And from his many operations, including loan sharking, which had been one of his specialties since his early days in his childhood neighborhood, the Patch, his total monthly take was four million dollars, and tax free as long as the IRS didn't know about it. He was always very generous with his underlings, but in at least one case, one that he didn't believe was doing his share of the workload, was paid only ten percent of his normal monthly take to get him back in line.

Then in 1966, Chicago law enforcement was making it too hot for Mooney, so he moved to Mexico City. He was introduced to Mexican President Luis Echeverria by Richard Cain, a former Chicago cop turned gangster who had contacts in Latin America and served as Mooney's Spanish interpreter. And Mooney was accepted by the President as a welcome alien guest of Mexico. Mooney lived in a posh Mexico City apartment for some time, then moved to a massive, luxurious estate in Cuernavaca, some twenty or thirty miles south of Mexico City.

Mooney met with Meyer Lanky at least one time and set up gambling in Latin America. And for eight years in Mexico City and Cuernavaca, Mooney smuggled millions across the Mexican and other borders by way of a Catholic priest courier they called "Father Cash."

The connections I made with my profile of D.B. Cooper from information in the Giancanas' book were:

1. Mooney lived in Mexico City, or nearby Cuernavaca when Cooper skyjacked Northwest Airlines Flight 305 and ordered the flight crew to fly him to Mexico City, then bailed out over Portland, Oregon.

2. Mooney had a fondness for loan sharking with its fifty percent interest compounded daily, weekly or monthly.

3. Mooney controlled all Mafia loan sharks for thousands of miles.

4. Mooney had no respect for gamblers, and with one look to his lieutenant, one pleading debtor was later found in a ditch, brutally slain.

5. Mooney made many trips to Las Vegas and registered in hotels under various fictitious names.

6. Frank Costello had Hoover in his pocket as a result of Hoover's addiction to horse race gambling.

7. Meyer Lansky was blackmailing Hoover with evidence, and probably photos, of his homosexuality.

Of these, the most relevant to me was Mooney living in Mexico City, or near that city, which convinced me beyond any doubt that Cooper's demand to be flown to Mexico

City was the second part of his coded message to his hitman tormentor, most likely Tony Spilotro, who loved to sadistically kill.

The only missing connection to my profile of Cooper in the Giancanas' book was no mention at all of Tony Spilotro. But that is understandable, because Mooney had been in Mexico City for five years when Spilotro was sent to Las Vegas to manage Mafia affairs in that city. And Mooney was well reputed to be completely close-mouthed about Mafia operations, except in his private, confidential discussions with other Mafioso and Chuck. And it is certain that Mooney would not discuss confidential Mafia matters over a phone or in a letter. Also, because Chuck, his gorgeous wife, and two sons had been rejected by neighbors, and his boys tormented by schoolmates for being Giancanas, Chuck had their last name changed in 1969, and distanced himself from the Outfit. This destroyed his relationship with Mooney, and they did not speak again. Mooney apparently thought Chuck had crossed him, but his only punishment for his younger brother was alienation.

Then after being a welcome alien guest of the President of Mexico for eight years, the unimaginable happened. On the evening of July 18, 1974, three weeks before President Nixon resigned the presidency on August 9, 1974, Mooney was grabbed by Mexican Immigration agents in the walled garden of his security-guarded massive estate to deport him as an undesirable alien. Wearing only a bathrobe and slippers, he was taken to the local jail and incarcerated overnight; then the next day, he was taken to Mexico City and flown to the port of entry at San Antonio, Texas, where he was pushed across the border into the arms of the FBI and served with a subpoena to appear before a Chicago grand jury.

The Giancanas repeatedly wrote in their book that Mooney said the Mafia had owned all of the Presidents since Teddy Roosevelt, and he told Chuck that Nixon was on their side. The timing of Mooney's ambush deportation opened up another big can of worms in my Cooper investigation. So I scribbled a note about that extremely surprising event and filed it with the dozens of other notes I had written since starting on the Cooper case in 1993. It amused me to think that Harry invited me to join him in his Cooper case investigation solely to confirm his theory that Cooper's wildlife-scattered remains are on a Columbia River island. And now I had apparently followed the paper trail all the way to the Nixon White House.

But anything Nixon would do did not surprise me. One of my dozens of San Diego cousins was a California assemblyman in the late 1950s, and Governor Pat Brown appointed him as a municipal court judge in 1959. My cousin has always been a staunch Republican, was a native of San Diego, had been shot down over Germany in World War II, and was in a German POW camp for the last fifteen months of the war. With the latter two credits to his name, he was elected as assmblyman of a Democratic section of San Diego. So, Governor Brown appointed him as a judge to get rid of him so he could be replaced by a Democrat.

Being a staunch Republican and being in an elected position, my cousin and his wife were very active in the Republican Party. In a conversation I had with him in 1968, when

Nixon was running for president against Hubert Humphrey, he told me to be wary of Nixon. He said Nixon was self-serving, acted as though he was "Mr. Republican," and so arrogant that he treated the Party workers as though they were his slaves.

Even with that inside appraisal, I painfully voted for him, but only because I was voting against Humphrey, as he was vice president under LBJ, who created "The Great Society" social giveaway programs. And it really pained me to have to vote for Nixon, because I was also well aware of his nickname, "Tricky Dick."

Then when I was a California Highway Patrol lieutenant in the South Los Angeles office in late 1969, a sergeant and I drove Senator Barry Goldwater from the Long Beach Hyatt House to the LAX Airport. Goldwater was a true American, and we had just entered the I-405 Freeway when he said, "If the people only knew what was going on in Washington, they would revolt." And Nixon had been in the White House for less than a year at that time.

So, with all of that knowledge I had acquired about Nixon, and the Giancanas reporting about Nixon being involved with Mooney, and the Mafia in general, it did not shock me that there could be a direct connection between Nixon, Mooney and the President of Mexico. And with the June 1972 Watergate burglary and ensuing congressional action to impeach Nixon being the top news story for over two years, the President of Mexico had plenty of warning that Nixon was through. And with that, Mooney would no longer be of any use to him.

Most of all, based on all that the Giancanas had reported

about Mooney in Mexico City and smuggling millions across the border, it gave me the impression that Mexico City was the money-laundering capital of North America. And as long as Nixon was president, he could have Mooney take care of the President of Mexico as long as the money flowed like cheap street wine. But with Nixon gone and no longer able to do whatever he was doing for the President of Mexico, Mooney could only become a part of Mexico City history.

Then a few years later, I viewed a TV showing of the movie *All The President's Men*, based on the book of the same title authored by Carl Bernstein and Bob Woodward, *Washington Post* reporters who investigated and broke the Watergate case. At one point in their story, one or both of them made a comment that the case was about money.

So, I quickly went to a used bookstore and bought a copy of *All The President's Men*, and studied and highlighted the critical parts, as I had done with all of the Cooper case–related books.

What I discovered was very interesting, and perhaps related to the Cooper case in a big way, so I will cover that part of the confused, apparently far-reaching Cooper case later herein.

SEVENTEEN

Third Key Link Discovery

An Honest FBI Special Agent

S UMMERS WROTE IN HIS extensive book about veteran
FBI Special Agent M. Wesley Swearingen telling about
Hoover lying to the House Appropriations Committee
about how many wiretaps the FBI had at that time. Swearingen said the day before Hoover was to appear before the
Committee, FBI headquarters would call the Chicago office
where he was assigned, and tell them to reduce their wiretaps to only one, and that one was on the Communist Party
headquarters. They would then call the phone company
and tell then to disconnect all of the other wiretaps for one
day, until the day after Hoover appeared before the Committee, then reconnect all of them.

My first learning of Swearingen being an honest FBI special agent was when there was a concerted effort to prove
that Black Panther Elmer "Geronimo" Pratt had been

framed and falsely arrested, prosecuted, convicted, and imprisoned for the murder of a woman on a tennis court in Santa Monica. There was a TV documentary exposing the case to prove the FBI and LAPD had framed Pratt, because J. Edgar Hoover had sent a directive to the Los Angeles and some other FBI field offices to "neutralize," or put out of circulation, certain Black Panthers leaders, including Pratt. The TV coverage of the Pratt case was in about 1993, about sixteen years after Swearingen had retired from the FBI, and about twenty-one years after Pratt had been sent to prison. Swearingen appeared on the TV episode, and candidly stated that when he learned of the Pratt case after being transferred to the Los Angeles FBI field office, he searched for the file on Pratt's case and he couldn't find it. He then stated that in his over twenty-five years on the FBI, that was the only time he was unable to find a file.

Publicly revealing that on TV convinced me that Swearingen was definitely a completely honest FBI agent. Then I learned that he had authored and published his book, *FBI Secrets*, and I bought a copy, and researched and highlighted the critical, relevant information to the Cooper case, as I had done with all of the other books related to the Cooper case.

As it turned out in the Pratt case, from the time of murder to his arrest, he had an airtight alibi that he was in Oakland, the birthplace of the Black Panthers, at the time of the murder. But the husband of the slain woman positively identified Pratt as one of the two gunmen who murdered his wife and shot and severely wounded him. However, as it was later revealed, Pratt was the third suspect that the husband had positively identified as being the second gunman. So, Pratt was convicted and imprisoned for over twenty years, until his case was highly publicized and reviewed by a court, and he was exonerated and released when the truth was revealed. I will not claim that Swearingen's TV declaration of the Pratt file vanishing from the Los Angeles FBI field office made the case to exonerate him, but I do think it did get the attention of the right people who could pursue justice and closely review all of the evidence in the case and clear him.

Swearingen wrote extensively about Hoover's tyranical control of the FBI and his indiscriminate firing of special agents that he did not like or didn't think fit the FBI image. Swearingen reported that the final test to graduate from the FBI training school after nine weeks of recruit training was an audience with Hoover. And Hoover did not like "pinheads" or truck drivers, as his class was told by an inspector in the classroom before their audience with Hoover.

Hoover had reported two "pinheads" to the training school inspectors in the previous recruit class, but did not tell them the names of the recruits, so they checked the hat sizes of all of the recruits' fedora hats that were part of the dress code and fired the two with the smallest sizes. One recruit heard in advance about the hat size inspection, so he replaced his $6\frac{7}{8}$ hat size tag with a $7\frac{1}{2}$ size tag.

The cruelest part of this report to me is that Hoover waited until after the recruits had endured nine weeks of grueling training to give them their final test of being scrutinized by him for hat size, or whatever, and for only three minutes, as also reported by Swearingen. This dastardly process of elimination concocted by Hoover was not only cruel, it was also a waste of taxpayers' money to pay the rejected trainees nine weeks salary while they were in training. But it served to illustrate to all of those who passed and graduated as FBI special agents that he was in absolute total control and to never forget it.

Swearingen wrote about Hoover's 1958 published book, *Masters of Deceit: The Story of Communism in America and How to Fight It,* and how it had been written by more than a few special agents, including Swearingen, who had written parts on two of the characters in the book. In order for the book to be a success, Hoover issued a mandate that required that all special agents buy at least one copy. One Chicago field office special agent refused to buy a copy of the book because he thought it was FBI propaganda to scare the American people into believing that Hoover was the foremost expert on Communism. That special agent was soon transferred by his supervisor to the applicant squad. Swearingen wrote that he was happy the book was an office joke, even though Hoover received the royalties as the falsely alleged author, which was a violation of federal law.

Even before I read Swearingen's book in my investigation of the Cooper case, I became convinced that Hoover used his long crusade against the threat of Communism as a diversion away from the Mafia. He had prodded Senator McCarthy into holding his infamous Senate hearings on Communism and subversion in Hollywood that destroyed the careers and lives of many movie personnel by being falsely blacklisted.

It was also very interesting that Hoover's falsely authored book went on the market just the year after the 1957 Appalachian raid by the New York State Police on the Mafia summit meeting, which was highly publicized and reportedly embarrassed him.

Swearingen wrote that he had transferred from his first assignment in Memphis to Chicago because he had read in the Chicago newspaper of the one hundred gangland murders in that city a year. So, as a dedicated law enforcement agent, he prepared himself to do something about that carnage and requested a transfer to the Chicago field office.

But when he told a veteran special agent of his noble plan for Chicago, his fellow agent told him to forget it, because Director Hoover did not recognize the existence of the Mafia being in Chicago. He then told Swearingen that Meyer Lansky's organization had enough on Hoover and Tolson being homosexuals that Hoover would never investigate the Mafia. He then noted that when he was in the nine-week recruit training, there had not been any training about organized crime.

He then wrote about Hoover doing nothing about organized crime for thirty-seven years, until he was pressured to do so by Attorney General Bobby Kennedy in 1961.

Swearingen then quoted from the dust cover of Anthony Summers's book, which in so many words stated that because the Mafia bosses had information on Hoover's sex life, he never pursued them, and that greatly contributed to the Mafia getting their hold on America.

Considering all that I learned about Hoover and his relationship with the Mafia because of his addiction to horse race gambling and homosexuality in my investigation of the D.B. Cooper case, I had to conclude that Hoover had, for self-preservation purposes, aided and abetted in the murders of thousands of mobsters and many innocent people. And I believe one of the latter was D.B. Cooper, or whoever he was by any other name, because of Hoover's dictatorial command that allowed the Mafia to run rampant in the U.S., and for years after his death.

EIGHTEEN

Case Solved

The Hot Potato

IN THE NUMEROUS PHONE calls I made to Harry to keep him apprised of my progress in researching the three critical link books I had stumbled onto, Harry was convinced that I was right in my theory that the Cooper skyjacking case had never been reportedly solved by the FBI because it was a J. Edgar Hoover cover-up from the beginning.

The first time he acknowledged that I was right, he rather sadly said he was embarrassed that he hadn't seen it long before because of the absence of a report of tracking Cooper's skyjacked plane by the Portland International Airport traffic controllers. I told him that he shouldn't be embarrassed about anything, because he had focussed solely on determining where Cooper's remains were located and finding them, to the exclusion of all of the mishmash of contradictions and conflicting information in Tosaw's and

Himmelsbach's books. And he had given up on the case
when the Port of Portland refused to give him any more
access permits.

He asked me what I was going to do with my cover-up
theory findings, and I told him I was going to write a complete summary of the case, including his Columbia River
island theory and my Hoover cover-up theory, and send
copies to some publishers to find out if they would publish
it, as I had planned to do from the beginning if he found
Cooper's remains. He said that was the best thing to do, so
I started typing the summary.

It was only a few weeks before Christmas when we had
that conversation, so when my daughter asked me what I
wanted for Christmas, I said I would like a directory of
book publishers. When I acted surprised when I opened
that present from her and her family, which I had to do to
in the true spirit of Christmas, she said, "Now we can all
get rich." And that was over ten years ago, in 1999.

When I had completed the fifty pages of case summary,
including Sources in addition to over twenty-five pages of
illustrations, I mailed copies to over a dozen publishers that
were listed in the gift directory as publishers of crime stories. Then a few weeks later, I started receiving form letter
rejection notices, that in due time added up to the same
number of publishers I had mailed my summary to. That
was my introduction to the publishing world.

With that revolting experience, I decided to mail copies
of my summary to five carefully selected congressional
members with the hope that one or more would see fit to
conduct a hearing and investigation of the Cooper case.

One of my friends suggested I send a copy to Ted Kennedy, because there was no love lost between the Kennedy family and J. Edgar Hoover since the days when Bobby Kennedy was the Attorney General. So, I sent a copy to Ted Kennedy in addition to John McCain, Mary Bono, J.C. Watts and Christopher Cox, my own U.S. Representative. After my experience with the publishers, I decided to mail the summary to the five congressional members certified and return receipt requested U.S. Mail. The return receipts signed by aides of the five started arriving in my mail box, and that was the last there was of that exercise in futility. When I told Harry about my being stonewalled by all five, and all but Ted Kennedy were Republicans, we agreed that the Cooper case had to have a far-reaching impact on one or more persons in Washington, D.C.

In mulling it over, Harry and I agreed that Cooper may have been the black sheep of a very powerful elected Washington, D.C. politician. And in our numerous phone conversations in the years to follow up until his passing on in 2009, we became more and more convinced that it could be the case. That is, unless reports of Hoover's dossiers still being in the garage of a retired FBI employee or special agent included files on all five of those congressional members.

As Harry had done since 1993 when he invited me to join him in his Cooper case investigation, he sent me a copy of every news article related to Cooper's skyjacking. Then in July 2004, he sent me a newsclipping written by Oregonian investigative reporter Margie Boulé about a Florida real estate agent named Jo Weber, who had reported that her husband, Duane Weber, had told her on his deathbed that he was Dan Cooper. I phoned Harry, and he told me that Margie Boulé was an excellent investigative reporter. Boulé's name and office phone number were at the bottom of the article. I had received it on a Saturday, and after I phoned Harry, I then phoned Margie Boulé's office number. A recorder answered, and I left a message, saying to forget about Duane Weber as a suspect because D.B. Cooper had died in his jump, and the case had never been solved by the FBI because it was a J. Edgar Hoover cover-up from the beginning, and I hung up.

Three days later on a Tuesday, Margie Boulé phoned me, and she immediately said that numerous active and retired law enforcement officers had offered their theories about the Cooper case, but I was the first one who said it was a Hoover cover-up. I told her that I had actively investigated and researched the case for eleven years, including searching with my partner, and that the others who had contacted her had probably conducted their investigations from an armchair.

A few days later, I received a copy of Margie Boulé's *Oregonian* article about my telling her it was a Hoover cover-up. Later that night, I phoned Harry, and he told me that his neighbor had left a copy of the article at his door, and with a note that said, "Interesting." And Harry said he did not think the neighbor knew that he and I worked the Cooper case together, or who I am.

Then on August 5, 2004, I sent a letter to Margie Boulé' and I enclosed a four-page list of forty-nine questions for Himmelsbach, to answer in a video-taped interview, if she could arrange a meeting with Himmelsbach and me. The day before, on August 4, 2004, I had sent her a four-page cover letter with my fifty-five-page summary of the Cooper case. Knowing she was probably very busy with all else she had to do as an investigative reporter, I sent follow-up letters to her on August 8, 2004, August 10, 2004, August 30, 2004, and October 14, 2004, because of the interest she had shown in my cover-up theory.

She did not respond, and I thought she had just lost interest in my bizarre Cooper theory. Then after patiently waiting for over two months with no response, I told Harry about it during one of our numerous phone conversations. In the interim, I phoned Tosaw's office number that was listed on the first page of his book. The first time I phoned, the receptionist said he was not in the office. The second time I called, I told the receptionist my name and that I was calling about the D.B. Cooper skyjacking case, and she said he was there. Then, in less than a minute, she said he wasn't there.

When I told Harry about Boulé' not responding and Tosaw suddenly not being in his office after the receptionist said he was there just one minute earlier, Harry and I quickly came to the conclusion that the FBI had gagged both of them, and just like the flight crew members.

Tosaw's 1984 copyrighted book was the first D.B. Cooper book published, and it was self-published. And Tosaw had reported that he interviewed the entire flight crew, Northwest Airlines trouble shooter Paul Soderlind, and the flight crew had given him the handwritten notes documented during the skyjacked flight. And in lieu of our being able to get any response from any of the flight crew members, Himmelsbach's contact, J.T., had harassed Harry and tried to scare him away from searching the Washougal River watershed area, and tried to discourage him from searching the Columbia River islands. The only one involved in any way in the Cooper skyjacking that we were able to interview was Earl Cossey, the parachute rigger who owned the chutes provided to Cooper. And his demonstration and expert information and opinions were most valuable with respect to Harry's Columbia River island theory, but had nothing to do with what I much later discovered. In fact, after Boulé published my cover-up theory, I phoned Cossey and told him about my cover-up theory, and about Boulé's article. He immediately disagreed with me, because he said he had been contacted by numerous FBI agents who had worked so hard on the case.

Then while I was authoring this book manuscript, on December 10, 2009, I phoned Margie Boulé's old office number to find out if she was still an *Oregonian* investigative reporter, or if she had been fired on the demand of the FBI. Her answering machine announced that it was her number, so I left a message telling her that I had some new information on the D.B. Cooper case, and I would like to pass it on to her. She not only did not respond, her article about my J. Edgar Hoover cover-up theory was the last D.B. Cooper article by her that Harry sent to me, after his ten years of doing so.

Until Harry's passing on Septemmber 10, 2009, we had many times agreed that the FBI had gagged all of the players in the Cooper case except Earl Cossey. And they will not know until this book is published and on sale just how valuable Cossey was to our investigation to confirm Harry's theory of where Cooper's remains are located, and where they can be found if a county grand jury directs the local sheriff and Oregon State Police, not the FBI, to search all of the Columbia River islands.

Also, on August 11, 2004, days after Boulé's news article about my Hoover cover-up theory was published, I sent a letter to the U.S. Attorney in Portland, with a copy of her article, some other reports, and other material I had amassed in my then eleven years of investigation of the Cooper case, and explained that a federal grand jury should investigate the case. And I have never received a reply.

Prior to Boulé publishing my Hoover cover-up theory, on September 26, 2000, at the conclusion of an A&E TV *Biography* episode about Hoover, it was reported that Senator Harry Reid was attempting to have Hoover's name removed from the FBI headquarters building in Washington, D.C. And as I recalled, it reported that Senator Reid had introduced a Senate bill to officially and legally remove Hoover's name from the building. As it happened, it was also in the year of 2000 that a bill was introduced in congress to change the name of the Washington National Airport in Washington, D.C., to the Ronald Reagan Airport. That bill was passed unanimously by vote of congress, but there was never any other report of Reid's attempt to remove Hoover's name from the building.

Based on that A&E TV espisode, I sent a three-page letter to Senator Harry Reid on September 27, 2000. Therein, I enclosed copies of my letter to FBI Director Louis

Freeh and the FBI's letter of response. I then explained the most irregular and suspicious reported issues in the Cooper case that my partner and I had discovered in our investigation as:

1. The list of 10,000 ransom bill's serial numbers not being released to the press for two years.
2. No report of Cooper's skyjacked plane being tracked on radar by Portland international Airport air traffic controllers.
3. No publicized report of an official FBI profile of Cooper, and my profile of Cooper.
4. Hoover's cover-up of the Cooper case because he was being blackmailed by the Mafia.

I mentioned my fifty-five-page summary of the Cooper case, but did not enclose it for two reasons. One being that I had wasted my time and money in sending copies to the other five members of congress, and I figured if Senator Reid was sincere in his effort to remove Hoover's name, he would reply to my letter and request a copy of my Summary. And just like the no-responses from the flight crew, the other five members of congress, Margie Boulé, and the Portland U.S. Attorney, I have never received any response from Senator Reid. And because I did not receive any response from the other five congressional members, I did not send my letter to Senator Reid via certified and return receipt requested mail. I just sent it first class U.S. Mail.

With all of these no responses, in our many ensuing phone conversations, Harry and I totally agreed that the

Cooper case had to have some far-reaching impact on any number of powerful Washington, DC officials.

In a later phone conversation, Harry and I discussed in detail my not getting any responses from the congressional members and the U.S. Attorney. We then agreed that the only way to officially solve the case would be to present it to the Attorney Generals of the States of Washington and Oregon to hold a county grand jury investigation into the state crimes of grand theft and kidnapping. We agreed that in California taking any amount of money over $400 was grand theft, and kidnapping is taking a person by force or fear into another country, state, county, or any part of the same county. And Cooper clearly committed both of those crimes. So if the laws of Washington and/or Oregon are essentially the same, they would be grounds for the case to be presented to a county grand jury for investigation.

May 12, 1999

Senator Edward M. Kennedy
U.S. Senate
Washington, D.C. 20510

Senator John McCain
U.S. Senate
Washington, D.C. 20510

Representative Mary Bono
House Office Building
512 Cannon
Washington, D.C. 20515

Representative Christopher Cox
House Office Building
2402 Rayburn
Washington, D.C. 20515

Representative J.C. Watts
House Office Building
1210 Longworth
Washington, D.C 20515

Honorable and Distinguished Congressional Members:

You were each carefully selected to receive the enclosed
"D.B. COOPER SKYJACKING CASE SUMMARY," based on my perception
of your dedication to serve all national interests, and with
dignity and integrity. And with my belief that your particular
assigned committees would be able to provide the specialized
expertise essential to resolving the many complex issues in
the case, as reported in the case summary sources listed.

Also, because this case has no political partisan issues, only
law-and-order truth and justice interests, I believe crossing
party lines to involve those who may have a particular interest
in this case would best serve to resolve it. And I sent it to
all of you, hoping at least one of you would find it worthy
of investigation.

Any or all of you may seriously wonder why two old cops would
spend years investigating and analyzing an ancient unsolved
skyjacking. Well, there are several reasons. One is, we don't
like playing golf, don't play golf, and will never play golf.
Another is, we are from the "Old School" of cops who believe
every criminal should be apprehended and face justice. And in
our generation of cops, we weren't paid overtime to get the
job done right. We just did what we had to do on our own time,
and the satisfaction of doing it right was our compensation.

-1-

We also believe putting our mental faculties to good use is
a form of "mental exercise" that will keep us from getting old,
vegetating, and talking to ourselves. There are other reasons,
but I hope these will suffice for now.

Despite our donating our time to do the job right, I will mention
this only to illustrate our profound interest in solving the
D.B. Cooper case. After retiring from active law enforcement,
both my partner and I were private investigators for a few years.
And my attorney-accepted expert witness and private investigator
hourly fee was $50 an hour, plus mileage and other expenses.
My total hours expended on the Cooper case have exceeded 1,000
hours, amounting to over $50,000, plus expenses for office
supplies, copying, mileage, and flying to Vancouver, etc.
I do not know how many hours my partner expended for sure, or
how much he spent on special search equipment, mileage, etc.
But it was a "labor of love" for both of us, and we donate this
case summary in the sole interest of truth and justice, with
no expectation of compensation, whatsoever.

I mention these time and monetary expenditures only in the hope
that at least one of you will deem solving the Cooper case worthy
of expending up to $50,000 to at least conduct a preliminary
investigation, as outlined under "CONCLUSION" in the enclosed
case summary.

And because I am certain said preliminary investigation will
show more than sufficient cause to conduct a complete
Congressional Committee investigation and hearing.

I have also enclosed copies of three letters to prove I did
achieve something, and served in an extremely responsible
position during my 31-year police career. The latter was during
my last year before retiring, coordinating with the Secret
Service to protect President Reagan, and the Queen of England.

Your timely reply of interest and contemplated action, or
otherwise, would be greatly appreciated. And if this letter
and enclosed case summary is or will be made a part of the
Congressional Record, and be protected by law as "Legislative
Privilege." Although I am certain I did not defame any living
person in my case summary, this protection would be comforting.

Respectfully yours,

George C. Nuttall, Captain, California Highway Patrol, Retired

enclosure
cc: file, partner, attorneys

-2-

SENDER:
- ☐ Complete items 1 and/or 2 for additional services.
- Complete items 3, 4a, and 4b.
- ☐ Print your name and address on the reverse of this form so that we can return this card to you.
- ☐ Attach this form to the front of the mailpiece, or on the back if space does not permit.
- ☐ Write "Return Receipt Requested" on the mailpiece below the article number.
- ☐ The Return Receipt will show to whom the article was delivered and the date delivered.

I also wish to receive the following services (for an extra fee):
1. ☐ Addressee's Address
2. ☐ Restricted Delivery

3. Article Addressed to:
SENATOR Edward M.
KENNEDY
U.S. SENATE
WASHINGTON, D.C. 20510
(D.B. COOPER Summary)

4a. Article Number
Z 267 938 126

4b. Service Type
- ☐ Registered   ☒ Certified
- ☐ Express Mail   ☐ Insured
- ☐ Return Receipt for Merchandise   ☐ COD

7. Date of Delivery
MAY 1 8 1999

5. Received By: (Print Name)

8. Addressee's Address (Only if requested and fee is paid)

6. Signature (Addressee or Agent)

PS Form ... mber 1994   102595-99-B-0223   Domestic Return Receipt

Is your RETURN ADDRESS completed on the reverse side?
Thank you for using Return Receipt Service.

SENDER:
- ☐ Complete items 1 and/or 2 for additional services.
- Complete items 3, 4a, and 4b.
- ☐ Print your name and address on the reverse of this form so that we can return this card to you.
- ☐ Attach this form to the front of the mailpiece, or on the back if space does not permit.
- ☐ Write "Return Receipt Requested" on the mailpiece below the article number.
- ☐ The Return Receipt will show to whom the article was delivered and the date delivered.

I also wish to receive the following services (for an extra fee):
1. ☐ Addressee's Address
2. ☐ Restricted Delivery

3. Article Addressed to:
SENATOR John McCAIN
U.S. SENATE
WASHINGTON, D.C.
20510
(D.B. COOPER Summary)

4a. Article Number
Z 267 938 128

4b. Service Type
- ☐ Registered   ☒ Certified
- ☐ Express Mail   ☐ Insured
- ☐ Return Receipt for Merchandise   ☐ COD

7. Date of Delivery
MAY 1 8 1999

5. Received By: (Print Name)

8. Addressee's Address (Only if requested and fee is paid)

6.

PS Form 3811, December 1994   102595-99-B-0223   Domestic Return Receipt

Is your RETURN ADDRESS completed on the reverse side?
Thank you for using Return Receipt Service.

SENDER:
- ☐ Complete items 1 and/or 2 for additional services.
- Complete items 3, 4a, and 4b.
- ☐ Print your name and address on the reverse of this form so that we can return this card to you.
- ☐ Attach this form to the front of the mailpiece, or on the back if space does not permit.
- ☐ Write "Return Receipt Requested" on the mailpiece below the article number.
- ☐ The Return Receipt will show to whom the article was delivered and the date delivered.

I also wish to receive the following services (for an extra fee):
1. ☐ Addressee's Address
2. ☐ Restricted Delivery

3. Article Addressed to:
REPRESENTATIVE Mary Bono
HOUSE Office Building
512 CANNON
WASHINGTON, D.C. 20515
(COOPER Summary)

4a. Article Number
Z 267 938 125

4b. Service Type
- ☐ Registered   ☒ Certified
- ☐ Express Mail   ☐ Insured
- ☐ Return Receipt for Merchandise   ☐ COD

7. Date of Delivery
MAY 1 8 1999

5. Received By: (Print Name)

8. Addressee's Address (Only if requested and fee is paid)

PS Form 3811, December 1994   102595-99-B-0223   Domestic Return Receipt

Is your RETURN ADDRESS completed on the reverse side?
Thank you for using Return Receipt Service.

SENDER:
- Complete items 1 and/or 2 for additional services.
- Complete items 3, 4a, and 4b.
- Print your name and address on the reverse of this form so that we can return this card to you.
- Attach this form to the front of the mailpiece, or on the back if space does not permit.
- Write "Return Receipt Requested" on the mailpiece below the article number.
- The Return Receipt will show to whom the article was delivered and the date delivered.

I also wish to receive the following services (for an extra fee):
1. ☐ Addressee's Address
2. ☐ Restricted Delivery

3. Article Addressed to:
REPRESENTATIVE Christopher Cox
House Office Building
2402 Rayburn
WAShington, D.C. 20515
(D.B. Cooper Summary)

4a. Article Number
Z 207 938 123

4b. Service Type
☐ Registered   ☒ Certified
☐ Express Mail   ☐ Insured
☐ Return Receipt for Merchandise   ☐ COD

7. Date of Delivery MAY 17 1999

5. Received By: (Print Name)
_____ ssee or Agent)

8. Addressee's Address (Only if requested and fee is paid)

Is your RETURN ADDRESS completed on the reverse side?

Thank you for using Return Receipt Service.

PS Form 3811, December 1994   102595-99-B-0223   Domestic Return Receipt

---

SENDER:
- Complete items 1 and/or 2 for additional services.
- Complete items 3, 4a, and 4b.
- Print your name and address on the reverse of this form so that we can return this card to you.
- Attach this form to the front of the mailpiece, or on the back if space does not permit.
- Write "Return Receipt Requested" on the mailpiece below the article number.
- The Return Receipt will show to whom the article was delivered and the date delivered.

I also wish to receive the following services (for an extra fee):
1. ☐ Addressee's Address
2. ☐ Restricted Delivery

3. Article Addressed to:
REPRESENTATIVE J.C. Watts
House Office Building
1210 Longworth
Washington, D.C. 20515
(Subject: D.B. Cooper Summary)

4a. Article Number
Z 267 938 127

4b. Service Type
☐ Registered   ☒ Certified
☐ Express Mail   ☐ Insured
☐ Return Receipt for Merchandise   ☐ COD

7. Date of Delivery MAY 18 1999

5. Received By: (Print Name)
_____ or Agent)

8. Addressee's Address (Only if requested and fee is paid)

Is your RETURN ADDRESS completed on the reverse side?

Thank you for using Return Receipt Service.

PS Form 3811, December 1994   102595-99-B-0223   Domestic Return Receipt

September 27, 2000

U.S. Senator Harry Reed
528 Hart Senate Office Building
Washington, D.C. 20510

Honorable Senator Reed:

At the conclusion of the September 26, 2000, A&E TV episode
"Biography: 'J. Edgar Hoover; Personal & Confidential,'",
it was stated that you were attempting to have J. Edgar Hoover's
name removed from the Washington, D.C., FBI Headquarters
Building. And as I recall, I believe it was stated that you
had introduced a Senate bill in an attempt to do so.

As a 31-year-veteran California peace officer and private
investigator of the 1971 D.B. Cooper skyjacking case, I applaud
you for your honorable effort in this matter. And I would like
to assist you in any way possible to bring this matter to a
successful conclusion.

The enclosed copies of my May 24, 1995, letter to FBI Director
Freeh, and the FBI's July 25, 1995, letter of reply will
hopefully indicate to you my intense interest and involvement
in the unsolved D.B. Cooper skyjacking. Please pardon the blanked
sections, but my partner wishes to remain anonymous, as explained
in my letter to Mr. Freeh. And at age 79, my partner recently
learned by diagnosis that he has a severe heart condition.

From the beginning of our active Cooper investigation in 1994,
strange events started occurring. Unlike Richard Tosaw, author
of the first D.B. Cooper book published in 1984, and who reported
the full cooperation of the flight crew and other witnesses,
none replied to our inqueries. All except Earl Cossey, who packed
the Cooper chutes, and retired FBI Special Agent Ralph
Himmelsbach, who has been publicly represented as the Cooper-
case agent since the time of the skyjacking. And the latter
is a mystery in itself, because Himmelsbach was assigned to
the Portland FBI field office, and the Cooper case has been
assigned to the Seattle FBI field office since the time of
Cooper's skyjacking. And you can readily see from the enclosed
FBI letter of reply, my letter was forwarded to the Seattle
field office.

However, these events are only the tip of the iceberg, and may
appear to be inconsequential to one who does not know all of
what my partner and I experienced and uncovered. Actually, there
are dozens of reported and real events that do not make any
sense to us as experienced criminal investigators. And so much
more, that my Cooper-case summary is 55 pages in length,

-1-

including one full page of sources, plus 27 pages of supporting
exhibits.

And the most obvious strange reports we detected from the outset
of our early investigative research were:

1. J. Edgar Hoover reportedly waited 8-15 days after Cooper's
skyjacking to release the list of 10,000 serial numbers of the
$20 ransom bills, and then only to banks and other financial
institutions. Then his successor did not release the list to
the media for publication until two years later. And the Secret
Service estimates that the lifetime of a $20 bill is 18-24
months.

Obviously, that list should have been released to the media
the night of Cooper's crime. Why wasn't it released then?

2. Published reports, including Himmelsbach's 1986 copyrighted
book, "NORJAK," states that the Cooper-skyjacked aircraft was
tracked on radar by Seattle; McChord Air Force Base; and Auburn,
Washington. And they are all located about 100 miles to the
north of the Columbia River and the adjacent Portland
International Airport.

However, there is no report of the aircraft being tracked on
radar by the Portland International Airport FAA air controllers.
And despite reports that they thought the skyjacked plane was
on automatic-pilot-course Vector-23, which passes directly over
the west runway of Portland International Airport.

Furthermore, one Cooper publication states that the FBI had
a skyjack plan at that time, which included the immediate
dispatch of "Team One" to the control towers of airports in
or near the flight path of skyjacked aircraft.

Then it was not learned by the FBI until after the find of $5,800
of the ransom money in 1980 that the Cooper-skyjacked aircraft
was being flown manually, not on automatic pilot, and had drifted
an unknown distance to the east of Vector-23.

Why wasn't the skyjacked aircraft reported to have been tracked
by the Portland FAA air controllers? And why didn't the FBI
know from the night of the skyjacking that the aircraft was
being flown manually, not on automatc pilot or on Vector-23?

3. Himmelsbach reported in his 1986 copyrighted book, "NORJAK,"
that the FBI was profiling Cooper. Himmelsbach then personally
profiled Cooper as a burned-out ex-con, trying for one last
big hit.

However, despite the FBI Academy Behavioral Science Unit profile
specialists reportedly profiling criminals since no later than

1979, to my knowledge, the FBI has never published an official
profile of the skyjacker known only as "Dan Cooper" and "D.B.
Cooper."

And based on six consistently reported facts, and one of
questionable validity, I soon profiled Cooper as a compulsive
gambler, loner within his own element, and over his head in
debt to Las Vegas Mafia loan sharks. And they had given him
his last warning to pay up or else. Also, from my seven years
of researching this case, I'm certain Cooper was a former Green
Beret and served in Vietnam.

If my profile is correct and valid, and I'm certain it is, it
is the crucial link to ultimately proving the Cooper case was
a Hoover cover-up to protect himself from his Mafia associates.
It has been repeatedly reported that Hoover was an addicted
horse-race gambler, and got tips on fixed races from Frank
Costello. And that Hoover bet with Mafia bookies. And when his
horses won, they paid him the winnings, and when his horses
lost, they forgave his losses.

Then there are the reports of Hoover's homosexuality, and his
being blackmailed by Meyer Lansky with proof of Hoover in a
homosexual act.

Some or all of this may sound far-fetched, but my seven years
of research, investigation and evaluation have convinced me
beyond any doubt whatsoever that my theory of a Hoover cover-
up of the Cooper is absolutely accurate and valid. And my partner
agrees with me wholeheartedly.

So, if you want Hoover's name removed from the FBI Headquarters
Building as much as I do, please reply or call at any time,
and I will send you a copy of my 55-page case summary and 27
pages of supportive exhibits.

However, I must warn you, the paper trail could very well lead
to the Nixon White House, based on information Bob Woodward
and Carl Berstein reported in "All The President's Men." And
from my personal knowledge of Hoover and his annual summer visits
to Clint Murchison's La Jolla Del Cerro Hotel and the Del Mar
Race Track. And much, much more.

Most sincerely,

George C. Nuttall, Captain, California Highway Patrol, Retired

enclosures
cc: file

-3-

D.B. COOPER

SKYJACKING CASE SUMMARY

CONTENTS

D.B. COOPER

SKYJACKING CASE SUMMARY

by

George Clifton Nuttall
Captain, California Highway Patrol, Retired

INTRODUCTION

As briefly explained in the enclosed copies of my May 24, 1995,
letter to FBI Director Freeh and the FBI letter of reply, I
investigated the unsolved D.B. Cooper skyjacking of Thanksgiving
Eve, November 24, 1971. My case partner had "armchair" analyzed
it from 1986 to 1993, and concluded Cooper's remains and evidence
of his true identification are on one of the Columbia River
islands. And most likely scattered by wildlife within 100 yards
of the north shore of Government Island.

In 1993, he urged me to join him in analyzing his collection
of Cooper case materiel to refute, modify, or support his
conclusions. Always fascinated by unsolved cases, and the Cooper
case in particular, I agreed to independently analyze his data.
Without delay, he mailed his seven-year collection of books,
news articles, maps, tide tables, and photos to me.

In reviewing, comparing, and analyzing three published Cooper
case books, listed herein under "SOURCES," they reported three
distinctly different theories on Cooper's fate and location
of his remains. They were: 1. That Cooper was believed to be
April 7, 1972, ransom skyjacker Richard Floyd McCoy, Jr., who
escaped from prison and was killed in a shootout with FBI agents
in 1974. 2. That Cooper landed safely in the Columbia River,
drowned, and remains there. 3. That Cooper landed injured in
the woods of southwest Washington and died of hypothermia, or
in the Columbia River or a tributary. (See enclosed copy of
November 24, 1988, edition of The Oregonian).

All three of these theories appear to propose that Cooper was
able to deploy the military NB-8 emergency pilot parachute he
used. Richard T. Tosaw, self-published author of "D.B. Cooper
Dead or Alive?," and parachute packer/expert parachutist Earl
Cossey reported Cooper used the NB-8 chute in preference to
three civilian models provided.

As explained herein under "COLUMBIA RIVER ISLAND THEORY," my
partner and I are certain Cooper was unable to deploy his chute,

-1-

based on our June 18, 1994, interview with Earl Cossey, and
free fell to his instant death.

Like others presented herein, this is our opinion, based solely
on our over 70 years of combined public law enforcement
investigative experiences in varied fields and specialties and
published reports and/or personal interviews conducted by one
or both of us.

Likewise, my independent personality/psychological profile of
the skyjacker most commonly known as D.B. Cooper is my own
opinion. And is based on my over 50 years of criminal-behavior
study, including the Mafia, and over 30 years as a California
law enforcement investigator, and from sources listed herein.

In June 1994, after sending a few inquiries to persons named
in the Cooper source books, I spent nine days with my partner
and his wife in Vancouver, Washington, to conduct my own
independent investigation. But even before I flew to Vancouver,
some strange events started occurring, and are explained herein
under "STRANGE EVENTS."

However, long before June 1994, based on my above related study
and experience, I profiled Cooper as briefly stated in my letter
to Director Freeh: a compulsive gambler hopelessly in debt to
Las Vegas Mafia loan sharks, and had been given his final warning
to pay, or else! And explained herein.

This personality/psychological profile was, and is, the sole
crucial link to my casual discoveries in 1998 that prompted
me to conduct research of published reports on J. Edgar Hoover
and his Mafia associations.

Three books listed under "SOURCES" herein report on Hoover's
association with New York Mafiso Frank Costello, with respect
to Hoover's alleged "addiction" to horse-race gambling, and/or
his being blackmailed by Mafia gambling kingpin Meyer Lansky.
All three books report that Lansky had blackmailed Hoover for
decades with evidence of his "closet" homosexuality. And it
was reportedly believed Lansky had one or more photos of Hoover
engaged in a homosexual act, in which Hoover was clearly
identifiable. These sources and specific reports on Hoover are
explained herein under "J. EDGAR HOOVER."

Although Retired FBI Special Agent Ralph P. Himmelsbach wrote
in his 1986 copyrighted book, "NORJAK: the Investigation of
D.B. Cooper," that the FBI was developing a profile of Cooper,
as late as 1991, no official FBI profile of him was reported
in any of the three Cooper case source books. And as late as
the November 24, 1988, edition of The Oregonian, Himmelsbach
was quoted as saying Cooper was "probably a burned-out ex-con."
And, "He used atrocious language - vile, vulgar, obscene, the

-2-

kind convicts use." As above stated, a copy of that edition is enclosed.

Now-Retired FBI Special Agent John E. Douglas, the most publicized FBI profiler, as in "The Silence of the Lambs," coauthored a book, "Mindhunter: Inside the FBI's Elite Serial Crime Unit." Therein, he related the development of FBI profiling dating back to 1972.

He wrote that FBI Special Agent Howard Teten actively explored profiling by 1972. And at an earlier unspecified date before 1972, Teten had consulted with Dr. James Brussel, a New York psychiatrist who had solved the serial "Mad Bomber" case in 1957. He did so by precisely profiling the bomber, including that he most likely wore a double-breasted suit, and with coat buttoned. Based solely on Dr. Brussel's complete profile, the police soon identified, located, and arrested the serial bomber. And when they arrested him, he was reportedly wearing a double-breasted suit, and with coat buttoned.

Douglas wrote of many cases, and that in 1979, the FBI profiling unit received about 50 requests to profile criminals, and the requests doubled each of the two following years.

Despite these reported profilings, the three Cooper case source books listed herein do not report an official FBI profile of Cooper. And they were copyrighted in 1984, 1986, and 1991, respectively. And as late as 1988, Himmelsbach, coauthor of the 1986 copyrighted book, was quoted as above herein stated in the November 24, 1988, edition of The Oregonian.

Therefore, an official profile of Cooper by FBI profiling and Mafia experts, and John E. Douglas, is most crucial to many published and reported case issues presented herein.

As reported by Douglas, the FBI profilers have accurately profiled numerous criminals, and based on far less information than I used to profile Cooper from published reports. And to the extent that the FBI profilers coach or instruct police interrogators how to question each category of profiled suspect.

Concurrence with my profile by FBI experts or not, the location of Cooper's remains and identification is a different, but directly related, issue. And will be explained herein under "COLUMBIA RIVER ISLAND THEORY."

What is presented herein must not in any way reflect unfavorably on FBI Director Freeh, the present FBI, or its administration. To the contrary, in my brief, limited contacts with active FBI personnel in this matter, they have been most forthright, informative, and helpful. So much so, I'm certain they have no idea of what I discovered and submitted in this summary.

-3-

However, if a Congressional Select Committee or Commission were
to investigate the D.B. Cooper case and the FBI's management
of the investigation, cause may be shown to rename the FBI
headquarters building in Washington, D.C.

When Congress changed the name of the Washington National Airport
to the Ronald Reagan Airport in 1998, the media reported Congress
debated removing J. Edgar Hoover's name from the Washington,
D.C., FBI building. But reasons were not publicized by the media,
that I can recall.

If for any reason a name change were to be made, I respectfully
suggest it be named the "FBI SPECIAL AGENT'S MEMORIAL BUILDING,"
in honor of the about 30-40 agents killed in the line of duty.
And with a prominent monument displaying their names at the
main entrance.

Two of the Cooper case source books were coauthored or one person
was the writer and the other researched the material. Both
included a retired FBI special agent, and will be referred to
as the author herein for clarity and brevity. They are: Ralph
P. Himmelsbach, coauthor of "NORJAK: the Investigation of D.B.
Cooper;" and Russell P. Calame, researcher of "D.B. Cooper:
The Real McCoy."

The third Cooper case source book, "D.B. Cooper Dead or Alive?"
was authored, copyrighted, and self-published by Richard T.
Tosaw. Therein, Mr. Tosaw wrote that he was a FBI special agent
from 1951 to 1956, then a Ceres, California, real estate
attorney, then an investigator of major unsolved crimes.

To avoid copyright infringements, I have stated all reported
information in my own words without distortion of the actual
content. In all cases except from "NORJAK: the Investigation
of D.B. Cooper," which grants some liberty in its copyright
protection, and stated as, "except by a reviewer, who may quote
brief passages in a review."

I hereby declare that all information presented herein is based
on published or produced sources, or by credible oral sources
from my own experiences, or that of another and identified by
name or other means.

In that the multitude of reports on many aspects of this case
were/are complex and conflicting, I will summarize and address
them in priority order of importance.

To protect my personal assets and interests in writing and
submitting this case summary as a public service, I consulted
with copyright and Constitutional Law attorneys for guidance.
And to the best of my ability, I have written this summary in
terms to avoid defamation and copyright violations.

-4-

PURPOSES FOR CONGRESSIONAL INVESTIGATION

A Congressional investigation of the unsolved 1971 D.B. Cooper
skyjacking case could serve the American public in more than
one way.

In his book, "NORJAK: the Investigation of D.B. Cooper," Retired
FBI Special Agent Ralph P. Himmelsbach wrote that of all the
skyjacking of the 1960s and 1970s, Cooper's was the only unsolved
case, and his was number 2,111.

This, of course, makes the D.B. Cooper skyjacking case unique,
and most likely the most highly publicized. To some, he has
remained a folk hero who "beat the system." At least one
fictional movie, "Pursuing D.B. Cooper," was released in about
1986, starring Robert Duvall. And as of late 1998, a sports
bar in Los Angeles remained to be named after him. To the best
of my recollection, it was, and probably still is, the "D.B.
Cooper Saloon and Restaurant."

Based on my investigation of the D.B. Cooper case, I sincerely
believe it can be solved only by Congressional investigation.
And that said investigation would serve the following, but not
all inclusive, purposes:

1. Primarily to solve the case, including a law enforcement
and/or infrared heat sensing photography search of the Columbia
River islands east of the I-205 bridge.

2. If cause is revealed through investigation and hearings,
it may justify renaming the FBI headquarters building in D.C.

3. The media recently reported a Congressional Commission on
Gambling Report was due to be delivered to Congress in 90 days,
or about July 1, 1999. If that report discloses the devastating
impact on American families of addicted gamblers and/or organized
crime involvement, it is my opinion a Congressional investigation
would serve to support the Commission's findings.

4. To illustrate that retired qualified police investigators
could be a valuable asset to public agencies in solving difficult
or unsolved crimes. Most actively employed police investigators
are overburdened with cases, and are frequently or constantly
interrupted by many intrusions while on duty. Many years ago,
a FBI agent told me agents had to carry up to 60 active cases
at all times.

Hundreds or thousands of retired expert law enforcement
investigators no longer serve the public. Some are private
investigators, and most are idle or otherwise uninvolved.

-5-

About two years ago, a TV program reported only about 17 percent of major crimes in the U.S. are successfully investigated and prosecuted. If that figure is accurate, the major criminals have over 4-to-1 odds of escaping detection and penalty.

Over a total of 13 years, my partner and I expended a combined total of about one year on the Cooper case. And much of that was duplication of time and effort, and without official case records. However, we had the luxury of uninterrupted time in quiet surroundings, no peer or media pressure, or career setbacks if we failed to resolve and close the case.

If our investigation, and opinions presented herein prove to be valid and of assistance in solving the Cooper case, I suggest Congress address a program to employ proven qualified expert retired law enforcement investigators to assist active law enforcement in complex, difficult, and/or unsolved crimes. A monetary benefit being that most retired law enforcement investigators receive health insurance and other benefits from their past employing agency. Costs could be limited to non-hazard wages, worker's compensation insurance, and only retirement contributions to Social Security.

5. The media reported the presence of the Russian "Mafia" in the U.S. And that FBI Director Freeh traveled to Russia to sign and agreement with Russian law enforcement to coordinate efforts to pursue this menace.

If the opinions presented herein prove to be correct, either by hearings or search of the Columbia River islands east of the I-205 bridge, or both, it would illustrate the extent to which organized crime can impact innocent persons. And the need for additional Congressional support of the FBI in the relentless pursuit and prosecution of all major organized crime elements.

MY PERSONALITY/PSYCHOLOGICAL PROFILE OF D.B. COOPER

My profile of D.B. Cooper was formulated based on my over 50-year study of criminal behavior, including the Mafia, and over 30 years as a California peace officer, supervisor, and administrator, and from reports in the published sources listed and identified herein.

1. Himmelsbach wrote that Cooper must have been really desperate to jump as he did.

Reports are that Cooper was wearing a business suit, raincoat, and slip-on, loafer-type shoes. And he jumped into about a 200-220 mph headwind in about 25 degrees Fahrenheit temperature in reportedly one of the worst storms in 24 years. He could not know the location where he jumped into darkness and dense cloud cover over mountains, forests, thorny blackberry vines, rivers, lakes, Interstate highways, power lines, farms, and some heavily-populated areas. Flying the aircraft manually, not on automatic pilot, and unable to see the glow of city lights over Vancouver and Portland due to the dense cloud cover, even the flight officers did not known their exact location when Cooper jumped at about 8:13 p.m.

Considering all of these reported conditions, and Cooper's reported familiarity with 727 aircraft and parachutes, it is apparent to me that he knew he was jumping to his near-certain, instant death. Or worse, to severe injury, and long, agonizing death in the wet, freezing wilderness. And with the potential of hungry wildlife, including cougars, attacking him while he was still alive and defenseless.

These reported conditions and events compelled me to agree with Himmelsbach's belief that Cooper must have been really desperate. But to a much greater degree. I did, and do, believe Cooper had to be extremely desperate, and to the level of self-sacrifice or to avoid a much worse death.

The only worse death I could envision from my over 50 years of criminal study was, and is, Mafia style: by slow and savage torture.

Examples of Mafia killings were written by Sam Giancana, godson, and Chuck Giancana, brother, of Chicago Mafia boss Sam "Mooney" Giancana, in their 1992 copyrighted New York Times bestseller, "Double Cross." One was the gruesome murder of Gus Greenbaum and his wife. Greenbaum reportedly managed the Las Vegas Riviera for Mafia gambling boss Meyer Lansky. Lansky reportedly allowed his underlings to skim reasonable amounts. But by 1958, Greenbaum was skimming far too much, and losing as much as $20,000 a week gambling. Giancana decided Greenbaum had to go, and Lansky agreed. The gruesomely mutilated bodies of Greenbaum and his wife were found in their Phoenix home, and with their throats neatly slit.

Another reported by the Giancanas was alleged to be the cruelest in Chicago Mafia history. And as an example. Mooney Giancana reportedly thought a Mafia loan shark had turned FBI informant. The suspected traitor was reportedly forcibly taken to a meat-rendering facility, hung from a meathook, and sadistically tortured nonstop for two days until he finally died in extreme agony. Then as reportedly ordered, photos of the gruesomely mutilated corpse were taken to warn others of the consequences of those who talked with FBI agents.

Both reportedly served to warn all others of what happened to those who crossed Sam Giancana, in any way. And they reported Mooney controlled loan sharks over thousands of miles.

The Giancanas also wrote that Chuck had been told by some of
Mooney's Chicago Mafia associates that Mooney had moved millions
of dollars across the Mexican border.

Compulsive gamblers, or "addicted gamblers" as they are now
labelled, reportedly have a severe mental disorder. As shown
on more recent TV documentaries and talk shows, they have no
perception of losses and ultimate consequences. The risk and
excitement of winning big with the next hand, roll, spin, race,
etc., drives them. Losses are only a run of bad luck, and it's
bound to change. Baseball great Pete Rose was identified as
a compulsive gambler on a TV talk show a few years ago. Most
recently, a TV documentary special was about a Texas millionaire
who lost over $2,000,000 at Louisiana casinos. He lost
everything, including his wife and children, as a result. He
said he couldn't control himself, and had to gamble.

Another most recent TV special was on females addicted to casino
video-poker machine gambling. One interviewed said playing the
slots was her escape from the real world, despite her losses,
and much like drug addiction.

My initial gambling education started in about 1943. That was
when a very experienced, streetwise father of a friend of mine
told a group of us the facts of gambling. He said, "It's human
nature that people can stand to lose, but can't stand to win.
If they win, they'll keep playing to win more until they lose
all of it. And the house will always win in the long run, because
the odds are always in its favor, and it has the bankroll to
cover all short-term, and even long-term, losses. But gamblers
don't." He cited his experiences, and proved his point to us.

Meyer Lansky reportedly always ran straight, honest gaming.
Reportedly a "genius" in his gambling specialty, he never ran
crooked games. He didn't have to, because he most certainly
knew the above facts of gambling, and won millions from many
levels of society without cheating. And most likely much of
it from compulsive gamblers who could not win it back in the
long run.

And nobody knows this better than loan sharks. They know when
a gambler borrows in desperation to cover losses, he or she
can never win it back to pay them off, plus their reported 50
percent or more rates of interest, compounded monthly, weekly,
or daily.

Considering the improbable odds, most, if not all, borrowers
will have to commit a crime to pay it back, or get the money
from a very benevolent, understanding, trusting family member
or friend. And most compulsive gamblers do not have either for
very long. Especially family members who are well aware of the
borrower's lifestyle.

This is the only predicament I can envision that could have
driven Cooper to jump as he did in all of the reported conditions
he had to encounter. Also, one of his reported acts that I
believe supports my opinion of his state of mind.

That is, Calame and Tosaw wrote that when Cooper allowed Flight
Attendants Alice Hancock and Florence Schaffner to deplane in
Seattle, along with the other 36 passengers, Cooper reportedly
offered each of the two attendants a packet of $2,000. These
author's versions of what Cooper said to the two differs, but
is not of great importance. The act in itself could indicate
at least two possibilities: One, that like most compulsive
gamblers reportedly perceive money, it is not important. The
anticipation "rush" of winning on the next bet or bid is what
drives them. And two, that he knew his odds of surviving the
jump were nearly impossible, and even if he did survive and
escape, somebody else was going to take most, or all, of the
$200,000 ransom money.

Himmelsbach did not write of this peculiar incident in his book.
And some of his other writings conflicted with or omitted those
reported by Calame and Tosaw. Overall, Tosaw's book proved in
our investigation to be the most complete and accurate. However,
Calame's book was primarily about McCoy and his skyjacking,
and included much less about Cooper than those authored by
Himmelsbach and Tosaw.

Other conflicting or omitted reports in the three Cooper case
source books are:

A. Calame and Tosaw wrote that Cooper sat in seat 18E. That
is the center seat of three to the right of the aisle in the
last row, counting from the left, facing forward in the passenger
cabin. Himmelsbach wrote that Cooper sat in seat 18C, the aisle
seat to the left of the aisle.

B. Himmelsbach wrote that Cooper was wearing a pearl stickpin
in his narrow, black tie. Pearl is the June birthstone, and
not widely worn by men. Considering all possibilities, I suggest
that Cooper's birthday could be in June, or the stickpin may
have been part of a service uniform, as later discussed herein.

Himmelsbach did not write of Cooper leaving the pearl stickpin
and black tie on a seat, and abandoning them when he jumped.

But Calame wrote that Cooper removed his clip-on tie and mother-
of-pearl tie clasp and left them on seat 18E. And that both
McCoy's mother-in-law and sister-in-law identified the two items
as belonging to McCoy. Despite this, Calame wrote that in 1990,
none of the Reno FBI agents who searched the skyjacked plane
after it landed in Reno, with Cooper missing, could recall
anything about the tie clasp and tie being on the plane.

CASE SOLVED [215]

Calame also wrote that the FBI had withheld information about the tie and tie clasp being left on the plane for 20 years, to screen the usual number of publicity-seeking loonies who confess to being the perpetrator in high-profile cases.

Calame also reported that the Reno FBI written reports of the search of skyjacked Flight 305 by four special agents did not include any mention of the tie and tie clasp.

Of greatest importance in Calame's report of the tie and tie clasp confusion is that the two items were eventually located at the Seattle FBI Field Office. And he briefly wrote that the Seattle FBI office was the office of origin and jurisdiction in the Cooper case. Therefore, the tie and tie clasp had been sent to that division office by the Reno FBI office.

This, in addition to other reports and events later addressed herein, is of importance because Himmelsbach wrote in his book that he was assigned to the FBI Portland division office in 1962, and he did not report his being transferred to another FBI office or division up to the time he retired from the FBI in 1980.

C. Himmelsbach wrote that Cooper rejected military parachutes, and demanded civilian chutes instead. Himmelsbach then wrote in parenthesis that Cooper apparently knew the type of military chutes suggested would open automatically after about 200 feet, as opposed to civilian skydivers and acrobatic pilots models that allowed the chutist to free fall any distance desired.

Although we are not parachutists, my partner and I have never figured out how an inanimate parachute can know when it has fallen 200 feet or is in a car trunk, on a shelf, or is moving or stationery. The only automatically controlled deployment of military chutes we have seen in movies and on TV shows are paratroopers with their chute ripcords tethered to a "Static" line to equally space their jumps and deployment of their chutes to prevent midair collisions of two or more paratroopers.

Himmelsbach also wrote that when skyjacked Northwest Airlines Flight 305 landed in Reno, without Cooper aboard, two parachutes were missing. One was a dummy training chute that was sewn shut so it wouldn't deploy. The other was a back pack made by Earl Cossey about six months earlier, and had not been tested.

However, Tosaw wrote that when Flight 305 was searched after landing in Reno, three civilian chutes were found on the aircraft. And the only chute provided and missing was the military NB-8, an emergency pilot model.

To resolve this reporting conflict, on May 17, 1994, I sent a letter to Cossey, including six pertinent questions.

-10-

Cossey graciously returned the questionnaire with detailed
answers, and offer to provide any further answers I needed.
And he included his home phone number and best hours to call.

Cossey's written answers were that the only parachute not
returned to him was the "Navy NB-8 Military 28' white nylon."
And the three civilian chutes were returned, including the
non-functional training chute, and with some of its shroud lines
cut up.

Also, in a telephone conversation with Cossey in mid-1998, he
told me that the training chute container was not returned with
the three civilian chutes. He said it had been his belief since
they were returned that Cooper had placed the bank money bag
in the chute container for additional securement of the money.

In response to my further questioning, Cossey said the container
was made of heavy cotton canvas, and would severely rot under
water over a period of a year or more. But the chute shroud
lines and canopy were made of nylon, and would not rot.

In early 1999, I phoned a parachute instructor in Perris,
California, to clarify two issues I had not discussed with
Cossey. One was if parachute containers were waterproofed.
He, name and phone number in file, said military chute containers
are normally waterproofed, but it could become less effective
over a period of years. In our ensuing conversation, he confirmed
Cossey's opinion on nylon not rotting. He said it would not
rot because it was made of plastic. Initially, I had briefly
explained my reason for calling was my investigation of the
D.B. Cooper skyjacking case. He was very interested, so I
described all of the conditions Cooper encountered in his jump.
He said he had been involved in sports parachuting for over
ten years, and from his experience and what I told him, he
concurred with Cossey's opinion that Cooper had to have plunged
to his death in a free fall.

And the most interesting information this parachute instructor
offered was that a person in a vertical position could free
fall at speeds up to 150 or 180 mph, depending on conditions.
My partner and I had assumed Cooper would have free fallen at
about 120 mph, from our early years of learning the earth's
gravitational pull. If this parachute instructor's information
is accurate, it should further support any theory that Cooper
free fell to his instant death. And should further support my
partner's "Columbia River Island Theory," with which I concur,
and explained later herein.

I was very impressed with this parachute instructor's apparent
expertise, but the 150-180 mph speeds should be confirmed by
specialized military experts. If confirmed, it should be further
proof to discount any theory that Cooper survived his jump.

-11-

2. The reports by Calame and Tosaw that Cooper chose the military chute over the civilian models, and other reports presented herein, lead me to believe Cooper was a former military paratrooper. And most likely a former Army Special Services Forces Green Beret Ranger, as reportedly believed by others.

Himmelsbach and Tosaw wrote about Cooper's knowledge of Boeing 727 aircraft and parachutes. One being that Cooper ordered the flight officers to fly with the landing gear down, flaps down 15 degrees, and under 10,000 feet, after taking off from Seattle SEA-TAC Airport. This degree of flaps was reportedly known only to 727 experts and flight officers, and somewhat confidential. Cooper also reportedly used technical aircraft terms for the rear stairway and plane's inner-communications telephone system. And Flight Attendant Tina Mucklow reported that Cooper tied the money bag to his waist with about a 6-foot tether of shroud line cut from one of the parachutes. Tethering in this manner was reported to be a paratrooper practice, so the weight of the load would land before the chutist, and not as additional weight upon landing.

Himmelsbach also wrote that the CIA had used 727s in the Vietnam War to drop agents and supplies behind enemy lines. The 727 was reportedly the only commercial model aircraft with a rear stairway parallel with the fuselage that could be lowered in flight and provide a platform for dropping and parachuting therefrom. Himmelsbach also wrote that when Cooper bought his one-way ticket from Northwest Airlines Ticket Agent ⬛⬛⬛⬛⬛⬛, he asked if Flight 305 was a 727.

A mid-1998 TV documentary I did not identify disclosed by interview with a former Green Beret that the CIA used Army Special Forces to assassinate foreign enemy military and political figures during the Vietnam War, and for some time thereafter. Another TV documentary reported the assassination of enemy military and political figures was banned in 1975 by Executive Order of President Ford.

The enclosed copies of portions of the July 28, 1998, edition of The Orange County Register corroborates these covert actions. Also the close-knit bond of Green Berets that was essential, as they had to trust each other with their lives, and keep their covert missions a secret until death. The headline of the continued page is, "HEBLER: Former assassin now spends his time saving lives." The article explains some of his past Green Beret activities, and his reluctance or refusal to talk about nearly all of them. It also reports that Hebler's admirable work is assisted by members of a Portland, Oregon, church. This location, along with other reports presented herein, raises the question in my mind of Northern Oregon and the State of Washington being attractive to former Green Berets. And much like Idaho and Montana are to retired LAPD officers, from many reports.

-12-

These reports strongly indicate that the covert nature and codes of the Army Special Forces and Mafia are much the same. The most sacred mandates of the Mafia have been widely reported to be: A. "Omerta": Code of Silence. B. "Honor." C. Loyalty to "Family," be it by natural blood relation, or blood-letting initiation or accepted association. D. Never harm an honest law enforcement officer or innocent person. And the Mafia penalty for any violation of these codes can be death as earlier related herein.

Of course, the Mafia's objectives and criminal activities are destructive to U.S. interests and security, as opposed to the noble, courageous mission objectives of the Army Special Forces. Only the covert nature of both organizations makes them similar with respect to their necessary codes. And making this comparison herein is not intended in any way to imply otherwise.

However, in addition to codes, from all publicized reports, members of the Mafia and Army Special Forces share a common potential threat of detection and death, frequently or constantly. In other words, they are both of the nature to live at risk, and what is referred by some as "Always living on the edge." Cooper most certainly manifested this unusual personal characteristic. And, in my opinion, in a way that indicates he was one who could easily cross the line from noble Green Beret to Mafia involvement to satisfy his compulsion for risk and "rush."

Another late-1998 TV documentary, "Green Berets," was on the exhaustive specialized training and testing they must successfully pass to graduate and be awarded their Green Beret. The reported passing rate is only about 30 percent. Those who are "washed out" are returned to their original Army units, and the successful graduates are looked upon as the elite.

This documentary reported that all trainees received paratrooper training. And their final test was to bail out in the total darkness of night, not being able to see where or how they would land. And much like Cooper did. Except he was not reported to be wearing the protective clothing, including high, laced jump boots. He was reportedly wearing slip-on, loafer-type shoes, which, by all reported expert opinions, would have been torn from his feet in the about 200-220 mph headwind the moment he jumped.

And one of the aforementioned strange events occurred in May 1994. Along with other query letters to witnesses named in the books by Himmelsbach and Tosaw, my partner and I both sent letters to Himmelsbach. In his book, he wrote in several parts that he had been assigned as the Cooper case agent in the FBI Portland office, had been on the case the longest and had been the closest to it. And he was contacted by Continental Airlines

Tom Bohan, who wanted to discuss a theory he had with the Cooper case chief investigator. Captain Bohan's theory will be addressed later herein under, "CONTINENTAL AIRLINES CAPTAIN TOM BOHAN AND INFRARED HEAT SENSING."

My partner sent his letter to Himmelsbach on May 9, 1994. After about two weeks of no response, and anticipating my mid-June trip to his Vancouver home, my partner became impatient. So he called directory assistance, got Himmelsach's business phone number, and called.

Himmelsbach's daughter answered, and my partner said she was very interested in our Cooper case investigation. She told my partner her father had been out of town for about two weeks, and was to return that day, or the next day. She said he would return the call as soon as he returned. My partner then gave her his well-protected, unlisted phone number to give to Himmelsbach.

My partner protects his identity, whereabouts, phone number, and even his current existence as a special precaution, although his name and personal data have been on file at the Seattle FBI office since August 1995. And to the extent that to this time he does not have "Call Waiting," or an answering/message recorder, and calls to his number must be preceded by *82, so the caller will show on his "Caller I.D.," before he or his wife will answer.

These precautions stem from his being seriously threatened by younger-generation Mafia hoods he successfully investigated in 1975. As his last of three law enforcement positions that spanned 41 years, he was an investigator in the San Diego County District Attorney's Organized Crime Unit. His investigation resulted in their convictions, and they threatened his life. Knowing the younger Mafioso are unlike the older generations, whose code was to never harm an honest police officer, and are more emotional, reckless and cocky, he considered the threat to be serious. And that is why I refer to him herein as "my partner," rather by his name.

In giving his phone number to Himmelsbach's daughter, he did not think it was necessary to tell her not to give it to anybody other than her father. And in that Himmelsbach was a retired FBI agent, my partner presumed it would be secure with him.

And rightfully so. No later than the mid-1960s, when law enforcement officers became known as "Pigs," and radical militants were snipe-shooting cops and bombing police facilities, police officer's addresses and phone numbers became confidential. Perhaps a bit paranoiac, nevertheless, they have been highly confidential since that time. And anyone requesting that information is viewed with suspicion to this day.

-14-

At that time, "Caller I.D." and "Star 82" were not yet available.
Later that day, or the next day, my partner received a surprise
phone call from a complete stranger. My partner said the caller
identified himself as ███████████████," age 42, and
retired Army Special Forces sergeant. The caller first told
my partner that Himmelsbach would be calling him. ██████ then
told my partner he didn't work, and spent his time searching
for Cooper's remains. And at that time, he was searching the
Washougal watershed area, based on Himmelsbach's "Washougal
River" theory that Cooper landed there. ██████ said he lived
in Washougal, and readily volunteered his phone number, which
was, ████████.

My partner said when he told ██████ he was searching the Columbia
River islands for Cooper's remains, ██████ replied that he had
searched all of the islands, and found nothing. Being skeptical,
my partner said he quizzed ██████ on his knowledge of the
terrain, activities, and landmarks on and around the islands.
He said from ██████ grossly inaccurate descriptive responses,
he quickly concluded ██████ was not familiar with the islands,
and had not searched any of them.

My partner said ██████ emphasized the danger to strangers in
the Washougal, and all areas of the Pacific Northwest, posed
by marijuana growers. He said the pot growers protected their
crops from detection like "Moonshiners" guard their stills.
But all of the growers knew him, and what he was doing, so he
was safe. But others, such as my partner, would be risking their
lives roaming anywhere near marijuana crops.

Well aware of illegal growers from Northern California to Canada,
my partner was not impressed with ██████ warning of doom. Most
of all, because he also knew that deer and bird hunters, and
stream, river, and lake fishermen frequented most public-access
areas in the region. And in his 8 years living in Vancouver,
he had never read or heard a report of a person being harmed
by a pot grower.

However, the threat of same did become a reality the following
summer, and reported in the enclosed copy of the August 16,
1994, edition of The Oregonian. As reported, it was on Government
Island, the primary target area of my partner's planned search.
And, like all of the Columbia River islands, owned by the Port
of Portland, and access allowed by permit only.

My partner had years earlier discounted Himmelsbach's Washougal
theory, which is later explained herein under "The Washougal
River Theory," and he considered ██████ to be somewhat simple-
minded, at that time. But in the following days and weeks, ██████
repeatedly phoned my partner at different hours of the day and
night, and very soon became a nuisance. One night, he phoned
at about 11 p.m., two hours after my partner had gone to sleep.

After that late call, my partner started phoning ▓▓▓▓ at his convenience in an attempt to ward off any more late calls from ▓▓▓▓. As when ▓▓▓▓ phoned him, my partner said the background noise sounded like a "Hippie Commune." And when he called ▓▓▓▓, he said sometimes the phone was answered by people other than ▓▓▓▓, and sometimes by women.

Half joking, my partner threatened to give my Laguna Hills, California, phone number to ▓▓▓▓, so he could call me in the middle of the night, and at long-distance rates. My partner reminded me that it was my bright idea to write to potential material witnesses, and ▓▓▓▓ was all my fault.

My first evening at my partner's Vancouver home, I had my partner phone ▓▓▓▓ so I could talk to him. In addition to repeating his previous warning to my partner about marijuana growers, I recall ▓▓▓▓ trying to convince me that Cooper's remains had to be in the Washougal region. And he had found some items that proved to him Cooper had landed there. One I clearly recall was his description of a pair of wire-rimmed RAY-BAN sunglasses, like aviators and sportsmen wear, and with the lenses missing. By all published reports, Cooper wore wraparound, plastic-rimmed dark glasses, like worn by new-age entertainers, et al.

At the conclusion of the conversation, I agreed with my partner that ▓▓▓▓ appeared to be a harmless, happy Cooper hunter. And much like the two of us, seeking some excitement in his boring retirement after his death-defying life as a Green Beret for about 20 years.

However, after my casual 1998 discoveries, I had my partner phone ▓▓▓▓ ▓▓▓▓. The area code has since changed, but my partner made the local call, and a man answered. My partner told me the man said he did not know a ▓▓▓▓, and had that number for some length of time. From the lack of any loud background noise, as in 1994, my partner was certain the number had been reassigned.

To my recollection, my conversation with ▓▓▓▓ was the last between my partner and ▓▓▓▓. But his reportedly being a retired Army Special Forces sergeant may be of significance, or perhaps just coincidence.

Nevertheless, as ▓▓▓▓ told my partner he would, Himmelsbach phoned my partner not long after he terminated his conversation with ▓▓▓▓.

My partner later told me that Himmelsbach was very congenial, forthright, informative, and interested in our Cooper investigation and findings. And as he was in our phone conversation, later, when he phoned me on June 14, 1994, the evening before I flew to Vancouver.

My partner said they discussed many aspects of the Cooper case,
and exchanged theories of the where Cooper's remains could be
most logically found. From this discussion, my partner was
certain Himmelsbach agreed that Cooper had not survived his
jump, and his remains could be located by search. But where
was the only difference of opinion. My partner said he offered
the many known and reported facts and expert opinions that had
convinced him it was improbable that Cooper had landed in the
Washougal watershed region. And he explained to Himmelsbach
all of the known and reported factors that caused him to form
his opinion that Cooper's remains were on an island. With that,
my partner said they agreed their theories were quite different,
and the conversation was soon terminated.

Calame wrote extensively about April 7, 1972, United Airlines
ransom skyjacker Richard Floyd McCoy, Jr., being a former Army
Special Forces Green Beret. And his serving in the Vietnam War
as a helicopter pilot, and his being awarded a decoration for
bravery in one mission.

Considering all of these reports, it is my opinion that Cooper
was most likely a former Green Beret. And possibly retired from
that service, or separated with other than an honorable
discharge.

3. Another report I factored into Cooper's profile was the name
he provided for the flight manifest.

All published reports state he gave the name "Dan Cooper" to
Northwest Airlines Ticket Agent ███████████. And Himmelsbach
wrote that Cooper gave it in Agent 007 manner as "Cooper. Dan
Cooper."

As it happened, an anxious UPI reporter reportedly heard the
name "D.B. Cooper" at the Portland Police Bureau, and quickly
put it on the UPI wire. And he has been popularly known by that
name since that time, except to the better informed readers
and viewers.

Webster's Encyclopedic Unabridged Dictionary of the English
Language defines "Dan" as: "Archaic. a title of honor equivilent
to master or sir." And one definition of "cooper" is: "3. to
furnish or fix (usually fol. by up)."

Of the tens or hundreds of thousands, or perhaps a million or
more, of given and surname combinations Cooper could have used
as an alias, I had to conclude that this was a coded name. And
to someone that he was indeed honorable and would fix something.
And, with his skyjacking for $200,000 of ransom money, it was
most likely a very large monetary debt. Despite the UPI
reporter's error, other media reports of Cooper's acts and
demands could have provided the intended message, in my opinion.

Historically, back to the 1920s, descriptive nicknames, and
sometimes coded names, have been used by gangsters and the Mafia.
And used by the military and law enforcement for secret agents,
operations, and missions. The decades of publicity of these
names are common knowledge, and to the extent that explanation
should not be necessary herein.

And, as earlier explained herein, the strict Mafia codes of
conduct are well reported to be punishable by gruesome death.
Among them, "Honor" is reportedly one of the most sacred codes.
Like the above mentioned nickname and coded name uses, they
have been widely publicized in books, movies, and in TV
documentaries for decades. And long before and since "The
Godfather."

Therefore, it is my opinion that "Dan Cooper" was a coded name
to Mafioso that he was honorable and would fix his debt to them.
And based on all conditions and expert opinions reported in
the Cooper case source books listed herein, it is most likely
Cooper knew he wouldn't survive his jump. If so, I also speculate
that his tormentors may have been holding one of his friends
or loved ones hostage. And survive or not, he was telling them
he was trying to square the debt, for whatever good it would
do.

4. Calame, Himmelsbach, and Tosaw all wrote that Cooper demanded
to be flown to "Mexico City." And even though it was 2,200 air
miles from the Seattle SEA-TAC Airport, where he was asked,
and he was told it would require refueling stops at Reno and
Yuma. He was also told Seattle was the last stop of the flight
crew's shift, and they were tired. Despite these advisories,
Cooper demanded he be flown to Mexico City.

Himmelsbach wrote that this demanded destination surprised the
FBI, because it was obvious Cooper intended to jump as soon
as possible, which he later did. And soon proved that he had
no desire to fly to Mexico City, much less as far as Reno or
Yuma.

Chuck and Sam Giancana wrote that Chicago Mafia boss Sam "Mooney"
Giancana had moved to Mexico City in 1966. And he had lived
in a lavish apartment for a year or two, then moved to a new
massive estate in the posh Las Quintas section of Cuernavaca,
which is about 20-30 miles south of Mexico City. And had lived
there until July 18, 1974, when he was taken into custody by
Mexican immigration agents, and incarcerated. The Giancanas
reported Mooney was later flown to San Antonio, Texas, where
waiting FBI agents served him with a subpoena to appear before
a Chicago grand jury.

Chuck and Sam Giancana also wrote that, while in Mexico City
and nearby Cuernavada, Sam Giancana set up gambling junkets

-18-

in Latin America, and met with Meyer Lansky at least one time.
And that Mooney Giancana specialized in extremely profitable
narcotics and munitions smuggling, and money-laundering schemes,
while in Mexico City and Cuernavaca. Also, as mentioned earlier
herein, the Giancanas reported Mooney Giancana controlled loan
sharks over thousands of miles, and Chuck Giancana had been
told Mooney had moved millions across the Mexican border.

The Giancanas also reported that the FBI learned of Mooney
Giancana's whereabouts no later than the summer of 1967.
And, of course, this would have been over four years before
Cooper's November 24, 1971, skyjacking.

5. Although questionable because of conflicting reports, I
factored in the denomination of currency bills Cooper reportedly
demanded, or did not specify.

Himmelsbach wrote that Cooper specifically stated, "Denomination
of bills not important." And that $20 bills were obtained and
provided at the urging of the FBI.

And Himmelsbach wrote that the flight crew was told the money
was coming from several Seattle banks. He then wrote that all
of the bills were run through a "Recordak," and microfilmed.
Calame also wrote that the FBI counted and recorded the serial
numbers of the bills, then packed the $200,000 in a bank money
bag stenciled, "Seattle First National."

However, Tosaw wrote a different version. He wrote that the
FBI knew the Seattle First National Bank had a fund of recorded
$20 bills for humanitarian service, in the event of a ransom
kidnapping when all banks were closed, as they were that
Thanksgiving Eve. And that is where the entire $200,000 was
obtained, and the money bag was stenciled, "Seattle First
National."

The 10,000 $20 bills and bank money bag were reported to weigh
21-22 pounds. In 1971, $50 and $100 bills were rarely used by
the general public, and would have been difficult to pass without
unwanted attention. And 42-44 pounds of $10 bills in two bank
money bags would have most likely been very difficult for Cooper
to manage under the reported conditions. Obviously, $5 and $1
bills would have been extremely bulky and heavy, and nearly
impossible to handle.

Most published reports stated that Cooper demanded the ransom
money be in old $20 bills. This factor is solely dependent on
Himmelsbach's report of "Denomination of bills not important."
Like many other conflicting published reports in the Cooper
case, in my opinion, the only means of qualifying all reports
in this case would be by Congressional investigation, hearings,
and search and analysis of the Cooper case file.

6. Himmelsbach wrote that of the hundreds of calls from
citizens wanting to help, none proved to be of value in
identifying Cooper, either as a suspect or missing person. And
despite the national TV coverage and a published composite
drawing of the skyjacker. However, in my recent phone
conversation with Seattle FBI Special Agent Don Glasser, the
Cooper case agent in 1995, he told me there were four different
composites of Cooper at that time. I will later herein report
Glasser's August 1995 phone call to me, and what he candidly
related to me that should be investigated by a Congressional
Select Committee.

Himmelsbach's report that nobody reported Cooper as a suspect
or missing person strongly indicated to me that he came from
a place where people did not talk to or help law enforcement,
regardless. And because of their activities or lifestyles, or
stark fear of being discovered as a police informant, or both.
Along with Cooper's reported dark, olive, or swarthy complexion,
as darkened by the sun, and the reported Mafia influence at
that time, Las Vegas stood far above all others that I could
envision. A place where everybody minded their own business,
didn't ask questions about things that shouldn't concern them,
and didn't talk about people and events that could make them
look like they knew too much and talked too much.

And based on my overall profile of the skyjacker, a place where
anybody who knew, or knew of, "Dan Cooper," would not report
him as a suspect or missing person. Also, because of the
transient nature of so many in gambling resorts, especially
Las Vegas at that time, it is most likely few would notice his
absence, other than his close associates. And from his reported
conduct, dress, and nature of his crime, it is extremely doubtful
that he associated with anyone who would dare report him as
a suspect or missing person to the FBI, anonymously or otherwise.

Cooper's reported dark, olive, or swarthy, complexion also
suggests to me that he could have been of Italian descent. If
so, or not, I also entertain the possibility that he could have
acted as a Mafia flunky to pay off his loan shark debts, until
his gambling debts far exceeded his ability to work them off.
And he knew what had happened to Gus Greenbaum and his wife.

7. As earlier described herein, Cooper was reportedly wearing
a dark, narrow-lapelled business suit; white dress shirt; narrow,
black tie; pearl stickpin (or mother-of-pearl tie clasp); low-
cut, slip-on, loafer-type shoes; and black raincoat.

In 1971, I bought two suits of the latest fashion at that time
to attend a six-week, live-in police-community-relations course
in San Diego. Then in 1972, I flew once a month from LAX to
Sacramento to instruct the same subject at the California Highway
Patrol Academy. My suits, and those I observed worn by most

-20-

men were broad-lapelled, light- or medium colored; shirts were
pastel-colored; and ties were wide, colorful, and with floral
or other designs.

And a suit I bought in 1961 was broad-lapelled, and as early
as 1965, ties were wide and with more subdued colors and designs.

To the best of my recollection, narrow-lapelled suits and narrow
ties were a short-lived fashion of the conservative 1950s.

From my above experiences and recollections, when I first read
Himmelsbach's book, I quickly formed the opinion Cooper's dress
was unusual, and most likely a service uniform. And like worn
by limo drivers, and waiters and bartenders and other service
employees in higher-class hotels and restaurants, and in lavish
casinos, as in Las Vegas.

In response to my May 1994, letter to him, Himmelsbach phoned
the evening of June 14, 1994. He was most gracious, forthright,
informative, and helpful. Of the many Cooper case issues we
discussed, some of which will be addressed in other parts herein,
he expressed his opinion that Cooper was wearing a "service
uniform." And before I mentioned my same opinion, which I then
expressed to him. I then explained my above related experiences
and recollections regarding men's styles, and he readily agreed.
And that I had concluded Cooper's reported dress style went
out of fashion in about 1960, with which he also agreed.

Profile opinion summary: Of the seven elements factored into
my profile of Cooper, based on reports and my experiences and
human-behavior and criminal study, the only one I believe is
questionable, as earlier stated, is denomination of bills
demanded, or not specified by Cooper.

Nonetheless, based on the other six elements, and my over six
years of review and analysis of this case, I am confident my
profile of Cooper is accurate and valid. And without any doubt,
whatsoever.

J. EDGAR HOOVER

In his 1993 copyrighted book, "Official and Confidential: The
Secret Life of J. Edgar Hoover," Anthony Summers wrote about
Hoover's homosexuality, addiction to horse-race gambling,
association with Mafia boss Frank Costello, and his being
blackmailed by Mafia gambling boss Meyer Lansky. And with 46
pages of "Source Notes."

To a much lesser extent, and without source notes, Chuck and

Sam Giancana wrote of Hoover reportedly being in Costello's
pocket, and Sam "Mooney" Giancana controlling loan sharks over
thousands of miles and transporting millions across the Mexican
border. And Meyer Lansky blackmailing Hoover with evidence of
his "closet" homosexuality.

Summers wrote that Meyer Lansky had blackmailed Hoover for
decades with proof of his "closet" homosexuality, and it was
believed Lansky had photos of Hoover orally copulating an
unidentified man. And the photos were reported to be so clear
that Hoover could be readily recognized.

Summers also quoted Mafia boss Carmine "The Doctor" Lombardozzi
as saying in 1990 that the Mafia had Hoover in their pocket,
and they never had to fear him. Summers wrote that Lombardozzi
directed the Gambino family financial operations, and died before
1993, when his book was published.

Summers wrote that Hoover had a relationship with New York Mafia
boss Frank Costello for decades, and related to Hoover's
addiction to horse-race gambling. Costello reportedly gave Hoover
tips on fixed races, and other sure winners. And Hoover placed
bets at tracks and with Mafia bookies. Hoover reportedly never
lost money when betting with Mafia bookies. If he won, they
paid him the winnings. If his horse(s) lost, they overlooked
and forgave the debt.

Although organized crime and the Mafia were well publicized
since no later than the 1940s, Hoover reportedly denied the
existence of the Mafia, and even after Attorney General Robert
Kennedy declared war on organized crime in 1962. And despite
the 1951 Kefauver Commission Report that officially recognized
the existence of the Mafia, the 1957 New York State Police
raid on the Apalachian Mafia summit meeting, and the 1963
televised testimony of Mafioso Joseph Valachi about the "La
Cosa Nostra" before a Congressional Committee.

First-person experience with Hoover's position on the Mafia
was reported by Retired FBI Special Agent M. Wesley Swearingen
in his 1995 copyrighted book, "FBI Secrets: an agent's expose'."

Therein, Swearingen wrote that he was transferred to the Chicago
FBI field office in 1952. He stated he was aware from Chicago
newspapers that gangland-type killings averaged nearly 100 a
year. He planned to do something to correct it, but a colleague
told him Hoover didn't recognize organized crime in Chicago.
And that the mob had homosexual evidence on Hoover and Clyde
Tolson. And it was Meyer Lansky's people, and Hoover wouldn't
investigate them.

A March 16, 1999, "FBI Files" TV documentary on the Discovery
Channel was devoted to the FBI Gambino Squad in New York.

Therein, FBI Special Agent Bruce Mau (sp?), pronounced like
"cow," related the history of the FBI Gambino Squad, which he
headed. He said it was formed in 1980, and at that time, there
were no intelligence files, photos, or other information on
the mob. He said they had to start with nothing, and work from
there, even to identify the mobsters, including John Gotti.
Mau (sp?) then related how they had to begin by identifying
mob hangouts, and take telephoto shots of those standing in
front of and frequenting the hangouts. Then they had to spend
much time identifying those in the photos, including John Gotti,
who was shown in one photo aired.

Needless to say, this documentary illustrates that until as
many as eight years after Hoover's May 2, 1972, death, the FBI
had no investigative files on the New York Mafia Gambino Family.

My personal experience with this situation occurred when I
attended the 102nd Session of the FBI National Academy in the
summer of 1975. The session was composed of 250 law enforcement
personnel from throughout the Free World. The session was 11
weeks in duration, and involved over 300 hours of classroom
instruction, training, and lectures.

Of that over 300 hours, we received only two hours of lecture
on organized crime, which was solely on the Mafia. The FBI agent
Mafia expert lecturer had to speak in rapid fashion to cover
the subject. And his admitted limited knowledge was best
expressed when he said it took them over a decade to discover
why Mafioso Albert Anastasia was assassinated gangland-style
in a New York barbershop in 1957. And despite the later November
1957 Apalachian Mafia summit meeting that was reportedly called
because of inner-organization problems, including the failed
assassination attempt on Frank Costello and assassination of
Anastasia, who was reported to be Costello's chief protector.

In my first review of books by Himmelsbach and Tosaw in 1993,
the most puzzling FBI action I readily noted was Hoover's delayed
release of the serial numbers of the 10,000 $20 bills of ransom
money.

Both books include a copy of the cover letter to distribute
the 34-page list, and signed by Hoover. The letter is dated
November 29, 1971, the Monday after the Wednesday afternoon-
evening skyjacking.

And Himmelsbach wrote that the lists were not distributed until
"Early in December 1971." And only "to banks and other places
where the bills were likely to be passed." Then Himmelsbach
later wrote the list "had been circulated to financial
institutions and money collection centers," at that same time.
And that the list was not released to the public until November
1973, the second anniversary of Cooper's skyjacking.

-23-

Himmelsbach also wrote that the average life of a $20 bill at
that time was 18 months.

In discussing the Cooper case with a Secret Service agent contact
of mine in 1994, he confirmed the average life of a $20 bill
was well-reputed to be 18-24 months. And to the best of my
recollection, which I wrote on a note at the time, and have
in file, he said there are normally one to two billion $20 bills
in circulation at all times.

As earlier mentioned herein, regardless of the source or sources
of the ransom money, the Seattle FBI agents should have obtained
the list of recorded serial numbers along with the money. And,
as reported, that would have been before 5:43 p.m., the time
Flight 305 landed at Seattle, after circling in a holding pattern
for over two hours as ordered by Cooper. He reportedly demanded
that the aircraft not land at Seattle SEA-TAC Airport until
after the ransom money and parachutes had been delivered to
the airport.

Needless to say, the list of serial numbers should have been
released to the media for publication no later than when the
aircraft landed in Reno without Cooper aboard. It reportedly
landed at 11:02 p.m., and it took less than 30 minutes to
determine for certain that he was not aboard, and that he had
jumped at about 8:13 p.m.

If Cooper had survived his jump, by "Early in December 1971,"
alone, those bills could have been circulated from coast to
coast in the U.S., and nearly impossible to trace back to the
originating source. And with about 48 years of experience as
FBI director at that time, Hoover certainly had to know his
delayed release of the list would seriously hinder the FBI
investigation, if Cooper survived and circulated the bills.

And the two-year delay in publicizing the list by his successor
in 1973, could be of little value, if any, considering the
reported 18 month lifetime of $20 bills. Or even 18-24 months,
as confirmed by my Secret Service agent contact.

The only imaginable purpose this two-year-later release could
serve would be to attempt to establish that Cooper had in fact
survived his jump and circulated at least one of the bills.

Hoover's reputation for dictatorial direction of the FBI and
collecting harmful intelligence on anyone who he wanted to
control to protect himself and his position is well reported
in detail in Summers' book.

And Summers extensive reporting about Hoover's dictatorial
control of the FBI served to confirm what most informed U.S.
law enforcement officers were told by FBI agents dating back

to the early 1950s, that I am aware of. Some more candid, daring, and frustrated FBI agents spoke openly of Hoover's arbitrary transfer of agents to "punishment" locations on his whim. And the most notorious frequently mentioned was "Butte, Montana," and "Big Jack," as Hoover was privately called by some, was feared, not respected by many, or most. Summers' writings support or confirm all of these reports, except "Big Jack."

Based on Hoover's about 48 years of reported dictatorial control of FBI agents and the Bureau's management and operations, it can be reasonably expected that he would have been much involved in the widely-publicized case. And until his reportedly unexpected death on May 2, 1972, slightly over five months after Cooper's "beat the system" skyjacking.

And as reported by Himmelsbach, and addressed in part later herein, the FBI, law enforcement, and at least 200 Army troops conducted massive organized searchs for Cooper for at least 37 days, and in the wrong areas. And, as Himmelsbach wrote, at a cost of thousands of manhours, hundreds of thousands of taxpayer's money, and perhaps millions of dollars spent on publicity of the case. And Himmelsbach wrote that the search mistake was not discovered until about eight years after.

Himmelsbach reported the last massive FBI and Army search ended on April 25, 1972. And Summers wrote that Hoover died on May 2, which would have been eight days after that last organized search ended. From all published reports, by that time, the Cooper investigation was in a state of confusion, and remained so until the $5,800 was found on a bank of the Columbia River on February 10, 1980. And that find proved the searches had been in the wrong areas, supported the belief of most experts that Cooper had not survived his jump, and prompted new theories on where his remains could be most likely located.

PARACHUTE PACKER/EXPERT/INSTRUCTOR EARL COSSEY

As earlier reported herein, Earl Cossey packed the chutes provided for Cooper. And Cossey replied to my letter with six pertinent questions included.

By earlier arrangement, my partner and I interviewed Cossey at his Woodinville home, east of Seattle, on June 18, 1994. His son and daughter-in-law, of Utah, were visiting, and were present during the informative and somewhat humorous exchange of opinions and data.

Cossey began by telling my partner and me that he thought we were crazy for wasting our time and money on the Cooper case. He then said we were about the twentieth person or persons to contact him in the then 23 years since Cooper's skyjacking.

Near the end of the interview, he reinforced his opinion of
our wasting our time, by describing the events and activities
at and after the time of Cooper's skyjacking.

Cossey said for weeks after the skyjacking, law enforcement
officers and FBI agents scurried about in what appeared to him
to be best described as being a "Chinese Fire Drill." He said
it was nothing short of mass confusion with no appearance of
organization, whatsoever. His description of the activities
and confusion sounded much like Jonathan Winters frantically
repeatedly yelling, "We've got to get organized," in the movie
"The Russians Are Coming. The Russians Are Coming."

Cossey, about 45 at that time, and a mid-school Algebra teacher,
explained in detail why he was certain Cooper could not have
deployed the NB-8 military emergency pilot chute. To begin with,
he said Cooper would have "spun ass over teakettle" jumping
into the 120 mph headwind. Apparently assuming Flight 305 was
traveling at about 100 mph, based on a 727 Stall Speed Chart,
copy enclosed, he was certain even that lower speed would spin
Cooper as above stated. However, all published reports were
that the skyjacked aircraft was traveling at about 167 to 195
mph when he jumped. Maps show it is over 120 air miles from
the Seattle SEA-TAC Airport, where it reportedly became airborne
at about 7:36 p.m., to Portland, where Cooper was reportedly
believed to have jumped at about 8:13 p.m. Calculating 120 miles
in 37 minutes amounts to about 195 mph. Plus the initially
reported believed to be 20-40 mph, would have created about
a 200-220 mph headwind, nearly twice that of Cossey's assumed
headwind. And as later reported herein under "CONTINENTAL
AIRLINES CAPTAIN TOM BOHAN AND INFRARED HEAT SENSING," Bohan
related to Himmelsbach that his aircraft was about 4,000 feet
above skyjacked Flight 305, and about four minutes behind it
headed for Portland. And his aircraft had 80 knots of southwest
wind at about 14,000 feet. If that could indicate the southwest
wind at about 10,000 feet was greater than 20-40 mph, the
estimated headwind Cooper jumped into may have been more than
200-220 mph, and perhaps as much as 220-240 mph, or more.

In any event, we believe Cossey's expert opinion about Cooper
spinning was, and is, qualified and valid. Cossey then said
the NB-8 military chute Cooper used was not easy to deploy in
the best of conditions. He said the ripcord handle was in a
pocket, high on the right back, below the shoulder. He said
with Cooper's reported raincoat and 6-foot tethered 21-22 pound
money bag violently flapping around him, and freezing temperature
numbing his hands and fingers, he was certain Cooper could not
have deployed the chute. And in the same about 40 seconds, get
into a stable face-down or near-face-down position he would
have had to assume to effectively deploy the chute. Cossey said
those positions were essential to avoid becoming entangled in
the shroud lines or 28-foot canopy, or both.

Standing upright, Cossey demonstrated the face-down positions
he said were essential to the effective, safe deployment of
a chute to avoid entanglement.

In answer to our question, Cossey said Cooper would have drifted
about 1/8 mile to 1 mile to the northeast in the reported
20-40 mph southwest wind at 10,000 feet, in a free fall, without
chute deployed. And he would have drifted about 3-5 miles to
the northeast, if he had effectively deployed the chute at about
9,500 feet elevation. He again emphasized his qualified opinion
that Cooper could not have deployed the NB-8 chute, based on
the reported conditions, and from his over 20 years of
parachuting experience.

Cossey also said all parachute packers have their individual,
unique construction methods, and he assured us he could
positively idenitify any chute parts found as being his, or
that of another packer. He then took us to his garage, where
he showed us some parachute hardware and other parts to
illustrate those he used, and could identify as his own, if
found.

Cossey's detailed explanations and demonstrations soundly
convinced my partner and me that Cooper had plunged to his
instant death.

Also, considering that Cooper would have attained the long-
reported gravity pull of about 120 mph within seconds, he would
have had hit the ground in less than 60 seconds, jumping from
about 10,000 feet elevation. Or less, if the parachutist I spoke
to in 1999 was correct in saying Cooper could have free fallen
at up to 150 or 180 mph. And considering that Cooper would have
had to effectively deployed the chute in no more than about
40-50 seconds after jumping.

Based on these opinions, and the $5,800 of ransom money found
on a bank of the Columbia River in 1980, as next explained,
I had to agree with my partner's "COLUMBIA RIVER ISLAND THEORY."

FEBRUARY 10, 1980, FIND OF $5,800 OF COOPER RANSOM MONEY

On Sunday, February 10, 1980, eight-year-old Brian Ingram was
reportedly clearing a small area for a fire to roast wieners
at a family outing, when he uncovered $5,800 of $20 bills later
confirmed to be part of the Cooper ransom money. It was at Tena's
(or Tina's, as variously reported) Bar, a sandy bank of the
Columbia River, about 16 miles downstream from the I-205 bridge
and west end of Government Island.

Himmelsbach wrote in his book that the FBI later excavated the
same area, and found fragments of $20 bills as deep as 3 feet.

And Tosaw included photos of the backhoe excavation by the FBI in his book.

Himmelsbach wrote that a Portland State University geologist concluded that the $5,800 had been matted together in water for a long time, which explained its being stuck together in one mass. And when Himmelsbach phoned me on June 14, 1994, among other issues we discussed, he said the FBI laboratory experts had analyzed the packets of $5,800. And they estimated that the $5,800 had been the center portion of about $14,000 compressed together under water for a long time.

Tosaw wrote in detail about the October 1974 dredging of the Columbia River deep-water ship channel by the Army Corps of Engineers at Portland. And Tosaw expressed his certainty that the $5,800 had been dredged onto that north bank of the Columbia by the Corps of Engineers during that dredging operation.

My partner and I agree with Tosaw's dredging theory, despite different theories offered by others. We also theorize that the balance of the $200,000 was dredged onto the bank with the $5,800, and much or most of it flowed back into the Columbia River in a large stream of murky water, sand, and debris. And that much of it was eaten by river and ocean fish.

As also reported by Tosaw, a bulldozer follows the large dredge pipe, and smooths and slopes the banks for proper drainage.

And, as reported in Himmelsach's book, there were opposing expert opinions on the banks of the Columbia eroding versus building with the accumulation of sand.

My partner and I believed the sandy banks would erode, not accumulate with sand. To resolve this issue, my partner located an elderly couple that had lived next to the Columbia for over 40 years. And she had walked the north bank, daily, including Tena's Bar, for 40 years, weather permitting. This couple confirmed that the banks eroded into the Columbia, and explained, that was why the Corp of Engineers had to dredge the river, every so often.

This made sense to us, so we factored it into my partner's river island theory as a minor part. But the most interesting part of my partner's contact with the elderly couple was their demand for anonymity, when he told them he was privately investigating the D.B. Cooper skyjacking case. After he identified himself with his retiree I.D. cards, and assured them he would never divulge their names, he said they were most cooperative and helpful. But he said his initial mention of "D.B. Cooper," and what he was doing, caused them to slightly withdraw from him. We will never know why, for certain. If one or both were wanted fugitives, they would have most likely shunned him altogether,

[234]   GEORGE C. NUTTALL

especially after he showed them his retiree I.D. cards from
three law enforcement and investigative agencies.

The only reason we can imagine for their demand for anonymity
is that D.B. Cooper remains to be a folk hero who "beat the
system" to some in parts of the Pacific Northwest, and they
didn't want to be identified as helping anybody in finding him.
Or his remains, which would shatter the myth that he survived,
escaped, and lived happily ever after on "The Establishment's"
money. And recent media reports that the highest concentration
of "White Supremists" and anti-government radical militants
is in the Pacific Northwest may add support to our reasoning.

We will probably never know, but was included herein to
illustrate the impact the name "D.B. Cooper" still has on some
folks in the Pacific Northwest.

In any event, Brian Ingram's uncovering the $5,800 of Cooper
ransom money was a major event in the case, and quickly became
the base for the theories later explained herein.

LOCATION OF MARCH AND APRIL 1972 FBI SEARCHES FOR COOPER

After Northwest Airlines Flight 305 reportedly landed in Reno
at about 11:02 p.m., without Cooper aboard, it was estimated
he had jumped at about 8:13 p.m. That was when the flight
officers observed rapid changes in some panel instruments and
felt a rush of air in the cockpit. A later experiment with the
same simulated conditions produced the same rapid changes, which
confirmed the time Cooper jumped.

However, due to the darkness, extreme storm, and dense cloud
cover, the flight officers did not know their location at 8:13
p.m. Also, because of the configuration of the aircraft with
landing gear down, flaps down 15 degrees, and flying at 10,000
feet, it was being flown manually, not on automatic-pilot-course
Vector-23. But, as reported in the enclosed copy of the November
24, 1988, edition of The Oregonian, Himmelsbach and the FBI
did not learn that Flight 305 was being flown manually, and
had drifted some unknown distance east of Vector-23, until 1980,
nearly 8 years after the massive searches.

And, as also reported in the enclosed November 24, 1988, edition,
Himmelsbach is quoted as saying, "We lost an opportunity to
conduct an effective search."

As the edition article explains, it was over two weeks after
the $5,800 was found that the copilot, who had been flying
skyjacked Flight 305, visited Himmelsbach and told him he had
been flying the plane by hand, not on automatic pilot. And that
the aircraft had drifted east of its planned flight path, and

-29-

probably over the Washougal River watershed. It should be noted
that all reports were that the planned flight path of Flight
305 was automatic-pilot course Vector-23, and that maps show
the western edge of the Washougal River watershed to be at least
15 miles east of Vector-23. And maps show the west fork of the
Washougal River to be about 20 miles east of Vector-23. This
will be further explained under "WASHOUGAL RIVER THEORY."

Himmelsbach wrote that Paul Soderlind, a Northwest Airlines
executive at the corporate headquarters in Minneapolis,
calculated Cooper's potential drop zone by computer. And by
using Cooper's 8:13 p.m. jump time, and reported FAA radar
tracking of Flight 305 on Vector-23. However, it was never
explained how the FAA tracked the aircraft on Vector-23, when
the copilot eight years later reported the plane was not on
automatic pilot, and had drifted an unknown distance east of
Vector-23 in the southwest headwind.

Himmelsbach wrote that Soderlind used Vector-23 as the west
boundary of the plotted potential drop zone. Then factoring
in Cooper's estimated drift with and without deployed chute,
plotted a 28-square-mile area.

Himmlsbach described the plotted area as 28-square miles, and
spanned from near Ariel Dam on the east, and ran southwest to
the Heisson area near Battle Ground on the East Fork of the
Lewis River.

Tosaw wrote that the plotted area of Cooper's probable landing
zone spanned for about 20 miles from Woodland, Washington, at
the north boundary, to Portland, Oregon, as the southern
boundary. And included Vancouver, north of the Columbia River.

In one part of his book, Himmelsbach wrote that Flight 305 was
tracked on radar by FAA air controllers in Seattle. He later
wrote that the skyjacked aircraft had been tracked on radar
by the FAA Flight Control Center at Auburn, Washington.

However, Tosaw wrote that Soderlind later used all flight data,
including from the plane's flight recorder and radar readings
from McChord Air Force Base, to confirm Cooper's 8:13 p.m. jump
time. And from all of this data, Soderlind was certain Lake
Merwin was within Cooper's possible drop zone. Lake Merwin is
on the Lewis River at Ariel, about 25 air miles north of the
Columbia River at Portland. And Vancouver, Washington, is across
the Columbia to the north of Portland and the Portland
International Airport.

Although Flight 305 was believed to be on Vector-23 on its
skyjacked flight from Seattle toward Portland, there is no report
of it being tracked on radar by FAA air controllers at Portland
International Airport. And despite maps showing Vector-23 crosses

the Columbia River in a southwest course that continues on a
path less than 2 miles west of the Portland International Airport
main terminal.

Himmelsbach wrote that a crowd of spectators who had heard media
reports of Cooper's skyjacking were waiting at Seattle SEA-TAC
Airport before Flight 305 landed at 5:45 p.m. And that two Air
Force fighter jets trailed Flight 305 from Seattle to where
Cooper reportedly jumped. Himmelsbach also wrote that there
were FBI agents all over Portland International Airport long
before Flight 305 landed at Seattle SEA-TAC Airport at 5:45.

My partner is certain Portland FAA radar would have routinely
tracked Flight 305 when it got within 10 miles of that airport,
even if it wasn't being skyjacked. And I completely agree that
all aircraft within 10 miles of an international airport should
be located and tracked on radar. Particularly when their
anticipated course is within 2 miles of the main terminal, and
in takeoff and landing air space.

With all of these reports, and no report of radar tracking by
Portland FAA, this raises another crucial question that could
be answered only by Congressional Committee investigation.

Crucial, because the lack of Portland FAA radar tracking most
certainly contributed to the law enforcement, FBI, and Army
searches of the wrong areas. And at great wastes of manpower
and monetary resources, as reported by Himmelsbach.

And by all published reports, because of the lack of Portland
FAA radar tracking, to this day, it is reportedly not known
where Flight 305 crossed over the Columbia River, which is
crucial to where Cooper would have most likely landed.

Then using Soderlind's computed 28-square-mile plotted drop
zone, Himmelsbach wrote that the FBI led a law enforcement search
of some areas within that zone. After weeks of futile searching,
Calame, Himmelsbach, and Tosaw wrote that the Army at Fort Lewis
was asked to provide troops for further searches. Tosaw wrote
that the Army agreed to provide 400 troops. And Calame and
Himmelsbach wrote in different terms that about 200 troops were
provided.

All three of these authors wrote that the FBI search with Army
troops was without success in finding Cooper or anything related
to his skyjacking.

And only Tosaw wrote that the Army troops did find two unrelated
bodies during the searches. And that both had been reported
missing for some time. One was that of a young woman found in
a mill pond. The other was a young man who had a broken leg,
and was believed to have died of starvation.

But Himmelsbach did not report the finding of these two bodies.
He wrote that the fact agents and soldiers didn't find another
body meant they could have missed Cooper in their search.

Himmelsbach wrote that the FBI agents and Army troops started
their combined search in mid-March 1972, lasted eighteen days,
and ended on March 30, 1972. This would have been from about
March 13 to March 30. He wrote that a second such search was
conducted from April 7 to April 25, 1972.

Himmelsbach wrote that the FBI and Army troops conducted a
painstaking, yard-by-yard search, and that the soldiers covered
every three to five feet of the area on foot. He wrote that
the heavy ground cover made it impassable in some sections,
and a person could pass within a foot of evidence in some places
and miss seeing it.

And Himmelsbach wrote the other body was "later" found by two
inquisitive housewives, and within the drop zone searched by
the FBI agents and Army troops.

Himmelsbach wrote that the body was that of an eighteen-year-
old Clark College student, and was floating in the bottom of
an abandoned grain mill cistern, when discovered by the two
housewives. And her body was found 33 miles north of Vancouver,
the location of Clark College. And that a medical examiner
reported the girl had been raped and stabbed to death, and had
been dead for about two weeks.

From when she was last seen alive, and being dead for two weeks,
her body could have been discovered as early as February 24,
1972, eighteen days BEFORE the first FBI and Army search started
on about March 13, as reported by Himmelsbach. In order to be
"later" than the searches, the girl would have had to be alive
and missing, or held captive, for at least two months before
she was killed. Homicide experts reports are that most kidnapped
and sexually assaulted women are murdered within 48 hours of
their abduction. This is another issue that could be confirmed
or refuted by FBI profiling expert, as most of their cases are
reported to involve serial killers.

Also, Himmelsbach wrote the body was discovered 33 miles north
of Vancouver. From the aforementioned descriptions of Cooper's
plotted drop zone, the northern boundary was no more than 25
miles north of Portland. With Vancouver being to the north of
Portland, across the Columbia River, 33 miles north of Vancouver
would have been at least 8 miles north of the March and April
searched drop zone, not in it.

Himmelsbach also wrote of other search difficulties. He wrote
that in 1975, a "brainstorming" session was held in San Francisco
to consider untried methods to solve the Cooper case.

Himmelsbach wrote that about 10 FBI agents with skyjacking
experience in general, and the Cooper case in particular, met
for two days. And the agents were from Portland, Seattle, San
Francisco, Los Angeles, Phoenix, Washington, D.C., Reno, and
Las Vegas.

Himmelsbach wrote that, among the numerous methods discussed
to try to find Cooper or to solve the case, one suggestion was
to again search the same projected drop zone areas searched
in March and April 1972. And he was asked what it would take
to search the previously searched areas to be certain Cooper
was not there.

Himmelsbach wrote that he replied, "Give me 5,000 men and five
years, and we can do it."

In my June 1994 nine-day search with my partner, we were able
to space ourselves about 50 feet apart, and effectively search
areas at least 100 feet in width on each sweep.

On the edges of dense forests and open areas where the widespread
blackberry vines are exposed to direct sunlight, they are 20
feet high, or higher, dense, and impassable. But it is not
difficult to see under them from near-ground level. In the
interior of the forests where the blackberry vines are seldom,
or never, exposed to direct sunlight, they are straggly and
easily passable. And due to the heat and humidity in the region,
by June, fallen leaves on the ground are decomposed to the extent
that the ground is nearly bare, and clearly visible. Discarded
beverage cans, other debris, and even a small occupied bird's
nest in a low bush, were easily seen by me.

Even in areas of deciduous trees that shed their leaves, allowing
direct sunlight to the blackberry vines, we were able to search
a 100-foot-wide area on each sweep, zigzagging through and around
the straggly vines. But due to the complete overhead tree cover,
I had to carry a compass to maintain a true, direct course.

Although we believe Cooper's remains were most likely scattered
by wildlife, we did not rely on finding Cooper's remains in
a wide-spread area. We searched in a manner that would ensure
finding his remains and undeployed parachute intact. Even with
this much smaller target in mind, we completely searched every
100-foot-wide sweep without difficulty, and with certainty.

Cooper's reported potential drop zone was 28-square miles. And
spanned about 25 miles north from Portland, and some distance
east of Vector-23. About 10-20 percent, or more, of this area
is flat and open, farming land, or developed and populated,
including Vancouver. Considering Cossey's calculated drift of
1/8 mile with undeployed chute, and up to 5 miles with deployed
chute, would make the width of the probable drop zone less than

5 miles wide and 25 miles long. Or slightly less than 125-square miles.

Spacing 5,000 men as close as 11 feet apart would span 55,000 feet, or over 10 miles. If 2,500 men in a line over 5 miles wide started at each end of the 5-mile wide plotted drop zone, and searched only one mile in length each day, they could effectively search the entire area in about 12½ days, in my opinion. And that area would include the city of Vancouver and 10-20 percent of other open and flat, farm, and developed and populated areas.

Or by spacing 50 feet apart, as my partner and I were, in my opinion, that same less than 125-square miles could be effectively searched by 55 men in no more than 125 days. And that is based on searching only a one-mile length of the width of the less than 5-mile-wide area each day.

Of course, as reported by Himmlsbach, his 5,000 men and five years estimate was offered by him in 1975, nearly five years before the $5,800 was found. And nearly five years before he was contacted by the copilot of Cooper-skyjacked Flight 305, and told he was flying the plane by hand, and had most likely drifted east of automatic-pilot-course Vector-23.

This very late reporting of that information may have been a result of the illustrated "debriefing" of the flight crew in Reno.

Tosaw's book includes a photo of the entire flight crew of six being debriefed. The six crew members are seated at a long table. The flight officers are in the foreground, and all with their arms folded across their chests. There are at least seven stand-mounted microphones on the table, pointed in their direction. And the photo is identified as being taken and/or provided by Wide World Photos.

"Debriefing" is a term that has been used for decades by the military, some law enforcement agencies, and especially the FBI, to define post-event meetings, including witness interviews.

One of the very basic rules of witness interviews and suspect interrogations is to separate them, isolate them in a relaxed, uninterrupted environment, and do not tell them what the other witnesses or suspects said. Witnesses may have to testify under oath from their own independent recall of persons and events. In an emotional event, as this was, and most are, the power of suggestion can severely influence and confuse recall of crucial events and descriptions of suspects. Especially when one or more present are of higher rank, and subordinates are not likely to publicly contradict any of them, as in this particular case. And at best, eyewitnesses are well-reputed

to be the weakest evidence in any criminal or civil trial,
and are well known to be the primary target for prosecuting
and defense attorneys alike, to discredit their testimony.

Also, Tosaw wrote that Flight 305 had originated at Washington,
D.C., the day of the skyjacking, and had stopped in Minneapolis,
Missoula, Spokane, Portland, and its final stop for the day
was Seattle. Furthermore, Flight Attendants Alice Hancock and
Florence Schaffner reportedly deplaned in Seattle, and obviously
had to be transported to Reno in order to be in the photo. And
after Flight 305 landed in Reno at 11:02 p.m., and it was
determined he was not aboard. It is about 500 air miles from
Seattle SEA-TAC Airport to Reno. Considering last-minute flight
arrangements, flight time, etc., a conservative estimate of
their arrival and debriefing would have been no earlier than
about 1:00 a.m. And after a very full day of cross-country flight
schedule, being skyjacked, and threatened with being blown up.

From our viewpoint as experienced law enforcement investigators,
this photo appears to my partner and me as being a major media
event, not a professional police witness interview. And factoring
in the reasonable assumption that the flight crew was exhausted,
or nearly exhausted, from their very long and very bad day,
this debriefing would have been less than effective. Especially,
if Cooper had been apprehended and prosecuted.

If the FBI debriefing depicted in Tosaw's included photo was
the only witness interview of the flight crew by the FBI, and
was in any way like most televised press conferences, it should
explain why the FBI did not know Flight 305's path of travel
at that time. And resulted in massive searches of the wrong
areas in March and April 1972.

Another significant event Himmelsach wrote about that revealed
misinformation at that time was his being contacted by
Continental Airlines Captain Tom Bohan about seven years later,
and as follows.

CONTINENTAL AIRLINES CAPTAIN TOM BOHAN AND INFRARED HEAT SENSING

Himmelsbach wrote that he was contacted by Continental Airlines
Captain Tom Bohan several months before the $5,800 of Cooper
ransom money was found on February 10, 1980. And because Bohan
wanted to discuss infrared heat sensing with the chief
investigator of the Cooper case.

Himmelsbach wrote of infrared heat sensing technology as being
one "that then was available," which tends to indicate that
it wasn't available at some earlier time. And he wrote that
Bohan was certain infrared heat sensing photography could locate
Cooper.

Himmelsbach wrote about Bohan's explanation of how infrared
heat sensing detects a "heat signature," because of different
material densities, which causes them to develop and retain
different levels of heat. And are readily detected as differing
from others in the area by infrared heat sensing photography
from aircraft.

In the late 1960s or early 1970s, aerial heat sensing photography
was widely reported to have been used to locate a dozen or more
bodies buried in shallow graves by serial killer Juan Corona.
And a recent TV documentary illustrated the use of infrared
heat sensing used by U.S. military in the Vietnam War to detect
supply movements from Cambodia. That episode also showed how
the Viet Cong foiled infrared detection by hanging metal objects
from trees in areas well away from their transportation route.

Sadly, when I attempted to contact Captain Bohan through
Continental Airlines regarding infrared heat sensing, a corporate
attorney graciously phoned to inform me that Captain Bohan had
passed on a few years earlier than then - 1994.

Calame, Himmelsbach and Tosaw did not write anything about the
use of infrared heat sensing technology to search for Cooper.
When this technology was first used by the military is another
issue that could be readily determined by Congressional Committee
investigation. And if it was ever used to search for Cooper.
And if not, why?

Himmelsbach wrote that Captain Bohan informed him that his
Continental aircraft was the first flight behind skyjacked Flight
305 heading south on Vector-23 toward Portland. And his aircraft
was four minutes behind and 4,000 feet above Flight 305.

And Bohan told Himmelsbach the storm that night was one of the
worst storm fronts he had encountered in his 24 years of flying.
Bohan reported he had 80 knots of wind from 166 degrees on the
nose of his aircraft.

Himmelsbach wrote that this surprised him, because the wind
factor they had used to project Cooper's landing zone was 20-
40 mph from 245 degrees.

Himmelsbach wrote that he then informed Seattle and Minneapolis
of Bohan's infrared heat sensing theory. And he then realized
from Bohan's information about wind and degrees that they had
miscalculated by as much as 80 degrees, causing them to waste
a great amount of manhours and money searching the wrong area.

FEDERAL GRAND JURY "JOHN DOE" INDICTMENT OF COOPER

Himmelsbach wrote that the Department of Justice "waffled"

-36-

until the last day of the five-year statute of limitations,
November 24, 1976, to obtain a "John Doe" indictment of the
skyjacker to preserve criminal prosecution.

And on November 24, 1976, a Washington, D.C., Department of
Justice official phoned the Seattle FBI office and ordered them
to present the case to the federal grand jury to obtain a "John
Doe" indictment. The DOJ official was not identified.

Himmelsbach wrote that the Seattle federal grand jury was not
sitting, so the unidentified DOJ official phoned the Portland
FBI office, and he took the call.

He then wrote that, that afternoon, he testified as the sole
witness to be called before the grand jury to obtain the
indictment. And as the one person closest to case, and who
had been on the case the longest.

Himmelsbach's reported "waffling" by the Department of Justice
raises more questions in this case. Summers wrote that Lansky
was blackmailing Hoover, and Hoover was blackmailing Attorney
General John Mitchell and President Nixon. Summers wrote that
Hoover had tape recordings of illegal wire taps of White House
Staff and news reporters, and authorized in writing by Mitchell.
And one reported wire tap was on Washington Post columnist Jack
Anderson's phone. Summers wrote that Anderson had written many
columns on confidential White House scandalous events, known
only to White House Staff members. And Mitchell had illegally
authorized the FBI wire taps to try to learn the source or
sources of the White House leaks. Summers wrote extensively
about Hoover's tapes and files that were the objects of searches
long after Hoover died. Summers also wrote that Hoover had
evidence of Nixon's relationship with a woman, that he used
to his every advantage, including keeping Nixon from terminating
his position as FBI director.

Aside from the delay of seeking the indictment, it raises the
question of why the DOJ official first called the Seattle FBI
office to obtain the indictment, when Himmelsach wrote that
he was assigned to the Portland FBI office from 1962 until he
retired in 1980.

And, as earlier stated herein, Calame wrote the Seattle FBI
office was the office of origin and jurisdiction in the Cooper
case.

WASHOUGAL RIVER THEORY

Like Tosaw's "COLUMBIA RIVER THEORY" and my partner's "COLUMBIA
RIVER ISLAND THEORY," explained to follow herein, Himmelsbach
reportedly based his "WASHOUGAL RIVER THEORY" on the location

of the $5,800 found on a bank of the Columbia River on February 10, 1980.

And rightfully so, as that is the only reportedly known location that can be used as a foundation to track back to theorize how it got there, and from where.

As in all theories presented herein, my partner and I had to form our opinions based on what we believe to be probable, possible, likely, reasonable, or logical, or to the contrary. And based on our over 70 years combined law enforcement investigative experiences, in addition to my partner's two-year experience as a San Diego City lifeguard from 1939 to 1941.

Himmelsbach's Washougal River Theory is that Cooper landed near the Little or Big Washougal River, or a tributary, was injured, and died of hypothermia. And that the money bag ended up in a stream or one of the Washougal Rivers, traveled down the Washougal River into the Columbia River, and down the Columbia for about 25 miles to Tena's Bar, where it was found.

We agreed to discount this theory for these reasons:

1. Maps show the west edge of the Washougal watershed to be at least 15 miles east of Vector-23. And maps show the west fork of the Washougal River to be about 20 miles east of Vector-23.

Although the copilot reported in 1980 that Flight 305 had drifted to the east of Vector-23 an unknown distance, if it had drifted as much as 10 miles, it should have been detected by at least one of the reported radar tracking stations. Cossey estimated Cooper's drift with deployed chute to be no more than 5 miles, therefore, Flight 305 would have had to be about 10 miles east of Vector-23 when he jumped.

2. Based on the expert opinions of Cossey, the Perris parachute instructor I phoned in '99, and of many reported in Himmelsbach's book, it was nearly unanimously concluded Cooper could have not effectively deployed his chute. And he most likely free fell to his death.

If so, he would have been killed instantly, not just injured to any extent.

3. If Cooper had effectively deployed his chute, he would have most likely landed in the tops of tall trees. And it is very unlikely that he could have removed the chute from the tree tops, whether injured or uninjured. The enclosed copy of the March 3, 1999, edition of USA TODAY illustrates the Washougal area. Also the enclosed photo copy viewing the Washougal area northwest from the highway near Multnomah Falls.

Also, even if Cooper had landed uninjured, it would have been at about 8:15 p.m. He would have had at least 8 hours of darkness in the heavy rainstorm and cloud cover to escape before sunrise. Therefore, my partner and I believe it extremely improbable that Cooper would have wasted time removing the chute to conceal it, even if he could.

And Himmelsbach wrote that he and others had flown over all of the areas where Cooper could have landed, in the weeks to follow, and a chute was never seen anywhere. Reports of smaller sheets of plastic, etc., were checked out, but there were no reports of the 28' canopy chute being sighted.

4. The head of the Washougal River is at least 20 miles north of the Columbia River. As shown in enclosed photo copies, both the Little Washougal and Big Washougal Rivers, which converge a few miles north of the Columbia, are rough, white-water-rapids rivers in many sections. And both rivers have many still-water inlet pools along the banks.

Most of all, as the enclosed photo copies illustrate, there is a lake at the foot of the Washoughal River that it flows through before entering the Columbia River. The lake is about one-half mile long, widens to at least fives times the width of the Washougal River, and has islands and sloughs. Although my partner and I do not know the depth of the lake, in June 1994, the water flowed through it so slowly, it appeared to be a still-water lake.

With all of these physical factors, we concluded it was highly improbable the money bag could traverse about 15-20 miles of rough, white-water-rapids river, without settling in a still-water inlet pool, cross a one-half mile still-water lake, into the Columbia River, and down the Columbia for about 25 miles, then settle to the sandy bottom in front of Tena's Bar.

In 1998, a 15-year employee of the Bank of America showed me a bank money bag. It was made of white, lightweight canvas, long and open on one end like a pillow case, and had no securing device on the open end. And she assured me that was the same standard type of money bag that has been used by all banks for decades, and long before 1971.

Even if Cossey's belief is correct, and Cooper placed the bank money bag inside the unreturned chute container, my partner and I believe it is not likely that the money bag in the container could have remained intact in either of the rough, rocky Washougal Rivers, crossed the lake into the Columbia River, and traveled another 25 miles downstream to Tena's Bar.

5. My partner assures me the wilderness areas of the Washougal watershed are open to public access. And are regularly frequented

by hunters, fishermen, hikers, and other outdoor types. From our experiences, and numerous reported cases, many bodies and evidence of crimes are accidentally discovered by outdoorsmen. Especially when not buried or otherwise concealed, and exposed, as Cooper's remains and parachute should be.

One Cooper-related find was reported by Tosaw. He wrote that after Flight 305 landed in Reno, the searchers of the plane noticed the 10' x 12' sign that instructed how to lower the rear stairway was missing. And it was found seven years later by a deer hunter, nearly directly under course Vector-23, several miles north of Woodland, Washington.

And Brian Ingram's well-publicized find of the $5,800 is another example of citizens discovering related evidence in public-access areas.

Considering all these known and/or reported factors, my partner and I believe Cooper would have been found in the over 27 years since his skyjacking, if in a public-access area.

___

McCOY-COOPER THEORY

Written by Bernie A. Rhodes and researched by Russell P. Calame, it is proposed in their book, "D.B. Cooper, the Real McCoy," April 7, 1972, United Airlines skyjacker Richard Floyd McCoy, Jr., and Cooper were the same person. And writer Rhodes wrote that he became convinced McCoy was Cooper as early as 1972. He also wrote in the "Introduction" that the book was about the one man who committed both skyjackings.

The book, with Calame identified as the author herein for clarity and brevity, reported McCoy's known travels and activities before and at the time of Cooper's skyjacking. These circumstantial events are quite convincing. But my partner and I are of the opinion the many reported known differences in the two men detract from this theory.

As Calame reported, McCoy was known to be a Mormon Sunday-school teacher, and did not drink, smoke, gamble, or use profanity. Cooper reportedly frequently smoked Raleigh filter tips, ordered and drank two bourbon-and-water drinks on the flight from Portland to Seattle, was profanely abusive to the flight crew, and had dark nicotine stains on one hand.

Calame also wrote that McCoy was known to be 29 years old. Although the other passengers and airline employees estimated Cooper to be anywhere from 30 to 55, it was best estimated he was 45 to 50 years old. Tosaw wrote that he had interviewed all of the crew members, and he reported Cooper to be middle-aged.

Also, McCoy was reportedly known to be dark-skinned, and blue-
eyed. And Cooper was reportedly described as dark, olive, and
swarthy complected, and had dark, piercing eyes.

With respect to these differences, including age, Calame proposed
that McCoy had used a disguise in his Cooper-role skyjacking,
and the reported nicotine stains on his fingers could have been
cosmetic make-up. And he could have changed his eye color.

The only reported physical similarity was the size of the two
skyjackers. Himmelsbach wrote that Cooper was described by
witnesses as being 5 feet 10 inches and athletic build. And
a FBI Wanted poster in Calame's book listed McCoy as 5 feet
10 inches.

However, Himmelsbach later wrote that McCoy was a lot smaller
than Cooper. And that McCoy and Cooper were psychologically
different, in that Cooper appeared to be more desperate.

And McCoy was known to have been a Green Beret, and Cooper was
reportedly believed by many to have been a Green Beret.

As in all theories presented herein, my partner and I considered
all reliable reports, and compared each against the thousands
of cases we worked in our over 70 years of combined investigative
experiences. In doing so, we discounted this theory as being
less likely than my partner's Columbia River island theory.

COLUMBIA RIVER THEORY

Like in the "WASHOUGAL RIVER THEORY" and "COLUMBIA RIVER ISLAND
THEORY," Mr. Tosaw reportedly used the location of the $5,800
find as the base for his theory.

With that, Tosaw wrote that he then based his theory on a FAA
aeronautical chart that showed Vector-23 crossed the Columbia
River about two miles east of the I-5 bridge that spans between
Portland and Vancouver.

For clarification, although not crucial, factoring Vector-23
into Waterways Chart C-12 shows Vector-23 to be about 2 nautical
miles, or 1½ statute miles, east of the I-5 bridge. However,
considering the many conflicting reports, and variables in
formulating any theory, this difference is insignificant.

Tosaw's apparent theory is that Cooper was able to deploy the
NB-8 chute, and landed uninjured in the Columbia River. Then,
being unable to free himself from the sinking money bag, he
sunk with it and drowned. His chute then snagged on something
in the river, and he remains somewhere in the murky waters of
the Columbia River. And over a period of time, the money bag

was freed from Cooper's body, and traveled about 8 miles
downstream and settled. Then, in October 1974, it was dredged
onto the north bank of the Columbia River by the Army Corps
of Engineers, where $5,800 of the ransom money was found in
1980. See enclosed- "Attorney renews search for D.B. Cooper."

Despite Tosaw's most accurate and complete reporting in his
book, I concurred with my partner's decision to discount this
theory for the following reasons:

1. As earlier reported herein, Cossey's detailed explanations
and demonstrations convinced my partner and me that Cooper could
not have effectively deployed the NB-8 military chute. And even
if Cooper had jumped into a 120 mph headwind, which by all other
reports and calculations, would have been about 200-220 mph,
as earlier explained herein. Or more, based on Captain Bohan's
report to Himmlelsbach the southwest wind at 14,000 feet was
80 knots, also explained earlier herein.

2. Cossey believed Cooper had placed the money bag inside the
civilian chute container not returned to him. This belief is
supported by Tosaw's report that Cooper demanded the $200,000
be delivered to him in a knapsack. But the knapsack was not
delivered. The $200,000 was reportedly delivered in only the
open-ended bank money bag, without any securing device.
Although it is not known if the unreturned civilian chute
container was waterproofed, Cossey stated it was made of heavy
cotton canvas. Whether Cooper used the container or not, the
bank money bag was reportedly made of lightweight cotton canvas.
And the 10,000 bills inside the bag would have been dry, or
nearly so. Dry quality paper is bouyant, and will even float
near the surface when saturated. So, even if the 10,000 bills
had been saturated, my partner and I believe the money bag would
not have been "dead weigh" to pull Cooper under water.

Much to the contrary, it is our opinion that the money bag would
have been buoyant long enough for Cooper to cut it loose, if
he foresaw it was going to pull him down. Or much longer. He
reportedly had a knife he used to cut the shroud lines he used
to secure the money bag, and should have had time to cut the
money bag loose in order to avoid drowning.

3. Cossey and the Perris, California, parachute instructor stated
cotton canvas would rot if under water for a long period of
time. But nylon would not rot under water. As explained by the
Perris chute instructor, nylon chute parts would not rot because
nylon is made of plastic.

Therefore, it seems most likely that the money bag would have
decomposed and spilled the money before the nylon chute shroud
lines would break loose from Cooper's body. Or ever break loose,

unless Cooper's skeletal remains separated after all of the
soft tissue had decomposed. And that is unlikely, because Cooper
was reported to be wearing a business suit, which, like most
suits, was probably made of wool, or a wool blend, fabric, that
would not rot as cotton does. Also, Cooper's remains would have
most likely been in the parachute straps, although made of cotton
canvas, and would have rotted in due time. But should have held
his skeleton together, until violently disturbed, such as by
the Army Corps of Engineers dredge.

4. Tosaw was also quoted in the enclosed news article from the
November 29, 1987, edition of The Oregonian, that he believed
Cooper's body and most of the $200,000 are at the bottom of
the Columbia River.

As earlier explained herein, it was believed by one independent
expert and the FBI laboratory experts that the $5,800 found
in 1980 had been under water for a long period of time. And
because it was stuck together in one mass, it had to have been
compressed for all of that time. Then finding fragments of $20
bills as deep as 3 feet in the same sandy bank, strongly
indicates that if the $5,800 was compressed under water, the
money bag and all of the $200,000 had to have been intact until
violently disturbed and dredged onto the bank. And as earlier
explained herein, in a large stream of murky water, sand, and
debris.

Therefore, it is most likely that all of the $200,000 that wasn't
recovered in the mass of $5,800, and other fragments uncovered,
flowed back into the Columbia River in packets or fragments.
And, no longer being protected in the money bag, probably eaten
by river and ocean fish.

So, in our opinion, it is improbable that most, or any, of the
$200,000 was on the bottom of the Columbia River as late as
November 29, 1987, or any time after the river was dredged by
the Army Corps of Engineers in October 1974.

5. Tosaw wrote that he based his theory on a FAA aeronautical
chart that showed Vector-23 crossed the Columbia River about
two miles east of the I-5 bridge that spans the river between
Portland and Vancouver. He also wrote in his book that he had
interviewed all six crew members of Cooper-skyjacked Flight
305. And they were all very cooperative, and most of all the
copilot, who, by all reports, was flying the aircraft when Cooper
jumped.

From these two reports by Tosaw, it is not clear to my partner
and me if he used Vector-23 as Cooper's jump location, or some
unknown distance east of Vector-23, as the copilot reported
to Himmelsbach in 1980. Although not of critical importance,
mentioned only as it pertains to further analysis herein.

-43-

If Tosaw calculated Cooper's jump location from a flight course
on Vector-23, he would have drifted over the west runway of
Portland International Airport, based on Captain Bohan's report
of 166 degree southwest wind. And based on Cossey's estimate
that Cooper would drift 3-5 miles to the northeast if he had
deployed his chute at 9,500 feet, Cooper would have drifted
across the west runway in a descent from about 2,500 to 1,000
feet in order to land in the Columbia River.

Despite the heavy storm and cloud cover, if Cooper had drifted
this low over the airport and populated surrounding areas, it
is quite likely someone would have seen him. Especially on a
Thanksgiving Eve with a crowded airport, and FBI agents all
over the airport, as reported by Himmelsbach, and media reports
of the skyjacking at least 3 hours earlier.

And based on the above analysis of reports by Captain Bohan
and Cossey, if Tosaw calculated Cooper's jump from as much as
1 mile east of Vector-23, Cooper would have drifted over the
airport main terminal area in a descent of about 1,000 to 500
feet or less in order to land in the Columbia River. And would
have landed in the area of Lemon Island, or near the far west
end of Government Island.

This drift course would have exposed Cooper to public and FBI
view more than the above calculation from Vector-23.

Either way, this again raises the question of no report of
Portland International Airport FAA radar tracking of Flight
305 in books by Calame, Himmelsbach, and Tosaw. If Portland
had tracked the skyjacked aircraft, it may be that the FBI would
have known when and where Cooper jumped within seconds. And
if he had been able to deploy his chute, or not. And preclude
massive FBI, law enforcement, and Army troop searches in the
wrong areas, as reported by Himmelsbach.

6. Cossey stated nylon would not rot. The Perris parachute
instructor also said nylon would not rot, and because nylon
was composed of plastic.

These opinions should indicate that the 28-foot nylon chute
canopy would be water-resistant or water-repellent, and would
most likely float. Accordingly, if the 28-foot canopy had been
deployed, it should have captured at least 1,000 cubic feet
of air under it, and served as a large buoy for at least a few
minutes. And long enough for Cooper to do whatever he had to
do to prevent his drowning.

Also, the chute should have been visible from the banks of the
Columbia River, and other nearby vantage locations. Himmelsbach
wrote that media coverage of the skyjacking started before Flight
305 landed at Seattle at about 5:45 p.m., and a large crowd

-44-

had gathered before Flight 305 landed at Seattle.

From my lifetime observations, including over 31 years of law
enforcement experiences at emergency scenes, I believe there
would have been many curious excitement seekers watching the
sky as Flight 305 flew over the Portland-Vancouver area. And
despite the extreme storm and cloud cover. If so, it seems likely
at least one of them would have seen Cooper's descending drift
or chute in the Columbia River.

7. To our knowledge, there were no reports of Cooper's body
ever surfacing in the Columbia River. And if it had, it most
certainly would have been much more newsworthy than the $5,800
find, which received national news coverage.

My partner and I grew up in San Diego where there were ocean
and lake drownings every year. And my partner was a San Diego
City lifeguard from 1939 to 1941, before joining the San Diego
P.D. He also grew up in the beach community of La Jolla. He
more than I, clearly recalls that all reported drowning victims
surfaced within days. Depending on the temperature of the water,
the bacterial action of the body causes it to bloat, surface
and float. The water temperatures in San Diego coastal waters
range from about 50 degrees in the winter to about 70 degrees
in the summer.

My partner moved to Vancouver in 1986. From then until this
time in May 1999, he has never known of a reported drowning
victim's body that did not surface within a week. And he follows
all TV and press reports of police and other emergency
activities. To the best of his knowledge, although not reported
in The Oregonian "Weather" section, the Columbia River water
temperature remains cold year-round at about 50 degrees.

The only reports we are aware of where bodies do not bloat and
surface are in one or more of the Great Lakes, and in the very
deep sections where the water is too cold for bacterial action.

The floating capability of bodies was reported in a recent TV
crime episode. In that case, a woman and her two daughters were
murdered while visiting in Florida. The killer reportedly tied
a 50-pound cinder block to a leg of each victim, and dumped
the bodies into the Florida coastal waters from his boat.

Despite the 50-pound dead weight attached to each victim, all
three bodies surfaced, were sighted and recovered, and led to
the successful detection and prosecution of the sex killer.

To the best of my knowledge from media reports, the Florida
Gulf Stream water temperature is about 80 degrees. However,
despite the about 50 degree temperature of Columbia River waters,
my partner and I believe Cooper's body would have surfaced.

The Columbia River up to the major port at the Port of Portland is heavily traveled by large freighters, and fishing and pleasure boats. And there are many who fish from the banks of the Columbia. From the news reports my partner has heard or viewed, all surfaced bodies have been readily sighted from boats on the mile-wide Columbia, or from one of the river banks.

However, we believe Tosaw's calculation that Cooper landed in the Columbia River area is most logical.

COLUMBIA RIVER ISLAND THEORY

As Himmelsbach and Tosaw reportedly did, my partner used the sandy bank of the Columbia River known as Tena's (or Tina's) Bar, where the $5,800 was found, as the base to calculate how it got there, and from where.

Using all of the aforementioned reports herein, my partner agreed with Tosaw's calculation that Cooper landed somewhere in the Portland-Vancouver area of the Columbia River. But on land, not in the river. And with chute undeployed, not deployed.

From that, in his seven-year "armchair" analysis, he developed his theory that Cooper had to have landed on one of the Columbia River islands east of the I-205 bridge, which was not built until after Cooper's 1971 skyjacking. And from my review and analysis of his seven-year collection of Cooper data, and my nine-day independent investigation with him in 1994, I concurred with his theory. He also had a large wall-mounted relief map and a satellite photo of the entire area where Cooper could have landed, chute deployed or undeployed, which helped me.

I concurred with my partner's island theory for the following reasons:

1. Based on our June 18, 1994, interview with Cossey and the find of $5,800, my partner and I are certain Cooper free fell to his instant death. This of course, is our opinion. This crucial aspect could be best supported, confirmed, questioned, or refuted, by Congressional query of military specialists.

2. The find of the $5,800 on the sandy bar of the Columbia River strongly indicates that the money fell into the river a reasonable distance upstream from where it was discovered. And considering the aforementioned analysis herein of the buoyancy of canvas and dry paper until both became completely saturated, we believe it could have traveled downstream 16 miles from the I-205 bridge, near the west end of Government Island. Then when the canvas and paper bills became saturated, the weight of the soaked canvas progressively pulled the money bag to the sandy bottom of the 40-foot-deep shipping channel. And it settled

in the bottom of the deepest part of the river. And dredged
in October 1974. Then at that time, the Corps of Engineers dredge
violently moved the intact money bag, causing the rotted cotton
canvas chute container and bank money bag to disintegrate. And
pieces of canvas and the 10,000 $20 bills were flushed onto
Tena's Bar in a large, or huge, stream of murky water, sand,
and debris. Then all except the matted bills and excavated bill
fragments flowed back into the Columbia in a large stream of
murky water. Or moved a considerable distance from the $5,800
find location by the large bulldozer that followed the dredger.
And possibly to a location beyond the area later excavated with
backhoes by the FBI.

3. As earlier explained herein, my partner and I discounted
Cooper landing in the Columbia River. From all other deductions,
also explained herein, Cooper most likely landed on land, either
on the mainlands to the north and south of the Columbia River,
or on an island. And in order for the money bag to travel any
distance, be it 8 miles as Tosaw theorized, or 16 miles from
the I-205 bridge and Government Island, we believe it had to
have entered the main channel of the Columbia.

We discounted the north mainland for these reasons: A. By all
reports of the southwest wind, Cooper would have drifted about
1/8 mile to 1 mile to the northeast in his free fall. If he
hit the ground at 120 mph, or more, and the money bag broke
loose from him, it would have been propelled to the north, away
from the Columbia. B. Like the south mainland, the north mainland
is public-access, flat, developed, and frequented by the public.
And if Cooper had landed on either the north or south mainland,
his remains would have been most likely discovered years ago.

And we discounted the south mainland for these reasons: A. The
same public-access and development factors as the north mainland.
B. The south mainland does not front on the main channel of
the Columbia in the most likely areas that Cooper could have
landed. From nearly a mile west of the prolongation of Vector-
23, before it changes to a southwest course, the south mainland
fronts on a secondary channel noted on Waterways Chart C-12
as shallow levels and "sand." Vector-23 changes course about
6 miles southwest of Battle Ground, which is about 20 miles
north of the Columbia River. The prolongation of the southeast
course of Vector-23, before changing near Battle Groud, crosses
the Columbia River at the I-205 bridge and west tip of Government
Island. Therefore, if Cooper had landed at 120 mph or more on
the south mainland, the money bag would have been propelled
into the secondary channel. And would have landed in shallow
water or on a sand bar, and remained there.

Considering Cooper's landing with chute undeployed, and drifting
northeast in his 120 mph or more free fall, we believe he had
to land on one of the Columbia River islands. And within 100

yards of a north river bank of one of the islands east of the
I-205 bridge. My partner is certain the trees on the islands,
and Government Island in particular, are deciduous, and would
have shed their leaves by November 24, 1971. We theorize that
Cooper crashed into tree tops at 120 mph or more, and the sudden
stopping impact tore the tethered money bag from his waist,
causing the bag to be propelled into the main channel of the
Columbia River. And Cooper's body fell to the ground through
the leafless tree branches, and into a high, dense, impassible
mass of blackberry vines.

My partner is certain the Columbia River flows at 5 mph. At
that flow, and the earlier herein analysis of the money bag
progressively sinking as it became saturated, be believe it
could have traveled the about 16 miles from east of the I-205
bridge to Tena's Bar. And even if it bounced and rolled for
some distance before settling to the deepest portion of the
river.

4. Unlike the Washougal River watershed area and other wilderness
areas that are open to public access, the Columbia River islands
are owned by the Port of Portland, and access is prohibited
except by written permit.

Despite this prohibited access, my partner knows that the Port
of Portland installs portable toilets only on the southwest
shores of Government Island each summer for boaters to use.
And he has frequently observed that few, if any, boaters use
the north shore of Government Island, apparently because of
the 5-mph flow of the Columbia River main channel, as opposed
to the slower south channel flow.

Therefore, the most unlikely places within Cooper's potential
drop zone where he could be accidentally discovered by hunters,
fishermen, or other outdoor types are on the access-prohibited
Columbia River islands. Even the Government Island caretaker
would probably not accidentally find Cooper and his chute in
a high, dense, impassible blackberry vine mass. And if by some
rare chance a marijuana grower found Cooper's scattered bones
and/or chute, he or she would most likely not report the find
to authorities. First, they would have to explain why they were
there, in a prohibited-access area. Second, persons involved
in illegal activities are not prone to contact the police in
matters that do not concern them personally, or in any event.
And, third, obviously, reporting a find could lead investigating
law enforcement to his or her marijuana crops.

Government Island is nearly 6 miles long, and nearly 1 mile
wide for about 5 miles of the center section. And from the center
section to the far east tip is well within Cooper's undeployed
chute drop zone, if he jumped from a flight course as much as
2 miles east of the prolongation of Vector-23.

Although we believe Cooper's body could have been scattered
by hungry wildlife, if it did fall into a high, dense, impassible
blackberry patch, it is possible that only scavenger birds could
get to it from the air. And that four-legged ground animals
could not reach it due to the height and sharp blackberry thorns.
If so, Cooper's intact skeletal remains and attached chute would
be that much more difficult to locate, especially in dense
blackberry vines on a prohibited-access island.

Cooper's location and identification opinion summary: From our
combined total of about 19 years of research and analysis of
available information on the Cooper case, my partner and I had
to conclude that his remains are located as above stated. And
being in one of the most remote, inaccessible locations within
his potential drop zone area, with or without deployed chute,
significantly supports this theory, in our opinion.

We also believe he would have been carrying his wallet containing
his true identification, for many reasons. Of others, the most
obvious to my partner and me is if he had been stopped by a
police officer and couldn't produce satisfactory identification,
he would have most likely been arrested, photographed, and
fingerprinted. And if he had been in the military or arrested
in the past, his fingerprints would have been in the FBI files.
And dressed as described, in what Himmelsbach and I agreed
appeared to be a service uniform, Cooper would have been more
obvious in a crowd or alone.

Also, based on my profile of Cooper, if his remains are located,
and his true identity is established, I am certain his residence
of record will be in Las Vegas, or another nearby Nevada city.

STRANGE EVENTS

Perhaps coincidence, based on our over 70 years of law
enforcement investigative experiences, my partner and I perceived
these events to be somewhat strange.

1. ███████████ obtaining my partner's well-protected, unlisted
phone number, and repeatedly calling my partner, and as late
as 11:00 p.m. Also, attempting to convince my partner he had
already searched the Columbia River islands, found nothing,
then tried to convince my partner and me that Cooper's remains
had to be in the Washougal area. And trying to convince us pot
growers would pose a serious threat to us, but not to him.

2. Although Tosaw wrote that he had interviewed all six crew
members of Cooper-skyjacked Flight 305, including Tina Mucklow
who was in an Oregon convent at the time, my partner and I were
unable to get any response to our letters to the most crucial
crew members, including Mucklow. And despite Tosaw writing in

-49-

his book that all crew members had been very cooperative, and had even given him their hand-written notes prepared by the crew while the skyjacking was in progress.

Providing Tosaw with the handwritten notes, as he wrote, also raises the question of why the crew, not the FBI, had the notes. And in that Tosaw copyrighted his book in 1984, and he apparently researched the material after the $5,800 find in 1980, he apparently interviewed the crew and obtained the notes about 1980-1984, nine to thirteen years after the skyjacking.

Our sole purposes in trying to contact the crew members were to reconcile the different and conflicting reports in the three Cooper case books, and most importantly, the most probable location where Flight 305 crossed the Columbia River, east of Vector-23. The latter being most crucial to any theory on where Cooper jumped and most likely landed.

Copies of the letters of reply to me from the FAA and Northwest Airlines are enclosed as supporting proof of my attempts to locate and contact the crew members. I also made at least two phone calls to a crew member's home, without success. And my partner, a devout Catholic, did not receive any response from his letters to Tina Mucklow through the Catholic Order. In that he believed Mucklow could be cloistered, I composed a list of questions with spaces for answers, so she could reply without outside contact. But he did not receive any reply, whatsoever.

3. As earlier addressed and analyzed herein, the "debriefing" of the six crew members by the FBI in Reno.

4. That Himmelsbach and the FBI did not learn Flight 305 was being flown manually, not on automatic-pilot, and had reportedly drifted an unknown distance east of Vector-23, until after the $5,800 was found on February 10, 1980.

5. The Port of Portland issued my partner a written permit to search restricted-access Hayden Island from June 14, 1994, to May 31, 1995. And my partner told me the Port of Portland employees were very cooperative and interested in his search for Cooper's remains.

He provided the Port of Portland personnel with evidence of his $1,000,000 umbrella liability policy. And even though the issued "Permit and Right-of-Entry" document has a "Special Insurance Requirements" section, and "None" was typed in the respective following space for insurance information.

Upon completing his search of Hayden Island in October 1994, he sent a letter to the Port of Portland, copy enclosed. As written, he expressed his plans to search other Port property upriver from Hayden Island in the future.

However, when he applied for a permit on October 27, 1994, to
search upriver islands, including Government, McGuire, Lemon,
and the two Sand Islands, he met with staunch resistance. He
was told the Port had a new legal counsel who was opposed to
issuing access permits. And in any event, one requirement was
that my partner would have to assign the Port of Portland as
the beneficary of his $1,000,000 public liability umbrella
policy.

This assignment would have deprived my partner and his wife
of their umbrella policy protection, so he couldn't do it. And
as late as February 1995, my partner had not received any written
reply to his written request. And his phone calls to the Port
of Portland office over the following months proved to be futile.

Despite the "None" entered after "Special Insurance Requirements"
on his June 14, 1994, to May 31, 1995, issued permit, seven
months before it expired, he was unable to obtain a permit to
search the other islands. We are still baffled by this change
of policy. This was especially strange, in that the Port did
not cancel his permit to further search Hayden Island, that
didn't expire until May 31, 1995.

Although I wrote in my letter to FBI Director Freeh that my
partner discontinued his search because of the hazards, the
real reason was his inability to get the necessary access permit
from the Port of Portland. But, at the time, I didn't think
it would be of importance. And thereafter, until my 1998
discoveries about J. Edgar Hoover in the source books by Anthony
Summers and the Giancanas.

Actually, despite some heart problems, and searching alone,
my partner had planned to buy a boat and cell phone service
to search the other islands. As he had said before and during
my June 1994 Vancouver visit and searches with him, "Searching
for Cooper really gets the juices flowing." And he said he had
lost about 20-30 pounds beating the bushes for Cooper's remains,
and hadn't felt that good since he was 30 years old.
Accordingly, it is an understatement for me to say he was
disappointed when he had to give up his searching for Cooper.
More importantly, we are both certain his search of the other
islands would have revealed Cooper's remains and true I.D. by
no later than 1996 or 1997.

6. The FBI letter of reply to my letter to FBI Director Freeh
is dated July 25, 1995. I received it on a Saturday, which was
about July 28, 1995. And I curiously noticed it said my letter
was being forwarded to the Seattle FBI office, not the Portland
FBI office where Himmelsbach wrote he had been assigned from
1962 until his retirement from the FBI in 1980. This was a
surprise to me, even though, as earlier mentioned herein, Calame
wrote that Seattle was the office of origin and jurisdiction.

At about 9:00 a.m. the Thursday after receiving the FBI letter
of reply, I received a phone call from Seattle FBI Special Agent
██████████. He said he was the current Cooper case agent, and
told me the Cooper case had been assigned to the Seattle FBI
office since the day of Cooper's skyjacking.

███████ was most candid, and said they had received a call from
Las Vegas. As I recall, ████████ said the caller told of a person
who reportedly planned to commit a major crime in the Pacific
Northwest. However, ████████ immediately changed to a more
revealing subject, and I did not learn if anything of value
resulted from the Las Vegas caller's report.

████████ changed the subject to former Seattle FBI Special Agent
████████, his role in the Cooper case, and his resigning
from the FBI after years of harassment by his supervisors.
████████ expressed his high regard of ████████ and his personal
achievements, including his graduating #2 in his Annapolis Naval
Academy Class.

Because I do not have documented evidence of our phone
conversation, my Constitutional Law attorney advised me not
to divulge the entire content of ████████ disclosures herein,
to avoid defamation of character libel liability.

However, I will only say, what ████████ told me may be crucial
to a Congressional Committee investigation.

At the conclusion of our conversation, I asked ████████ if he
would contact ████████, and ask him to phone me collect. He
assured me he would, but he was certain ████████ would not call,
because ████████ did not want to have anything more to do with
the FBI or Cooper case.

████████ did not call me. I phoned ████████ in early 1999, and
renewed the request. But ████████ did not contact me.

From what ████████ told me in 1995 and 1999, I believe both
████████ and ████████ could be crucial witnesses in an
investigation.

CONCLUSION

My interest and involvement in the Cooper case started as an
innocent attempt to assist my partner in validating his Columbia
River Island Theory. But it soon evolved into a search for
missing pieces in the complex, puzzling case. And the deeper
I searched, more unanswered questions surfaced. Then ████████
disclosures introduced more intrigue, which confirmed some of
my suspicions, but added to the mystery of the case. But with

absolutely no authority to pursue the case any further than
I had, I filed the case materiel.

Then in early 1998, a series of TV documentaries and biographies
were aired in rapid succession. They were about J. Edgar Hoover,
Meyer Lansky, Frank Costello, Sam Giancana, Bugsy Siegel, Las
Vegas, the CIA, and Army Special Services Forces Green Berets.

Vividly recalling my profile of Cooper, I then researched the
books by Anthony Summers and the Giancanas. Ironically, I had
them in my library, but had not found time to read either of
them due to other projects.

With my profile of Cooper as the crucial link, it wasn't
difficult for me to form the opinion that there could be a direct
connection between Cooper's ransom skyjacking and Hoover and
Mafia loan sharks. And the Giancana's report that Sam Giancana
lived in and near Mexico City from 1966 to 1974, controlled
loan sharks over thousands of miles, and moved millions across
the Mexican border, added that final factor to my profile of
Cooper. Also, in my opinion, it answered the question of why
Cooper demanded he be flown to Mexico City, when by all reports,
he had no intention of going there. And proved he didn't when
he jumped as soon as he could.

Along with his "service uniform" dress, and the name of "Dan
Cooper," I am of the opinion "Mexico City" was part of a coded
message to his loan shark tormentors that it was him, and he
would fix his debt to them.

But nobody will ever know for certain, and the Cooper case will
most likely remain unsolved forever, unless it is investigated
by a Congressional Committee.

And a Congressional Committee investigation of the Cooper case
may serve more purposes than merely solving that case, and more
than listed herein under "PURPOSES FOR CONGRESSIONAL
INVESTIGATION." If my theory is correct, and validated by such
an investigation, it could be instrumental in exposing the dire
consequences of compulsive, and otherwise irresponsible,
gambling. Most recent TV specials on casino gambling have
addressed the current concern and controversies of widespread
legalized gambling. And the devastating affects on the millions
in lower economic classes that deprive their families and
children of bare necessities to satisfy their gambling frenzies.

Needless to say, odds are that those deprived children can be
the future wave of criminals the next generation will have to
deal with, fear, and pay to apprehend, prosecute, and incarcerate
or execute. This may sound extreme, but my life and law
enforcement experiences tell me it is so true. And I believe
the Congressional Commission Report will say the same.

Based on my acquired knowledge of the D.B. Cooper case, I am
certain the following preliminary actions by Congressional
investigators would provide more than sufficient information
to justify a complete Congressional Committee investigation.

1. Submit a copy of this summary to FBI profiling and Mafia
experts, and to former FBI profiling expert John E. Douglas,
for their profiling of Cooper.

2. Interview FBI Special Agent ▆▆▆▆▆▆▆▆

3. Interview former FBI Special Agent ▆▆▆▆▆▆▆▆.

4. Subpoena the Cooper case file, and search for calls from
Las Vegas and directives from Director Hoover or FBI assistant
directors.

5. If still in file, subpoena Portland International Airport
FAA radar tracking records for November 24, 1971, from 2000
to 2030 hours.

6. Locate and subpoena retired Army Special Services Forces
Sergeant ▆▆▆▆▆▆▆▆▆ "

7. Subpoena the flight officers of Cooper-skyjacked Northwest
Airlines Flight 305.

8. Subpoena military parachute experts.

9. Subpoena Port of Portland Office Facility Manager ▆▆▆
▆▆▆▆

If these preliminary actions provide sufficient cause to justify
a complete Congressional Committee investigation, I strongly
recommend a preliminary infrared heat sensing aerial photography
search of the Columbia River islands east of the I-205 bridge.
And in the fall or winter, after the deciduous trees have shed
their leaves.

Then, regardless of detection of possible Cooper's remains,
that a foot ground search be conducted by Marine Corps explosive
experts, and with local law enforcement homicide investigators.
And starting with a search of the north side of Government
Island, and the area within 100-200 yards of the main channel
of the Columbia River.

Spaced 10-20 feet apart, in my opinion, 45 Marines and 5 local
law enforcement officers could search all of Cooper's probable
landing areas on all of the islands in no more than 10 days.

And finding Cooper's remains, and proof of his true name, could
expedite a Congressional investigation, in my opinion.

SOURCES

D.B. Cooper Dead or Alive? By Richard T. Tosaw. Copyright 1984
by Tosaw Publishing Co., Inc. P.O. Box 939, Ceres, CA 95307.

NORJAK: the Investigation of D.B. Cooper. By and copyright 1986
by Ralph P. Himmelsbach and Thomas K. Worcestor. Published by
NORJAK PROJECT, P.O. Box 567, West Linn, OR 97068.

D.B. Cooper the Real McCoy. By Bernie Rhodes; research by Russell
P. Calame. Copyright 1991 and published by University of Utah
Press, Salt Lake City, UT.

Official and Confidential: the Secret Life of J. Edgar Hoover.
By and copyright 1993 by Anthony Summers. Published by G.P.
Putnam's Sons, 200 Madison Avenue, New York, NY 10016.

Double Cross. By and copyright 1992 by Chuck and Sam Giancana.
Published by Warner Books, Inc., 1271 Avenue of the Americas,
New York, NY 10020.

FBI Secrets: an Agent's Expose'. By and copyright 1995 by
M. Wesley Swearingen. Published by South End Press, 116 Saint
Botolph Street, Boston, MA 02115.

All the President's Men. By and copyright 1974 by Carl Bernstein
and Bob Woodward. Published February 1975 by Warner Paperback
Library, 75 Rockefeller Plaza, New York, NY 10019.

Mindhunter: Inside the FBI's Elite Serial Crime Unit. By John
E. Douglas and Mark Olshaker. Copyright 1995 by Mindhunters,
Inc. Published by Scribner, 1230 Avenue of the Americas, New
York, NY 10020.

The Oregonian newspaper article "Attorney renews search for
D.B. Cooper." Edition of November 29, 1987. Copy enclosed.

The Oregonian newspaper article "Expert thinks Cooper died of
hypothermia." Edition of November 24, 1988. Copy enclosed.

The Oregonian newspaper article "Marijuana 'gardens' raided."
Edition of August 16, 1994. Copy enclosed.

The Orange County Register newspaper article "Saving Sergeant
Hebler," and continued page heading, "HEBLER: Former assassin
now spends his time saving lives." Edition of June 28, 1998.
Copies of pertinent sections enclosed.

[NINETEEN]

Mexico City Money Laundering

Nixon Connection

CARL BERNSTEIN AND BOB Woodward were the two *Washington Post* reporters who pursued and broke the June 17, 1972, Watergate burglary case, and authored and published their book, *All The President's Men*, which was made into a big screen movie.

Like my discovering Summers's book about J. Edgar Hoover's scandalous life and being blackmailed and controlled by the Mafia on a TV show, in watching the movie *All The President's Men*, I learned of Nixon's connection to a Mexico City bank through his secret Committee to Reelected the President (CRP).

In the movie, Dustin Hoffman played the role of Bernstein, and Robert Redford played the role of Woodward. What aroused my interest in the very involved movie was when Bernstein and Woodward discovered that money was the key to their very complex investigation. They had discovered $89,000 in cashier's checks that came from a Mexico City bank and in the name of a Mexican attorney. It was determined that the cashier's checks had been forged, which made me wonder if that attorney's decomposing body was in a ditch on the outskirts of Mexico City.

They then discovered that $750,000 had been sent across the Mexican border, and money was being sent back and forth across the border to Mexico City in a money laundering scheme. Although I had strong suspicions about a direct connection between Mooney Giancana, Nixon, and the President of Mexico when Mooney was arrested and deported only three weeks before Nixon resigned the presidency, after being in Mexico for eight years as a welcome alien guest, *All The President's Men* convinced me that it was true.

I also viewed another TV episode about Nixon that supported my Mooney Giancana and Nixon connection. After the six Watergate burglars were identified, one of Nixon's top staffers broke the bad news to him in the Oval Office. Nixon immediately asked how much it would take to keep them silent. The staffer replied six million dollars. Then in so many words, Nixon said without hesitation that it would not be a problem.

My reaction to that was, where could he get six million dollars at the drop of a hat, when six million in 1972 would be about thirty or sixty million of today's dollars? But I had clearly recalled Chuck and Sam Giancana writing that Mooney had a monthly take of four million dollars in 1958, fourteen years earlier, and no doubt increasing each and every year thereafter.

The only realization I had from that connection was that it could be why six congressional members and one U.S. Attorney had never responded to my Cooper case conclusions, including my case summary to five of them, and mailed certified and return receipt–requested U.S. Mail. Or could it be because Hoover's dossiers were still stored in a former FBI special agent's or secretary's garage. Or is the FBI still amassing dossiers on those they feel compelled to control for self-preservation.

Be it one, two, or all three of these suspicions of mine, I strongly believe that no Feds should be in any way involved, and the Cooper case must be exclusively investigated by a county grand jury in Washington, Oregon, California, or Nevada to get to the truth that I know it to be.

TWENTY

The Outsiders

The Beat Goes ON

A FTER BOULÉ'S AUGUST 2004 article about my J. Edgar Hoover cover-up theory, Harry continued to send me every D.B. Cooper newspaper article, but none were written by Margie Boulé'.

Then in our many phone conversations after I received no response from my 1999 and 2000 letters to the six congressional members and my 2004 letter to the Portland U.S. Attorney, Harry and I were certain our theories were valid, and we were the only two people in the world outside of the FBI who knew the truth about the Cooper case.

A few times in surfing the channels searching for anything worth watching on TV, I hit on another D.B. Cooper episode. I would quickly phone Harry to tell him about it, then hang up to watch another version, and they usually included Ralph Himmelsbach as the primary or sole

commentator. Then when they finally ended, after I had
yelled "bullshit" at the TV a few times, I would again phone
Harry to compare our impressions of the latest versions of
the Cooper case, and we always agreed that they were getting more ridiculous with each showing.

Then the first week of January 2008, I received a D.B.
Cooper article from Harry, dated January 1, 2008, and
published by the *Columbian*, not the *Oregonian*, about
Seattle FBI Special Agent Larry Carr, who was going to
renew the investigation of of the D.B. Cooper case. Then
the next day, I received a copy of the *San Diego Union Tribune* from old friend in San Diego. What immediately
caught my attention in the *Union Tribune* was that the
heading in that article stated that it was from the *New York
Times* News Service in Chicago. And an enlarged inset
stated "Intrigued agent asked FBI to give him the old case."

The "Chicago" initially intrigued me; then the article
went on to say that Larry Carr was a Seattle bank robbery
agent. It went on to say that technology not available at the
time of Cooper's jump was then at hand. That made me
laugh, because infrared photography was available at that
time, but the FBI did not use it to search for Cooper's
remains. The article also mentioned the mysterious tie that
Rhodes and Calame had claimed belonged to McCoy, and
DNA had been taken from it and compared to several men
who claimed to be Cooper. That made me think of the
many who claimed they knew who Cooper was, including
a man in Minnesota who reported that his brother was
most likely Cooper, and a woman in Texas. The problem
with the Texas woman's story that I readily recognized was

that she and her Cooper suspect husband were estranged and going through an ugly divorce. So, forget that one, I thought, in addition to my knowing for certain that Cooper had perished in his almost certain suicide jump.

Unable to control myself at that time about more Cooper FBI "Snipe Hunt" stories, I typed and mailed a letter to Agent Larry Carr. Therein, I enclosed a copy of Margie Boulé's article about my Hoover cover-up theory and told him that I had sent a letter to Boulé asking her to challenge Himmelsbach to an open discussion with me about the Cooper case, and I had not received a response.

I then wrote that a previous Seattle chief Cooper case agent had freely discussed the case with me, and when I made the regrettable mistake of letting the wrong people know, he was transferred to Jacksonville, Florida, and never again returned my calls to his office, as he had always done when he was in Seattle. I then wrote that if he wanted to discuss the case with me, he could phone me, and I would not tell a soul. I also wrote that he could go only two ways in his investigation, and that was to come to the same conclusions that Harry and I had theorized, and end his FBI career, or fake it and spin in circles, so to forget it. Then in the P.S., I said Cooper's remains are on a Columbia River island. Not surprising to me, I have never heard from him.

Then on March 25, 2008, I saw on the TV news that a parachute had been found in the area of Amboy, Washington, and FBI Special Agent Larry Carr thought it might be Cooper's chute. I looked at a map of Washington and located Amboy about ten miles east of Woodland, where dozens of FBI agents, local law enforcement officers and hundreds of Fort Lewis soldiers had searched for weeks in early 1972 and found nothing except two bodies not related to Cooper. Then after the $5,800 was found by Brian Ingraham on February 10, 1980, Himmelssbach openly admitted in his book that they had searched the wrong area, and at immense expense to the taxpayers.

I phoned Harry to discuss this latest alleged Cooper find, and we agreed that the chute was most certainly from World War II, when dozens of military pilots bailed out over or crashed on U.S. soil, which I had suspected from the time I first saw the newscast.

With that agreement from Harry, I typed and sent a second letter to Special Agent Larry Carr. Therein, I explained the flight path of Cooper's skyjacked plane, and our knowledge of the frequency of military aircraft crashes in World War II. Then I wrote that he should take the chute to Earl Cossey, who provided his chutes for Cooper's sky-jacking, and he could identify it as one of his, or eliminate it as a chute he had rigged.

About two weeks later, it was reported on the news that Earl Cossey had eliminated the chute as being one of his.

Then in January 2010, my son phoned me and said there was going to be D.B. Cooper episode on the Military Channel that next Wednesday at 8:00 P.M. I started checking the Military Channel, and for two weeks it reported that the Cooper episode would be aired the next Wednesday at 8/c7. I knew from seeing that time report many times before that the "c" meant Central time, and that it would be aired at 5:00 P.M. Pacific time.

When I convinced my son of the 5:00 P.M. time, he volunteered to tape it for me. I watched the episode on my TV, then the next evening I went to my son's house to watch it again so I could stop, rewind and replay many parts of it.

The episode started by stating that Cooper's skyjacked Flight 305 took off from Portland International Airport at 4:30 P.M. That was the first of many erroneous reports, because Tosaw wrote that it became airborne at 2:58 P.M., and Himmelsbach wrote that the flight officers had contacted Northwest Airlines headquarters in Minneapolis minutes before 3:15 P.M. while they were in flight. Then it stated that after a thirty-minute delay, Flight 305 landed at the Seattle Airport at 5:39 P.M., and Tosaw wrote that the flight officers had been instructed to go into a holding pattern over the Puget Sound, away from populated areas in the event the bomb exploded and they went down. And Tosaw wrote that Flight 305 landed at the Seattle Airport at 5:43 P.M. Furthermore, if the Cooper skyjacked plane had taken off from Portland at 4:30 P.M., and it was reported to be only a thirty-minute flight to Seattle, and delayed only thirty minutes, that would have given the FBI only one hour to get the $200,000 and four parachutes and deliver them to the Seattle Airport after all banks had closed at 3:00 P.M. And Tosaw wrote that Cooper ordered the flight officers to not land at Seattle until all of his demands were at the airport.

The episode showed Cooper sitting in a window seat to the right of the aisle, looking from the rear to the front. Tosaw wrote that Cooper had sat in seat 18E, in the middle seat to the right of the aisle, and that Cooper had ordered both Florence Shaffner and Tina Mucklow to sit next to him at different times. Himmelsbach wrote that Cooper sat in seat 18C, the aisle seat to the left of the aisle. If he had sat in that seat, it would have required two flight attendants to step over his legs and brief, or attaché, case to sit next to him, which he would have certainly not wanted them to do. And the many other TV episodes all showed Cooper seated in the middle seat to the right of the aisle, in the last row to the rear.

An attaché case was shown, and the narrator called it a briefcase.

It showed an illustration of automatic pilot course Vector-23 bending from southeast to southwest over Battle Ground, but did not show the continued southeast prolongation of Vector-23, indicating that Flight 305 was on automatic pilot and remained on Vector-23 and over the west runway of the Portland International Airport.

The narrator stated that the Cooper manhunt was the largest in FBI history.

The narrator stated that Jo Weber had been told by her husband, while on his deathbed, that he was Dan Cooper.

The narrator stated that 727s were only one of two jets that had aft staircases, when all other reports in books were that the 727 was the only commercial aircraft with an aft staircase, and were used by the CIA in Vietnam to drop supplies and personnel behind enemy lines.

It was stated that Cooper used a paratrooper-type parachute, and that military chutes automatically deployed. Tosaw wrote that Cooper used an NB-8 emergency military pilot chute, as Earl Cossey had confirmed when Harry and I interviewed him. Then later in the episode, it showed the aerial stuntman and parachutist star of the episode wearing both chest pack and backpack parachutes.

In that reenactment demonstration, the aerial stuntman and parachutist star of the show was shown wearing a chest pack and back pack, and with the money bag strapper tightly to his waist. But Tosaw wrote that Flight Attendant Tina Mucklow reported to him that Cooper tethered the money bag to his waist with about a six-foot length of shroud line he had cut from one of the other chutes. And Earl Cossey told Harry and me that one of the three chutes returned to him had some shroud lines cut from it.

Then in the reenactment demonstration, the star aerial stuntman jumped on a bright, sunny day onto a flat, level field that looked like a wheat field or one covered with tall weeds. He then performed the same jump at nighttime.

A narrator then stated that Cooper's jump would have been about five times more difficult than the aerial stunt-man's. That almost made me laugh, because there was absolutely no comparison, and Cooper's jump would have been about 100 times more difficult than the demonstration jump, due to the extremely different weather conditions, topography, and apparel.

The aerial stuntman then said he speculated that Cooper had a flashlight in his attachè case. That did make me laugh, because I had concluded in the very beginning of my investigation that when Cooper was about to jump, he would have had no more need for the attaché case and fake bomb, so he would have most certainly thrown it away before he jumped. It has never been reportedly found, so I speculated that it probably plopped into a body of water and sank to the bottom.

The narrator stated that the terminal gravity pull velocity is 126 miles per hour, and Cooper would have fallen about 1,000 feet to reach 126 miles per hour. Then thereafter, would have fallen 1,000 feet every five seconds.

The aerial stuntman then jumped from a high diving board into an Olympic-sized pool with large lettering of "USC" on a high wall in the background. Gray cardstock was used to simulate the twenty-one pounds of Cooper ransom money, and the money bag was again tightly strapped to his waist, not tethered as Cooper's reportedly was. The simulated money bag floated like a life raft for about four-and-a-half minutes, then dragged him down.

It was then stated that the life expectancy of a $20 bill was four years, not eitghteen months as reported by Himmelsbach, nor eighteen to twenty-four months as told to me by my Secret Service special agent contact.

It was inferred that Cooper could have landed in Lake Merwin with its water temperature of forty-eight degrees Fahrenheit. But Lake Merwin is due east of the Woodland and Lewis River area where the FBI, local law enforcement, and two hundred or four hundred Fort Lewis soldiers searched for weeks in 1972 and found nothing related to Cooper. And after the $5,800 of Cooper's ransom money was found, Himmelsbach admitted they had searched the wrong area, and at an immense expense to the taxpayers.

The narrator then mentioned that Jo Weber reported that her husband, Duane Weber, had told her on his deathbed that he was Dan Cooper. The FBI compared a photo of Duane Weber with a composite of Cooper, and it did not produce positive proof that they were the same person. So the photo and composite were taken to Security Research Development (SRD) in Las Vegas for facial recognition, and Weber was classified as number one match.

Based on that reported match, the narrator then speculated that Weber buried most of his ransom money in the woods, and that it was lost forever when Mount St. Helens erupted in 1980 and buried it forever. Needless to day, that did make me laugh. And to make it more ludicrous, shortly thereafter, he said that the authorities assumed that Cooper had been killed in his jump. If he was killed in his jump, how could he be Duane Weber in 1995, when he told his wife, Jo Weber, that he was Dan Cooper?

By the time I finished stopping, rewinding, and replaying certain parts of the episode for about two hours, in disgust, I concluded that they had finally turned the Cooper skyjacking case into a Ringling Brothers and Barnum & Bailey circus main attraction high wire trapeze act with a safety net.

Then I stopped and replayed slowly ahead to get a good look at the credits. And under "Special Thanks," along with some others, it read:

FEDERAL BUREAU OF INVESTIGATION
RALPH HIMMELSBACH

And the title of the show was: "D.B. Cooper, Unsolved History."

The narrator identified the aerial stuntman parachutist as being from Temecula, and I wanted to discuss the episode with him, so I looked up a retired CHP officer I knew who lived in Temecula and phoned him. I asked him if there was a skydive park in Temecula, and he said no, but there was one at Lake Elsinore, which is only several miles north of Temecula.

I then called directory assistance and got the phone number of the Lake Elsinore skydive park, and phoned it. A very helpful woman answered, and I asked her by the aerial stuntman's name given during the episode if he worked there as an instructor. She replied that he did not work there, but he had jumped there last June. It amazed me that she was able to immediately respond with the month he had jumped there. She then said I should call Perris Valley Skydive, because he might go there to jump, and she then quickly gave me the phone number of that skydive park.

In that he was not employed at or regularly jumped at Lake Elsinore, and it being the closest skypark to Temecula where he was reportedly located, it increased my curiosity and desire to talk to him. And to ask him how much of a role Himmelsbach played as a case advisor to the plot and script writer in that Cooper episode.

I then phoned the Perris Valley Skydive number, and another very helpful young lady answered. When I asked her by his given name if he worked or jumped there, she replied no, but his wife occasionally jumped there. I told her I would like to get in touch with the aerial stuntman. She said if I wanted to give her my name and phone number, she would give it to his wife the next time she came there to jump. I gave her my name and phone number and thanked her.

With time running out on authoring this book, I wanted to talk to him before I had completed my manuscript. So, I took a long shot and called directory assistance to get his phone number in Temecula. The directory operator quickly replied that the only listing by that name was in Carlsbad, and she switched to the recorded number and I wrote it down. I immediately phoned the number, and a recorder answered in a woman's voice. I hung up and decided to call again the next Saturday morning when he might be there and answer the phone. The recorder again answered in the woman's voice, so I stated on the message recorder my name, that I would like to talk to the name given about the D.B. Cooper case, gave my home phone number, and hung up.

My home answering recording refers to my cell phone number if I do not answer, but I have not received any return phone call, and that was over two months ago when I typed this page.

It didn't surprise me for more than one reason, because I was suspicious from the time my CHP retired contact told me that there not a skydiving park in Temecula. Then when I learned that he lived in Carlsbad, not Temecula as reported on the TV episode, I became very suspicious about his role in the circus-like episode.

So I thought, "What's new?" because only Himmelsbach and Cossey had ever responded to our requests for interviews, and that again confirmed my suspicions of what are they trying to hide. Then there was also the Seattle FBI special agent who phoned me in belated response to my letter to FBI Director Louis Freeh, but when I made the regrettable mistake of letting the wrong people know he had discussed the Cooper case with me, he was quickly transferred to the opposite corner of the country in Jacksonville,

Florida. And after that, he never returned any of my phone calls. And I sincerely apologize.

To make matters worse, I viewed a TV episode wherein that fine FBI special agent was one of the lead investigators in pursuing a Seattle area serial bank robber and appeared on the screen and spoke about the case. Also in that episode, a female FBI special agent was shown and identified as having the same rather uncommon surname. In fact, there are only six persons of that same surname in my South Orange County telephone directory. And South Orange County is fully developed and populated with hundreds of thousand of residents from the Pacific Ocean to the foothills of the Santa Ana Mountains. So I wondered if that female special agent was his wife, and if so, if she was also transferred to Jacksonville with him. Or if she was his wife and wasn't transferred with him, if that was another form of punishment for him because he had broken the FBI code of silence, which is much like the Mafia code of silence—"omertà."

One of Himmelsbach's passages in his book that stood out to me was his own profile of Cooper as being a burned out ex-con trying for a last big take, do or die. And that he publicly described Cooper as a "rotten, sleazy crook." Then at his retirement dinner, his fellow special agents presented him with a revolver and a T-shirt inscribed with "ROTTEN, SLEAZY CROOK."

That struck me wrong for more than one reason. One being that a cardinal rule of professional law enforcement is to never become personally or emotionally involved in a case or with a criminal suspect. To do so can easily cause the officer or agent to become biased and partial toward the case or suspect to the point of becoming overzealous in a prosecution and convicting an innocent person.

The other is that I have a totally different extended profile of Cooper, or whoever he was by his true name. First of all, I am completely convinced that he was a former Green Beret. And I believe that is supported by Rhodes's and Calame's report in their book that McCoy, a known decorated Vietnam War Green Beret, left his family on Thanksgiving Eve and Day to be in Las Vegas where I'm certain Cooper departed that afternoon for Portland. Also, J.T., a claimed retired Green Beret, hounded Harry to dissuade him from searching for Cooper's remains.

And if Cooper was forty-five years old or older, as the closest and most reliable witnesses described him to be, he would have been of an age to serve in World War II, the Korean War and the Vietnam War. With that to consider, I also theorize that if his remains are found and positively identified it could reveal that he was a highly decorated war hero and be interned at Arlington National Cemetery. So be it!

As far as "rotten, sleazy crooks" are concerned, the rottenest, sleaziest crook I could identify in my investigation was J. Edgar Hoover. Sam "Mooney" Giancana and Tony Spilotro and company were known to be the worst of the worst, but they had obviously never taken a sacred oath to protect and serve and to uphold the law and the Constitution of the United States of America as Hoover had sworn to do. And there is nobody more rotten and sleazy than a crooked cop. If you can't trust a sworn law enforcement officer, who can you trust?

It has been said that "Truth is stranger than fiction." Considering all of the fictional stories about the D.B. Cooper skyjacking case that have been published or produced, this true, exclusive report of the case should prove that adage to be absolutely true.

But this case can only be officially solved and Cooper's remains recovered and identified by a state attorney general or county district attorney presenting the case before a county grand jury in any one of the states of Washington, Oregon, California or Nevada.

And if none of those elected prosecutors do so, the D.B. Cooper skyjacking case should go down in U.S. history as the one that proved justice in America is not only blind, it is dead and buried.

With that, I present this case to all of them on a silver platter, after seventeen years of investigation involving thousands of manhours and thousands of dollars to bring the most publicized crime of the twentieth century to its official closure. And pro bono.

January 4, 2008

Special Agent Larry Carr
Federal Bureau of Investigation
915 Second Avenue, Room 710
Seattle, Washington 98174

Dear Special Agent Carr,

The enclosed photocopy of the San Diego Union-Tribune prompted
me to write to you.

Also enclosed are some photocopies of documents and sources
of identification to introduce myself.

You will also see the enclosed photocopy of The Oregonian article
by Marge Boule' that clearly states my Hoover cover-up theory
of the D.B. Cooper case. Although I did not include it herein,
I also sent a letter to Boule' asking her to challenge retired
FBI Special Agent Ralph Himmelsbach to an open discussion of
the facts of the case with me. I received absolutely no response.

Himmelsbach has widely publicized for decades that he was the
chief agent of the Cooper case, which was denied to me personally
by one of the previous Cooper case chief agents in Seattle.

Unfortunately, I disclosed that that agent discussed details
of the Cooper case with me to the wrong people, and he was
quickly transferred to Jacksonville, Florida and would no longer
answer or respond to my phone calls, as he did when in Seattle.

I will never make that horrible mistake again, but I do have
18 known or reported facts that clearly support beyond any
reasonable doubt whatsoever that the D.B. Cooper case was a
blatant J. Edgar Hoover cover-up.

Your reported volunteering to take the Cooper case baffles me
in that it is an open and shut cover-up, and you will commit
political suicide by reporting the true facts or go down in
flames for sadly failing. If you thought it would give you a
professional boost, forget it. You will spin in circles.

Call at any time if you want the real facts, and I won't tell.
In the interim, just fake it like you know what you're doing.

Most sincerely,

George C. Nuttall, Captain, California Highway Patrol, Retire

enclosures (7)
cc: file

P.S.: Cooper's wildlife-scattered
remains are on a Columbia
River Island. PERIOD!

March 26, 2008

Special Agent Larry Carr
Federal Bureau of Investigation
1110 - 3rd Avenue
Seattle, WA 98101

Dear Special Agent Carr,

As you can see from the enclosed letters to you I sent the two
letters and enclosures to you at the old address I've had for
about 13 years. I didn't know your office had moved to a higher
rent district.

Last night I saw on TV news that an old parachute was found
in the area of Amboy. I can only say that it could not have
been Cooper's because of that location. Based on the account
of the copilot that was flying Cooper's skyjacked plane, their
flight path was an unknown distance east of Vector-23 which
is where the automatic pilot course system is located. And
he did not fly on automatic pilot and drifted east of Vector-
23 in the strong southeast headwind of about 40-60 miles per
hour.

Therefore, the plane was always miles east of the Columbia River
where the $5,800 of ransom money was found about 8 years later.

Also, Cooper used a Navy Emergency Pilot chute. Many military
planes crashed in the U.S. during World War II, and that might
be from one of those crashes.

Earl Cossey provided the chutes for Cooper and he told my partner
and me he can identify every one of his chutes as his. So I
suggest you contact him to see if he can identify the one found
as being one of his and the one not returned to him. I believe
Cossey lived in Kirkland when my partner and I interviewed him
in 1994.

Good luck with it.

Sincerely,

George C. Nuttall, Captain, California Highway Patrol, Retired

enclosures
cc: file

TWENTY-ONE

The Final D.B. Cooper Episodes

The Whole Truth

THE DAY THAT MY publisher notifies me that this book is to be publicized and released for sale, I will send a letter to the Oregon and Washington States Attorney Generals along with my list of over twenty-five potential material witnesses. I will also state which of those potential witnesses should be called to testify first, and direct questions to ask them to possibly uncover the truth and bring this case to an abrupt truthful ending.

The authority of the Attorney Generals of Oregon and Washington extends to being able to investigate the crimes of grand theft and kidnapping of the four Flight 305 crew members. And possibly false imprisonment of the entire flight crew and other thirty-five passengers when their flight was delayed for two hours over Puget Sound as ordered by Cooper until his demands were at the Seattle Airport.

As I have previously stated, all witnesses scheduled to appear before a county grand jury should be given immunity from prosecution of obstructing justice, but not immunity from committing perjury. And all witnesses subpoenaed should be directed to not see or communicate with any other witnesses until after the conclusion of the grand jury investigation.

The grand jury should also issue an order for the Columbia River islands to be searched for Cooper's remains by the Multnomah County Sheriff and Oregon State Police, and with a clause to prohibit the FBI and any Green Berets, active or retired, from searching or encroaching on the islands.

In the event that the Attorney Generals of those two States choose not to pursue this investigation, then the D.B. Cooper skyjacking case can go down in U.S. history as the one that clasically proved that true justice is dead in America.

And if that proves to be the case, God help all of us.

BIBLIOGRAPHY

Bernstein, Carl and Woodward, Bob. *All the President's Men.* New York: Simon and Schuster, 1995

Douglas, John and Olshaker, Mark. *Mindhunter: Inside the FBI's Elite Serial Crime Unit.* New York: Scribner, 1995.

Giancana, Sam and Giancana, Chuck. *Double Cross.* New York: Warner Books, Inc.,1992

Himmelsbach, Ralph P. and Worcester, Thomas. *NORJAK: The Investigation of D.B. Cooper.* West Linn, OR: NORJAK PROJECT, 1986

Orange County Register, "Saving Sergeant Hebler: Former assassin now spends time saving lives," June 28, 1998

Portland Oregonian, "Attorney renews search for D.B. Cooper," November 29, 1987

Portland Oregonian, "Expert thinks Cooper died of hypothermia," November 24, 1988

Portland Oregonian, "Marijuana 'garden' raided," August 6, 1994

Rhodes, Bernie, and Calame, Russell P. *D.B. Cooper: The Real McCoy.* Salt Lake City: University of Utah Press, 1991

San Diego Union-Tribune, "Search for D.B. Cooper is on—again," January 2, 2008

Summers, Anthony. *Official and Confidential: The Secret Life of J. Edgar Hoover.* New York: G.P. Putnam's Sons, 1993

Swearingen, N. Wesley. FBI SECRETS! *An Agent's Exposé.* Boston: South End Press, 1995

Tosaw, Richard T. *D.B. Cooper Dead or Alive?* Ceres, GA: Tosaw Publishing Co., Inc., 1984

Vancouver Columbian, "FBI renews efforts to find D.B. Cooper," January 1, 2008

Breinigsville, PA USA
01 October 2010
246548BV00001B/1/P